The Business of Talk

The Business of Talk

Organizations in Action

Deirdre Boden

Polity Press

First published in 1994 by Polity Press
in association with Blackwell Publishers.

Editorial office:
Polity Press
65 Bridge Street
Cambridge CB2 1UR, UK

Marketing and production:
Blackwell Publishers
108 Cowley Road
Oxford OX4 1JE, UK

238 Main Street
Cambridge, MA 02142, USA

ISBN 0 7456 0291 6
ISBN 0 7456 1356 X (pbk)

A CIP catalogue record for this book is available
from the British Library and the Library of Congress.

Typeset in 10½ on 12pt Garamond Stempel
by Graphicraft Typesetters
Printed in Great Britain by Hartnolls Ltd, Bodmin, Cornwall

This book is printed on acid-free paper.

Contents

Preface and Acknowledgments

I used to make films for a living, in London and around Europe. Making films turns out to be mostly talk – in any language – with the camera running only occasionally and expensively. It would be a mistake, though, to think of film talk as separable from the action of cameras and crews. The casting sessions, production meetings, camera directions, on-film rehearsals, laboratory instructions, cutting room conferences, and final-cut projections are *all* talk and that's what makes movies. That early career in the British film industry taught me that though it may be true, in some sense, that "money talks" it does so through the people and conversations that make up the business day. Talk really isn't cheap; it is consequential and far-reaching, however ephemeral and epiphenomenal it may appear. In the cluttered cutting rooms and subterranean sound studios of Wardour Street and Soho Square, I learned not only to talk shop but to talk business and to do so under the guise of casual conversation. Over the years, in locations and languages as far scattered as Shepperton Studios on the Thames, Studios Les Victorines in Nice, Cinecittà in Rome and in the dusty hills above Beirut, I learned the same lesson over and over. People and their agendas meet at the level of everyday talk. This book is about that meeting.

The idea of studying talk in organizations as a fundamental way of understanding social order grew out of a return visit to London in 1981 (funded by a Humanities Graduate Research Grant from the University of California at Santa Barbara). As I found myself again talking with film technicians in crowded pubs and listening to the trendy chat at advertising agency parties, I was struck not only by the bright business patter but also with the fundamentally interactional yet organizational flavor of those conversations. These colleagues of my former career were not simply talking business. My curious ear seemed, recurringly, to hear advertising account executives, film producers, union shop stewards, editors, and production assistants "doing" their organizational activities not merely through the surface content and superficial topics of their talk, but through the very structure and organization of their exchanges. They were "talking" the organization. I decided to study that activity.

The personal and professional meet in still more ways. As a woman working in and with many organizations during the film production years and now, all the more, as an academic, I have often had the distinct feeling of being Alice – sometimes in Wonderland, more often in a looking-glass world of locally logical yet apparently exotic plans, decisions and outcomes. Even more central to the ideas explored in this book, the accounts provided by the mostly male organizational actors I meet in my wanderings, by way of sharing their agendas and explaining their actions, have also always had for me that oddly elusive yet logical quality of Lewis Carroll's clever dialogues. So often, too, have I danced the intricate steps or made the complicated moves of organizational dances and games that seemed distinctly lacking in either a clear beat or explicit rules, indeed with the "rules" changing all the time. Yet, the wonder of it all – no doubt the reason I became an ethnomethodologist – is that, just like Alice at the Mad Hatter's Tea Party, it so quickly makes sense. Garfinkel's considerable insight has been to locate and explicate the highly ordered and orderly reasonableness of everyday action. Lewis Carroll's talent was, as logician and writer alike, to make that same local logic child's play, and entertaining at that. This book is my own version of how talk creates its own logic and the reasonableness we demand of everyday experience.

Books themselves, I've discovered lately, take on a life of their own. This one is no exception. It represents not so much what I thought I had to say about the business of talk and the business that gets done through talk, but rather the things that were there to be said. The detail and density of human interaction tell their own story. As a sociologist, I am always amused when I present this sort of research to a typical gathering of social scientists. Trained in the postpositivist world of computer modelling and statistical sophistication, and with their self-conscious roles as "scientists," they view my world of talk rather as adults patronize clever children with favorite toys, or people praise poets with their rhymes, as amusing, stimulating but ultimately trivial. Not the stuff of science and discovery. Or rather, they do so until I turn on the tape-recorder. As the real world of real people explodes in their ears and they engage in the sort of sanctioned voyeurism that is every social scientist's dream, even the most committed positivist turns into an interpretive analyst. Here is "reality" – not a social scientist's or philosopher's construct – but the real world, really happening. Perhaps, in the end, I never stopped being a film-maker and storyteller because in the chapters that follow I am most concerned to achieve that "you were there" atmosphere of early documentary film-making and to weave a story that belongs to the talk, not to the sociologist. Whether I have succeeded is for the reader to judge.

Books also don't get written alone, however lonely and frustrating the process may seem at times. This one wouldn't exist at all if it weren't for an extraordinary degree of trust and enthusiasm expressed directly and indirectly by many friends and critics along the way. I have Lenville J. Stelle to thank for his insightful interpretation of a muddled collection of ideas about language and social order and for guiding me to the works of ethnomethodologists. It was love at first sight, although, then and now, I find the syntax of those early formulations daunting. Happily for the reader of this volume, I have yet to master the style!

I came to this work too late to know Harvey Sacks, but I have been fortunate enough to spend happy hours with Harold Garfinkel in recent years. Sacks's insights and Garfinkel's originality illuminate the pages that follow, though hardly as each might want.

The ideas that are presented here have been nurtured and nourished in many ways and places. I am particularly grateful to Don H. Zimmerman, Harvey L. Molotch, Thomas P. Wilson, and Leonard Broom for tolerating and even encouraging an early version of these ideas which, rather to my amazement, became a Ph.D. dissertation. Don Zimmerman has always provided singular and unwavering support and inspiration, coupled with a wry world-view. Impetus of another and welcome kind came later during a National Institute of Mental Health postdoctoral fellowship period at Stanford University, from Jeffrey Pfeffer, James G. March, and W. Richard Scott, who taught me how to study organizations and, more importantly, *why*.

The organizational community, both at Stanford and elsewhere, has shaped the key questions this study attempts to address. At the same time, the intense community Garfinkel likes to call "the Company" has also brought these pages alive in distinct ways. Neither the ethnomethodologists nor the wider organizational group will fully approve what follows but it is my hope that they will take it seriously and that it is worthy of their critique.

A number of colleagues have already taken that step. I would like especially to thank friends who have read and reacted to parts or all of the manuscript in its many forms, including Howard Aldrich, Michel Audet, Stewart Clegg, Ira Cohen, Frank Dobbin, Thomas Eberle, Richard Hilbert, John Flood, Brigitte Jordan, Annette Lareau, James G. March, Hugh Mehan, Jeffrey Pfeffer, Lucy Suchman, Henry Walker, Thomas P. Wilson, and Don H. Zimmerman. I owe a special note of thanks to several people who offered useful yet gentle correctives in the closing stages of the project: Paul DiMaggio, Douglas Maynard, and, especially, John Heritage. This book is, in many ways, a measure of the influence of Maynard's earlier study, *Inside Plea Bargaining* (1984), on my thinking, both in Santa Barbara and along the many roads I have taken since.

Never at a loss for wit or words, Harvey Molotch has shaped my thinking and my self-esteem probably more than he realizes. Our recent work together is refracted throughout many of these pages. In St Louis, Janet Gouldner Ver Plank, Karen Lucas, Larry Irons and other members of the local editorial panel of *Theory and Society* provided an important intellectual community in the erratic production of this book.

That there is a book at all is to the credit of one person. Through his own writings, uncomplicated friendship and encouragement, Anthony Giddens guided this book to completion. I am most grateful. Gill Motley, Debbie Seymour, Ann Bone and the Polity people have also always made me feel welcome, however far the distance from St Louis to Cambridge. In St Louis, the Sociology Department was cheerfully helpful in so many ways. It is an irony that a study of the local logic of organizational decision-making came to completion just when Washington University abolished a once-stellar department of sociology.

While I was writing this book, a little boy died tragically in a fire. He was a magical child, with a fine mind and an even finer eye for the delicate and contingent nature of the world. I like to think he would have liked this version. Because I love and miss him very much, this book is for my godson and nephew, Michael Kevin Boden, who would have been thirteen years old as I write these final lines.

Introduction

Talk is at the heart of all organizations. Through it, the everyday business of organizations is accomplished. People in organizations talk all day, every day. In meetings, on the telephone, at work stations, on the sales floor, at doorways, in corridors, at the cafeteria, in pairs and groups, from the boardroom to the janitor's closet, talk makes the organizational world go round. The recurring and recursive patterns of everyday talk in organizations are the subject of this study.

This book is about the relation between talk and what is generally called "social structure." The central premise is very simple: by directly observing people talking their way through the business day, we can locate, quite specifically, the *structuring* of organizations. We can observe structure-in-action. To study talk as structure has a dual purpose, a kind of phased approach. The immediate goal is to present an empirical study of the structure and interactional import of everyday talk in organizational settings. A broader and ultimately more important goal is to locate this analysis of the "business" of talk within the larger theoretical arena of organizational analysis and general social theory.

Throughout these pages, organizations are taken to be locally organized and interactionally achieved contexts of decision-making and of enduring institutional momentum, rather than entities that have corridors and conference rooms and are independent of the people that fill them. This is not, therefore, a book about organizations *per se* but of the ways in which they are constituted moment to moment, interaction to interaction, day to day – across the *durée* of institutional time. The force of this latter proposition is to move an apparently microsociological analysis of Erving Goffman's "interaction order" to the received and perceived macrolevel of current concern in social theory. This is not, however, to assert the primacy of one level over the other, nor certainly to reduce one to the other.[1] In fact, a major goal of this book is to propose to (and perhaps persuade) organizational researchers and sociologists more generally that there is no such thing as "macro" or "micro," nor should there be.

In the chapters that follow, I also wish to build explicitly on earlier, insightful work of Karl Weick on the basic "organizing" features of all organizations, and on the notion of the "enacted environment." Weick, in that slim volume of 1969 that still captures the citations if not the constant attention of virtually all organizational researchers, drew on the work of social psychologists, phenomenologists, and ethnomethodologists to develop a rather unique theory of organizations in action.[2] I am equally interested in developing a number of fundamental themes in the work of James March and his colleagues, especially notions of decision-making and something I term the "local logic" of organizational rationality. This is, in turn, coupled with the need to reflect on the considerable insight of some of Henry Mintzberg's work with managers, which showed the considerably fragmentary nature of managerial work and its dependence on verbal interaction and a constant updating of news and information. Information in organizations has also recently emerged as a subject in the work of Arthur Stinchcombe in a quite provocative and, for me, stimulating way. It is my hope to offer a useful advance in tackling what I take to be central problems of contemporary organizational analysis, using, for my own contribution, the grounded study of talk in organizational settings.

So in the analysis that follows I will be attempting to blend these organizational themes with the work of ethnomethodologists and conversation analysts. In particular, Garfinkel's work shapes each of these pages, though admittedly reflecting my own affections and affectations for his ideas. In particular, his interest in the inherently *orderly* quality of human life illuminates the ways in which this book attempts to use the framework of ethnomethodology and the grounded methods of conversation analysis to move both organizational theory and general social theory one tiny step further toward a more holistic and inherently *sociological* discipline.

At its best, sociology exposes and illuminates the fine, delicate, and largely hidden membrane that supports, connects, and binds social actors in a flexible web of patterned relations. It is an irony of language, in my view, and a consequential one at that, that we have come to call this complex phenomenon "structure": words carry a freight of meaning and, for social scientists, few terms are more quickly concretized and reified into a nearly immovable and insuperable object. The very semantic weight of solidness and separateness attributed to structure has had, it seems, extraordinary consequences in twentieth-century sociology, effectively driving a wedge between action and both its causes and its consequences. Indeed, the autonomy of social structure is a "domain assumption," characterizing a fundamental concept of the relation between the individual and society, and, as such, it is central to the basic premises of academic social science.[3] Thus the antecedent conditions of action and its multiple outcomes, whether intended or unintended, have increasingly and largely unthinkingly come to be treated as *the* topics of social science enquiry. That those "structural forces" do not, *pace* Marx, weigh evenly or with any constancy on the shoulders of the living has largely been forgotten. The result has been highly problematic in at least two general senses: (1) much social theory is currently driven by methodological conventions rather than genuinely empirical insights; and (2) the emphasis of structure "over" action has resulted in the invisibility of the latter in the shadow of the former.[4]

In the first case, no one can ever fully agree on what social structure "really" is (hardly surprising given the diversity of human conditions it is supposed to capture). As a result, analysts have increasingly carved out different domains of structure for themselves and built edifices occupied exclusively by the faithful of that particular persuasion. In the study of organizations especially, scholarship has become highly fragmented by virtue of a near-obsession with so-called "levels of analysis." Most simply, these amount to the individual and organizational levels of analysis; in practice, however, a finely layered system has emerged that is mutually exclusive to a large extent. Driven almost entirely by considerations that are rooted in methodological constraints rather than empirical evidence, quite a number of talented researchers critique or ignore each other's findings and theories based on essentially socially constructed, if methodologically tidy, distinctions that are features of data sets and statistical convention rather than properties of the real world. These many and separate levels are then treated as "structure" and assumed to shape the behavior of microscopic human actors. When these actors, in their turn, seem to choreograph elaborate organizational agendas to the apparent beat of many different drummers, their actions and interactions are taken to be variously operating on informal levels of social structure or are dismissed as "irrational." The fact that most organizations run in the "informal mode" *all* the time has not tended to deter organizational theorists and researchers bent on locating the "real" structures that determine people's behavior.[5] We will return to these themes in chapters 1 and 2, and recurringly to the conventional distinction between formal and informal organizational structures and practices, since it marks such an oddly taken-for-granted assumption in almost all research on organizations.

A number of interwoven elements only sketched here will be developed in some detail in the chapters that follow. I hope that the reader can tolerate the mild redundancy this strategy entails. To move beyond splintered approaches to the study of organizations, not – I hope – as a polemic but as an empirically grounded and theoretically relevant discourse, involves updating and occasionally rejecting a number of cherished but empirically unfounded assumptions in organizational theory and research. Some of these are explored in chapter 2, where a brief and highly selective overview of the field is presented. In chapter 3, I attempt to lay out a broad argument for the study of language-in-action and for the analysis of talk as structure.

The empirical sections of the book, chapters 4 to 7, then present a fine-grained analysis of talk and its essential *structuring* quality. I realize, only too well, that such a detailed approach to something like "structure" will take some patience on the part of many readers. Yet, as I shall hope to demonstrate, everyday talk is the primary medium through which human beings make sense of their world. That sense-making is rooted in language, and the meanings produced matter a great deal, not just to the particular actors, but to how the world unfolds as a collective collaboration.

Moreover, taking seriously central elements of social life such as language and meaning also entails reanalyzing the rather well-worn distinction between "objective" and "interpretive" approaches to social phenomena. Structural conditions, variables, and outcomes are really no more "objective" than the ongoing process that creates and carries them, though they are assuredly handy objects for quantitative analysis. All too easily, then, they take on a methodological life of their own in the so-called "quasi-experimental" manipulations of everyday sociology. These maneuvers are based on what Lieberson has dubbed "impossible assumptions,"[6] namely the compromises of convenience that occur at virtually every stage of any research, but in the case of sociology on the experimental assumptions of decidedly nonexperimental data. To study either structure or process (or both) *inevitably* involves the researcher in decisions on "what counts"; that distinction, always and everywhere, is a local judgment call – no more, no less – and it is thoroughly interpretive.

One serious result of the recent emphasis on structure "over" action has been an illusion of the importance of one domain "over" the other. In the process, sociologists all too often appear to think they are studying entirely different universes of social order. However, the world is of a piece, single and whole. This was ever the case and is all the more relevant in the closing moments of the twentieth century when we live in a world made tiny through the simultaneous mechanisms of capitalism, technology, telecommunications, and the delicate nuclear balance. While it is tempting to think of these consequences of modernity as "macro" and the discrete actions of individual actors as "micro," the spirit of this book, as indicated, will be to argue otherwise. In the pages that follow, a major theme will be to propose, in many ways, that there is no such thing as "micro" and "macro," but that our theories and analytic strategies try to make it so.[7] This state of affairs, so alien to the worlds of classical sociologists, is, in effect, part of what the philosopher Maurice Merleau-Ponty calls the "retrospective illusion," here applied to contemporary sociology, namely that having invented structure we take it to be the pre-existing condition of our research.[8] My suggestion will be to recognize both structure and action and to explore the ways that they are *codeterminative* of each other. The tiniest local moment of human intercourse contains *within* and *through* it the essence of society, and vice versa.

The second rather pervasive consequence of allowing structural analysis to push and pull the discipline of sociology follows from the foregoing discussion. In the rush to structure, what Pollner has charmingly dubbed "the extraordinary organization of the ordinary" (1987: xvii) is entirely lost. At its most extreme, structural analysis of even "interaction" can lead to reducing the remarkable density of daily life to mechanistic data points in mathematical matrices. At its best, the study of social organization as interlocking structures, disembodied and independent of human moments, can lead to a largely lifeless view of human society. Lost in the process is the important intersection of action and structure or, more simply, people and their history.

The agency/structure debate therefore provides an important backdrop to the discussions that follow. This issue has animated the recent works of a considerable range of writers, in sociology and beyond. Although it is hardly within the scope of this book to provide any new "theory" or "solution" to this problem, it is my hope to make a contribution to an arena of discourse that I take to be critical to any real advance in our understanding of social order and social life. It is a problem given to us from the writings of nineteenth-century thinkers, but one which has taken on a deepening urgency in the latter part of the twentieth century. The evolving and eclectic writings of Giddens, perhaps more than any other writer today, have repeatedly but critically returned to Marx's dictum than people make history, but not under circumstances of their own choosing. Giddens takes this problematic to be essential to the development of social theory in general and a major focus of his own theory of structuration. The theory of structuration, which has developed through both a sympathetic critique of historical materialism and a penetrating synthesis of major strands of classical and contemporary social theory, also owes much to the work of American researchers of the interaction order. The power of structuration theory, in my view, derives additionally from a critical and original reorientation of metatheorizing around the elemental dimensions of time and space, coupled with an intense focus on the dynamic and elastic tension between local and global forces in the affairs of modern human beings.[9] Ethnomethodology's central analytic interest lies in the finely ordered details of local action, while structuration theory provides a way of articulating those local moments on a scale with the global pace of history in the making.[10]

At the same time, it also seems critical for the development of ethnomethodology itself that practitioners begin to reexamine the consequences of their findings "in their larger social context and to consider their significance for a form of social life concerned with forms of social life" (Pollner 1987: xvi). This is to say that ethnomethodology needs to recognize and reflect on its *own* activities as a social practice located within sociology. As we shall see, with the work of younger ethnomethodologists and conversation analysts, this trend is already well developed. By the same token, it is my hope that with a book such as the present offering, Harold Garfinkel's considerable insights into the organization of experience and Harvey Sacks's command of the details of interaction will now reach a wider audience.

All social life is, first and finally, episodic. The essence of our humanness is contained and communicated through verbal interaction, face-to-face or, at stages and places removed, telephonic and even electronic.[11] Language and discourse are at the center of all human activity, realized in the many moments of daily routine. These everyday episodes, layered one upon another, occur contemporaneously across similarly interlaced institutional activities, constituting the immediate practices of daily life. People's everyday actions in concrete social situations *are* the stuff of social order and, as such, the constitution of society involves the mutual and simultaneous elaboration of structure and action across time and across space.[12] The business of talk is just that.

1

Talk and Organization

Organizations are people. When people come together in organizations to get things done, they talk.[1] This book is about the business that gets done through talk, as well as about the interactional business for which talk is the primary medium. Through the chapters that follow a single thread will be drawn: talk, I shall propose, is the lifeblood of all organizations and, as such, it both shapes and is shaped by the structure of the organization itself. Through multiple layers of ordinary talk, people in organizations actually discover, as a deeply collaborative and contingent matter, their shared goals, many agendas, environmental uncertainties, potential coalitions, and areas of actual conflict. That mutual discovery, moreover, makes the durable features of the organization come alive – not just as fleeting details of the moment but as the elaboration of structure-in-action. It is through the telephone calls, meetings, planning sessions, sales talks, and corridor conversations that people inform, amuse, update, gossip, review, reassess, reason, instruct, revise, argue, debate, contest, and actually *constitute* the moments, myths and, through time, the very *structuring* of the organization.

Throughout much of the social sciences, however, ordinary, everyday human action is more typically treated as a resource for understanding larger social processes and social structure, and not as a topic in its own right.[2] From the mathematically manipulated isolation of the concept of the Market, for example, economists look down and presume to understand the methodological actions of the individuals who constitute it. Sociologists, for their part, have constructed a Great

Wall of Structure comprised of the sedimented and often rather stolid actions of social actors. Even historians, not as preoccupied with universal laws and predictive modelling, have nonetheless tended to dismiss single events in favor of large sweeps of history. Throughout these traditions, discrete, local, momentary human action is used to explain these larger factors, and not treated as a *topic* for investigation and theoretical insight. It is, moreover, often the case that analysts actually confuse topic and resource. Because of the involvement of social scientists in the everyday world of experience – what Schutz calls the "attitude of everyday life"[3] – they draw on members' knowledge about society as a *resource* for studying the *topic* of their research, thereby confounding the two. Zimmerman and Pollner recommend instead that the everyday world of experience be treated as a research phenomenon in its own right, just because "the fundamental facticity of the social world" – its social structure – can be seen to be the lived, situated, practical accomplishment of social actors.[4] But, by using individual actions in the everyday world as analytic resources and not as topics, social scientists routinely engage in just the sort of commonsense theorizing their formal theories are designed to suspend, while smoothing the apparent sloppiness of daily life into those patterns and transformations of the collective level so firmly recommended by Durkheim. People are effectively, although rather magically, made to disappear from much social science theory and research. Indeed, as Wilson has recently rather creatively suggested, all too often human agency is actually "explained away"[5] in an effort to view structure all the more clearly in its solidity and sustained persistence.

By treating talk as central to what organizations *are*, rather than as passing and peripheral phenomena, two further, broad strands will be woven through the interactional materials and discussion presented throughout this study. One thematic element, already mentioned, addresses what is currently characterized as the agency/structure debate. The foundational features of this *conjuncture* have been developed best in the work of Giddens, Philip Abrams, and Pierre Bourdieu, and , with gathering momentum, picked up by a remarkable range of authors now pondering the role of agency given the overdetermined status of structure in sociology and other social sciences.[6] Surprisingly few of these treatments, however, get close enough to the fine structure of human action to be able to theorize its richness and the consequences of interactionally achieved actions and events. Thus a major task in these chapters will be to demonstrate just how such microscopic events as turns at talk embed *and* enact organizations and institutions and, in so doing, ground global issues in local conditions of concrete action.

The second theme I shall thread through these pages will be the essential, ubiquitous, and utterly unavoidable predominance of organizations in modern life. While this claim is hardly news and indeed comprises, in some form, the opening sentence of most books on organizations, I hope to introduce a useful twist. That twist involves a new and rather insistent emphasis on the need to study organizations *as they happen*. Virtually all organizational studies study events and decisions long after they occur. They depend on interviews, or questionnaires, or the residual records of the organizations themselves, losing entirely the dynamism that is such a central feature of *all* social organization. That dynamism is, to be sure, methodologically untidy, but it is central to what organizations *are*, how they *work*, and even why they don't. My suggestion to students of organizations will be that theories and research strategies that ignore the local dynamism of organizational life miss much of the innovation, change, and even inertia they hope to understand. Organizations in action are busy, even buzzing, places but they are also exciting and challenging analytically.

By studying organizations in action[7] I mean quite explicitly to suggest that, just as social theory stands at an important intersection in the examination of agency and structure, the study of formal and complex organizations is also at a critical impasse.[8] The relatively new field of organizational analysis has made remarkable progress since it grew out of the foundational musings of Max Weber and Chester Barnard. As with all progress, however, there has been a high cost, in that the field has been brought to a level of considerable methodological and analytic sophistication with little real theoretical advance. The camp fires of the various organizational paradigms burn brightly, to be sure, but they are scattered across the landscape with their camp followers often out of hailing distance of each other.

Connecting these two themes, then, is what I take to be a rather urgent need to put people back into organizations (and back into society). In organizational terms, I mean something a good deal more fundamental than the recent calls to bring people, firms, the state, and even society "back in."[9] Indeed, many of these pleas for inclusion of one or another level of analysis highlight just the methodological advances and theoretical impasse alluded to above. I am suggesting more broadly that we need to recognize, and take very seriously indeed, the practical activities of real people engaged in concrete situations of social action. That is to say that we need to put aside, as suggested earlier, the "macro" emphasis of much social analysis and peer thoughtfully through a sort of social microscope. Here I am building quite consciously on John Heritage's recent suggestion[10] that with Garfinkel's powerful if highly specialized ethnomethodological insights into everyday action, that microscope is now ready. By using it, I am further suggesting that, in the details of moment-to-moment human action, the social universe is revealed.

Agency, Structure, and Organizations

In making the agency/structure question central to this book, I draw on Giddens's frequent insistence that society is constituted through what he calls the "duality of structure."[11] Giddens argues that the production and reproduction of social institutions across time and space is accomplished through the "essential recursiveness of social life, as constituted in social practices."[12] The point of departure, therefore, for this study is the observation that social structure is both a resource for and a product of social interaction, and Maynard and Wilson's proposal that this reflexive interplay between social organization and social interaction is located in the turn-by-turn, moment-to-moment development of social life.[13] There is a bidirectional connection between social structure and social interaction that can be located, with varying degrees of explicitness, across many levels of social order. This formulation of resources restores the individual to the status of active agent, while neither reducing society to a mere collection of unit acts nor reifying it as an object independent of the individual.[14] Maynard and Wilson further identify and illustrate the possibility of using the techniques of conversation analysis to elucidate empirically the mechanisms of social structure as an essential context on which participants rely, in the turn-by-turn development of their interaction, and the way it is, at the same time, the product of that same interaction.

This position, in turn, depends still more centrally on the work of ethnomethodologists, and especially, as noted, on the writings of Harold Garfinkel and principles of conversation analysis developed by Harvey Sacks.[15] For ethnomethodologists, social structure is something humans do, rather than something that happens to them. At issue is the *enabling* as well as the constraining quality of the object we call "society." Since the notions of both "structure" and "agency" are used in a variety of ways throughout the social science literature, it will be useful here to provide a brief clarification of what it means to study organizations as they happen, and to do so with a theoretical agenda that combines the work of Garfinkel, Sacks, Giddens, and also Goffman.

Sociologists conventionally define social structure as some domain of orderly relationships between specified units that are regular, routine, and nonrandom in some systematic manner.[16] Though there is not a great deal of consensus on the details of this phenomenon, the "idea of social structure"[17] has great appeal to the inheritors of Durkheim's initial insights into, and insistence on, the importance of the collective *over* the individual. Structure is, moreover, assumed to be essentially larger than action; many interconnecting and seemingly independent structures of a given society *overarch* the rather small actions of individuals below.[18] As a result, a measure of scale is *built in* to sociological analysis.[19] Individual actions are thus played out in the vast shadows cast by organizations, institutions, and the nation-state. In Tilly's memorable phrase, we are confronted with "big structures, large processes and huge comparisons."[20]

At best, structure and process are seen as "mutually enriching" but, as Robert K. Merton argued, irreducible to each other. Researchers of organizations recognize the interrelationship of structure and action, although formulations vary widely and "[one] researcher's structure . . . is another's process."[21] More dangerously, all process is assumed to solidify into structure or, put more precisely, all important processual phenomena are presumed to sediment into durable and measurable aspects of structure. Structures are then taken to be *the* relevant empirical data for the explanation of social order.

Framed as external, constraining, and *big*, the discrete actions of situated actors are treated as "effects," that is, as indicators, expressions or symptoms of social structures such as relationships, informal groups, age grades, gender, ethnic minorities, social classes, and the like.[22] Social structure, in this conventional view, is taken to condition or "cause" social conduct, and social interaction itself can be treated as the intersection between structurally located actors and events. Viewed this way all human interaction in actual social situations is seen as a *product* of those social forces. Moreover, since social structure forms the presumptive context of activities of lesser scale, it is ultimately the fundamental explanatory resource and hence the arbiter of which research questions are interesting and important, and which are not.[23] Just as "macro" is too easily taken to subsume "micro," the agent of social action is presumed to be constrained and contained within pre-existing and largely determinative structural arrangements.

From an ethnomethodological point of view, on the other hand, the patterns of action and reaction that constitute "structure" are the *in situ* product of members of society. This is not to say that there *are* no pre-existing conditions of that action, nor does such a position intend an essentially ahistorical world, as Gouldner and others have so mistakenly suggested.[24] For Garfinkel, the structures of practical action are the observable, accountable, and irreducibly local instantiation of structure in action. Social life achieves its recognizable, repeatable and recursive quality through the routine and unremarkable ability of actors to *make sense* of their shared activities. In this way, human beings are knowledgeable agents in the production (and reproduction) of their lives and their history. That knowledgeability, which is central to Garfinkel's notion of membership, is achieved as a constant stream of necessarily intelligible and accountable actions that are the foundation of an intersubjectively accomplished social order. Through their actions in real places and under real and quite specific conditions of action, social actors instantiate those elusive and invisible structures of social science lore.

This conception of structure, which also plays a central part in Giddens's theory of structuration, thus requires a powerful notion of human agency. According to ethnomethodologists, it is in the accomplishment of accountable activities that agency emerges, not as a metaphysical principle or personal illusion but as an essential feature of the organization of social interaction. Indeed, ethnomethodology proposes that it is through making their activities accountable that members actually produce and reproduce the features of social structure, in particular, its cohort independence, facticity, and constraining character.

For the purposes of the discussions to be developed throughout these chapters, I take human agency to comprise the actions and inactions of social actors who are, *always* and *at every moment*, confronted with specific conditions and choices. Those conditions are not, again with due deference to Marx, simply historically given, but are instead made relevant (or irrelevant) as a local matter. In organizations, for example, the rules and regulations of standard practice, operational procedure, or even contingency planning are routinely and unproblematically adjusted, altered, and even ignored in the actual tasks and decisions of organizational actors. Thus so-called "informal" practices are not some alternative normative rule-set, but, as suggested earlier, they constitute "business as usual." They are Garfinkel's "structures of practical action," an evolving, temporally located, sequentially produced set of *relevancies* which *instantiate* the generalized organization as a real place. People achieve the relevance of their actions through their treatment of each other as agents, which is to say as accountable for those actions. It is tempting, in standard organizational research, to dismiss both the specificity of action and its conditions by focussing on contingencies. Yet the realtime qualities of human activities and their finegrained structure have *direct* consequences on conventional organizational variables and, eventually, on any interest in social scientific explanation and prediction.

In its routinely observable form – in interaction – human agency is displayed, enacted, and reacted to by human beings in the collaborative activities that make up daily life. This may seem a far cry from the sort of agency proposed by economists and economic theorizing, but it has, in effect, very much the same sort of moral quality; namely that social actors treat each other as *morally accountable for their actions*. In their collaborations, human beings must – as a central condition of existence and even survival – treat each other as reasonable and competent, as well as reasonably compliant and cooperative. This "reasonableness" is what I mean by agency. It is achieved through a deeply reflexive quality of human action and interaction – as Heritage describes: "via the reflexive properties of actions . . . participants – regardless of their degree of 'insight' into the matter – find themselves in a world whose characteristics they are visibly and describably engaged in producing and reproducing."[25]

It is, in other words, in their accountable activities that human actors both produce and expect agency in immediate and distant others who, *through their actions*, constitute the organizations and institutions of their society. Through their local activities and accounts, moreover, they create the facticity of "matter of factness" of the world, which they then treat as real and constraining. In phenomenological terms, social agents give to their collaborations a kind of retrospective illusion of solidity and facticity.[26]

These "accounts in action"[27] are not some flawed version of an otherwise objective "reality," or rationalizations of "irrational" or unreasonable strategies and decisions that are being given a gloss of "retrospective rationality"; they *are* the organization in action. Through language, most commonly through language-in-action as talk, we provide accounts of our actions, accounts which are, through and through, historical yet immediate and utterly tailored to local events and conditions. When people talk they are simultaneously and reflexively talking their relationships, organizations, and whole institutions into action, or into "being."[28]

Structure is thus realized *as action*.[29] In this sense, organizations and institutions exist through the actions, reactions, and inactions of their constitutive members, who embody and enact the history or spatio-temporally constituted set of relations we call structure. So organizations and institutions are not really cages that contain and constrain their passing members; they are more like fine and transparent mesh matrices, the threads of which are being woven and rewoven by current members with a considerable mix of old patterns and new stitches. That mix makes any human organization stable yet inherently unpredictable and utterly fascinating.

The conversational materials presented in succeeding chapters mark one way of capturing the evanescent quality of organizational life, while, through the structuring properties of talk itself, isolating some of the predictable properties of organizations. Organizations can be, and often are, busy yet boring places and that, too, is part of their fascination. We will be looking at the ways in which routine features of organizations are constantly and necessarily used to deal with new and contingent factors. Talk itself, for instance, has many recurrent and repetitive features that are simultaneously routine and innovative. Where talk and organizations meet is the sort of agency/structure articulation this study hopes to illuminate.

Talk and Organization

Throughout these pages, then, everyday interaction in organizations is taken to be a *constituent* feature of the setting of which it is a part, which is to say it is a primary mover in making organizations happen. This claim is central to all ethnomethodological work. Through the timing, placing, pacing, and patterning of verbal interaction, organizational members actually constitute the organization as a real and practical place. Furthermore, through a turn-by-turn analysis of organizational talk, it is possible to gain insight not only into how everyday business gets done at the level of talk, but also the interactional and organizational business that is accomplished *through* that talk. The structural and interactional properties of everyday talk are thereby reflexively tied both to the occasion of speaking and, simultaneously, through these recurrent patterned activities to the larger social order, in this case to the organization as a whole.[30]

Organizations have traditionally been defined as rational collectivities of social actors engaged in purposive, goal-oriented activities within the domain of a clearly defined boundary.[31] More recent organizational theory and research, had, on the other hand, tended to view the activities of individuals in organizations, as well as of organizations acting within and reacting to their environments, as *coalitions* rather than homogeneous collectivities, as groups of groups, interdependent to varying degrees along various dimensions and toward a variety of goals.[32] Conceptual revisions of Talcott Parsons's notion of legitimate bureaucratic authority and of collectivities engaged in the purposive pursuit of shared goals[33] has meant that contemporary theorists can therefore redefine organizations as "settings in which groups and individuals with varying interests and preferences come together to engage in exchanges."[34] The notion of coalition further suggests that individuals and groups within an organization are both interdependent and in competition, exchanging information, skills, services, and scarce resources in complex relationships of power and position. In the next chapter, I develop a rather idiosyncratic discussion of current work in organizations as a way of locating my position within it.

My approach, as already indicated, will be to suggest that organizational theorists and practitioners take seriously the role of language and everyday discourse in organizations, since it is through and with language that organizational members describe and provide accounts of their activities and decisions. Studies of corporate executives and middle-level management suggest that such individuals spend a great deal of their daily routines engaged in some kind of talk, whether in meetings, office interaction, or on the telephone.[35] Mintzberg, in developing his dynamic "structuring" models of organizations, for instance, notes the ways in which organizational decision-making is actually a rather fluid and staged exercise in "commitment to action" in which communication flow plays a vital role.[36] Gronn, in a qualitative study of school principals in Australia, argued that, in fact, talk *is* the work of managers.[37] But, with the exception of Gronn's study, most organizational interest in the role of language has focussed on descriptive accounts of lexical expressions or vocabulary, cognitive processing, or the general role of language in organizational culture.[38] Yet, overwhelmingly, the language of organizations occurs as everyday talk, which remains largely unstudied, although professional institutions such as legal, medical, and educational settings have been studied extensively by conversation analysts and others (see chapter 3 below).

To one concerned with the interface between talk and social structure, the systematic methodology of conversation analysis provides a vital analytic tool. Philosophers and linguists have long been interested in the essentially social role of language as a primary form of human behavior. Sociolinguists, in particular, have been concerned with the social patterns and organization of language[39] and psycholinguists have addressed the social psychological factors involved. Within sociology, Goffman has sensitized students of human behavior to the delicate balance of human interaction, with a specific emphasis on the centrality of verbal face-to-face exchange in his later work.[40] But Goffman was content, indeed insistent, to state that the "interaction order" is a domain in its own right, only "loosely coupled" to the larger social order.[41] I am not easily persuaded of this limitation although it is clearly important, for analytic purposes, to recognize and respect the fact that interaction has unique, locally managed contingencies and concerns that have their own self-organizing autonomy.

At the same time, however, the recurrent features of everyday life contain within them fundamental and irreducible elements of experience that not only ground but continuously renew the "larger" order. Talk and interaction are thus *both* a domain in their own right *and* the primary social location of all human experience, exchange, and events. Distinctions *between* the autonomous domain of interaction and the institutional domains it enacts need to be carefully drawn and may be independently analyzed,[42] but the linkage is undeniable and deserves quite deliberate if careful explication.

Conversation analysis, in contrast to other linguistic or sociolinguistic approaches, concentrates on the sequential and interactional properties of action. An insistence on the turn-by-turn analysis of interaction allows the researcher to uncover and understand how talk as social order is achieved across time and space. As organizations are, in one broad sense, social systems that explicitly "bracket" time and space,[43] we need to understand how this is accomplished. The systematic structuring of temporal and spatial dimensions so critical to modernity is, as we shall see, anchored in and articulated through everyday talk and the settings of talk, such as meetings, telephone calls, conferences, interviews and so forth. Moreover, conversation analysis allows the researcher to locate and track the accomplishment of what I will term *organizational agendas* that are woven in and through interactional settings. These agendas and accounts are refracted like so many shiny particles through the density of interaction itself and require careful explication and considerable detail of discussion.

This analysis of the many facets of interactional and organizational "business" that gets done through talk also introduces a new direction in conversation analysis. To date, a central focus on turn-*taking* has led to an insistence on exclusively studying the immediate adjacent ordering of talk. But in talk-based work settings – such as the many meetings and telephone calls studied here – variation in turn-*taking* reflexively embeds a variety of sustained aspects of turn-*making*, as actors use talk environments to advance or subvert the many policies and political moves of the organizational day. Conversation analysts have been pursuing an important distinction between everyday talk-in-interaction and "institutional" talk which occurs in various professional settings.[44] This study is, however, concerned with organizations in the broadest sense and with the intense interactional settings that animate and advance them.

The very density of interaction incorporates a further important element of all organizations because it is through talk that *information* is transmitted and, more importantly, transformed. No information, whether institutional, as, for example, in the law, or organizational as in news about competitors, is either static or neutral. Nor is it (nor ever can it be) simply "communicated," despite hundreds of textbooks and management articles that suggest just such simplicity of message, medium, and reception. And, while company reports and government policy stand as "official" records of past actions and future constraints, the gap between them and what "really happens" (or will happen) is considerable, as we all know. One suggestion of this study is that we need to take that gap more seriously if we are to understand organizations.

The gap occurs, in part, because of the dynamism of social life. But it is also the result of incomplete, imperfectly understood and unevenly distributed flows of information travelling not from A to B to C, and so on, but rapidly and in multiple directions at the same time. So *understandings* and how they are achieved are central to everyday life and to good social science. Understandings involve a *constant updating*, which, in turn, means that they are *constantly* shifting.[45] Moreover, meanings are embedded in ongoing action. Understandings of both information and action are therefore necessarily being transformed by immediate circumstances and local agendas.

Meanings, most importantly, do not occur as isolated cognitive phenomena in the heads of atomized individuals; they are constructed *interactively* and under quite pressing conditions of time and space. The "need to know" has a for-the-moment quality that is irreducible to individual cognition; nor can it be abstracted away from the concrete conditions of action and treated as an independent system. Let me give a very quick example of the sort of interactional intensity and density of realtime phenomenon the methods of conversation analysis can deliver. The following fragment of talk comes from a university council meeting. The first speaker (at line 1) breaks into the official meeting agenda on a so-called "point of information"; for his effective understanding – right there and then – of the larger drift of the discussion (and eventual decisions it projects), he needs to know what a particular acronym stands for. There is a description of all the transcription conventions used in this book in the appendix (see pp. 218–20) for now, note that square brackets denote overlapping speech, colons are used for "stretched" or drawled vowels, and pauses are indicated in tenths of seconds in parentheses. Throughout most of this study, these transcription devices have been greatly simplified to aid reading, but here they help to explicate the considerable inter-actional dance that talk entails. Note in this example, in particular, the collaborated and almost syncopated way several speakers move to answer "Rock's" question:

1.1 Council Meeting

```
 1   Rock:    Question?
 2                            (0.6)
 3   Chair:   Yeah?
 4   Rock:    What is the (0.3) C-PEC (0.1) stand
 5            for?
 6     →                      (1.1)
 7            (Wha-) (.) ⌈group is it?⌉
 8   Dean:                ⌊C a : : l i⌋ fornia,
 9                            (0.8)
10            ⌈⌈remember it?⌉
11   Lana:    ⌊⌊Po : s t    se⌋ con-
12   Mel:     Post Seco⌈:  n   d   a   r   y-⌉
13   Dean:              ⌊Post Secondary ⌈E:⌋ducation Co : mmission⌉
14   Chair:                             ⌊Po : st S e : c o n dary  ⌋
15                Educa : tion Commission.
```

This is also an especially dense strip of talk, the collaboratively achieved reply (lines 8–15) involving no fewer than four of the members present at this meeting. Rock's question is necessarily addressed to the Chair, not only because he is interrupting his report, but because such requests for turns out of order must be so directed. The Chair, either because he can't remember what "C-PEC" stands for or isn't sure quite what Rock is questioning, does not reply immediately. This produces the pause at line 6, causing Rock to recycle his question in more general terms. Pauses *predictably* produce reformulations of just this kind, and the Dean moves to answer. By "predictably" I mean that the turn-taking model for conversation predicts minimal gap and minimal overlap in talk.[46] Gaps (such as 1.1 seconds at line 6 or 0.8 at line 9) also predict that several speakers are likely to start up together; this occurs, with considerable coordination, when four speakers sequentially construct the full name of the organization: California Post-secondary Education Commission (CPEC). Note, too, that the development of the full title is both *iterative* and *interactional*, and that the Chair finally chimes in with his own version of the joint communiqué. In all, an elegant example of the kind of syncopation of interaction that was foreshadowed in the writings of both Garfinkel and Goffman and is revealed in detail by the tape-recordings of conversation analysis. We will return to this example later, but it serves here to introduce just the sort of phenomenon talk is and the dance it involves.[47]

In chapter 3, the relationship between language, action, and interaction is traced, and a detailed description of the methods and assumptions of conversation analysis offered. Here I want simply to stress the interactional and realtime nature of meaning, information, cognition and, ultimately, organizational action. Cognition is not an "individual" matter. Meaning is not simply located in the rules and rituals or organizations. Information is neither neutral nor readily grasped. As a result, actions taken in organizations and, in the final analysis, their overall effectiveness, efficiency, and success depend *utterly* on local understandings and local rationality.

Rationality Revisited

In the latter part of this study, I hope therefore to contribute to the growing debate over rationality. Ever since March and Simon elegantly isolated the notion of "bounded rationality" as an explanation of the cognitive limits whereby organizational actors are unable to live up to the rational model held over their heads,[48] sociologists, economists and political scientists have come up with ever more ingenious gradations of boundedness.[49] In some versions, the actor disappears completely, either as an artifact of aggregation or because every action is assumed to be programmed through systems of institutionalization.[50] Often what is quite mundane to our daily experiences disappears and the everyday actions of organizational members frequently become the "unexplained variance in the theories."[51] In still other approaches,

the limits of cognitive capacity and the inherently ambiguous properties of social life are assumed to lead to largely random actions on
the part of organizational actors. Or rationality is assumed to be
constructed *ex post facto* as a retrospective process of rationalization.
In most treatments, the limits of rationality are assumed to be largely
incurable and the result is seen as vaguely "socially constructed"
adaptations.

In a later chapter of this book, I hope to restore the notion of
"bounded rationality" to an active category of organizational analysis. Rather than conceiving of rationality as some singular and limited
cognitive and thus ultimately psychological phenomenon, I will suggest that it would be useful to think of it as an *interactionally
bounded* phenomenon. Bounded methods of *local* rationality produce
locally reasonable actions and even decisions which are *also* (indeed,
must be) accountable ways of solving some immediate problem so
that the solution stands the test of organizational needs and goals.
Anticipating the larger discussion, what I shall propose is that organizational actors fit current actions (and inactions) to some immediate
problem in ways that retrospectively mesh with earlier actions and
prospectively will be seen to adequately accommodate projected organizationally shared agendas. Their success at this varies, of course,
as do their strategies. Some solutions may seek problems, other problems may seek suitable actors to address them, still more local agendas seek both problems and solutions through which to weave their
own actions and often diverse and even diverging goals. Throughout,
both organization and environment are enacted as moment to moment
yet thoroughly accountable and thus "rational" entities.

In fact, to foreground a major conclusion of this book, organizational decision-making doesn't look much like the theories and many
discussions of it offered in the wide literatures of economics, political
science, sociology, and management. Like March and Olsen before
me, I have been "impressed by the ways the imagery of 'decision-
making' confounds an understanding of organizational phenomena."[52]
Rather than being the exciting "tilt points" and "critical moments" of
common parlance, actual decision-making is a diffuse, incremental
affair. Organizational members create decisions *from within* and
discover their sequential elements, collaborative stages, and even
"functional" parts *as they go along*. Rightly, March and Olsen point
out that ideas about "decisions" (as a set of outcomes) are confused
with "decision-making" (as a process) by a semantic presumption
that the latter is connected to the former in some nonproblematic
manner.[53] As we shall see, producing activities that approximate

accountable "goals" and "decisions" is *the* problematic of most organizational settings. As realtime phenomena, *decisions* are, in fact, largely invisible and thus empirically unavailable, whereas *decision-making* can be located in the fine laminations of actions and reactions that build, from one moment to another, into the organization.

As outcomes, decisions are real enough, of course, but only as long as a static, snapshot observation is made. But in the flux of organizational life, neither decisions nor their "reasons" stand still. Instead they are a fundamental part of the recursive yet constantly renewing properties of social organization. Layered one upon another, strips of decisions (and nondecisions) are sedimented into our experiences and into that retrospective illusion of social structure discussed above. As one incremental layer of action is created out of the last, the actions of individuals are guided by a local logic that is simultaneously responsive to the moment and inclusive of the collectivity. That local logic, in turn, is built out of a kind of cooperative competence. Local actions must not only make sense to their participants but must be seen as reasonable and, in organizations, reasonably efficient and cost conscious as well as adaptive and accountable.

Caught in the pressing necessity of choice, organizational actors move through a fluid mix of problem identification, goal negotiation, solution seeking, and decision-making that rarely displays those rather singleminded rational strategies and logical paths recommended in business schools. As ethnomethodologists insist, concrete conditions rarely if ever emulate abstract theorizing, yet choices are made and decisions are produced in an intricate interpenetration of local contingencies and global responsibilities. The very "process of decision does not appear much concerned with making a decision,"[54] yet decisions *are* made and are *made* to make sense. The *in situ* production and reproduction of social life is itself made possible through the local choices, micro decisions, and apparently minor moments of daily life *and nowhere else.*

In summary, the relation between agency and structure shapes the pages that follow. It is characterized as talk and social structure with, however, a critical caveat, namely that talk has its own structure and endogenously structuring properties. The locus of interest and analysis is at the level of talk. Talk is taken to be *the* most pervasive of all social activities, indeed central to what it means to *be* social, to be human. The "social" in this formulation is both Durkheim's collective and Garfinkel's member. Indeed the role of *member* lost in Parsons's transformation of the "unit act" is central to putting people back into organizations and into social theory.

And, to reiterate, rather than focus on the formal structure of organizations, I am concerned with what many have mistakenly called the "informal" practices of organizational members. I take the distinction between formal and informal organizational structures as simply another social science dichotomy. It is interesting when it explicates the perspective of organizational members, as will be seen in chapter 4. And it allows, to be sure, for certain kinds of research problems to be more easily served. But it also sidesteps the practical and, ultimately, profound fact that organizations *are* the people who comprise them.[55]

There is a well-worn dictum in the advertising business to the effect that 95 percent of an ad agency's assets go down in the elevator every evening. If we are to genuinely understand the nature of work and organizations in this rapidly changing period of high modernity and postindustrialism, we would do well to treat this participants' analysis quite seriously. Virtually every study of leadership and management confirms this hunch, as do recent studies that link the essential attributes and attitudes of top management to corporate communication and personal performance. What is at stake is the so-called "human factor" in all organizations. That human element is as ephemeral as it is essential. It is, nonetheless, what makes organizations "tick," what makes some succeed and some falter, some grow and others stagnate. Even in the "age of the smart machine,"[56] the human factor haunts every corner of every organization. However automated the work or standardized the procedures, people bring organizations to life. What people do – up and down the hallways and up and down the organizational structure, all day long – is *talk*, hence this study.

2

Organizations in Action

In a very real sense, organizations are us, and we are them. Circular
and simplistic as this may seem, it is also a fact of modern life. When
I lift the phone, turn on the television, open a can of soup, or brush
my teeth, I am connecting to corporate life and to capitalism. AT&T,
CNN, Campbell's and Colgate-Palmolive are the social facts of modernity; they connect me to far-off friends, information, nutrition,
and modern hygiene. They bring the latest and most public of technology into the intimacy of private life – in an instant, fibre-optic
telephone lines, satellite news, low-salt diets, and fluoride. Dressed in
clothes from Hong Kong, with a watch from Switzerland and shoes
from Italy, I climb into a German car, turn on a Japanese tape-deck
and play music from England. En route to a university endowed with
corportate millions, I stop at a bank cash machine and, through the
magic of plastic, receive old-fashioned paper money, itself the most
basic measure of modernity.[1] Virtually every interaction and transac-
tion of my day – and yours – is organizational.

The range and reach of modern organizations is such that no contemporary human community can truly be outside their influence.
The modern nation-state has guaranteed this in a way neither the
Catholic church nor the dense bureaucratic layers of ancient Chinese
society ever could. In traditional and premodern societies, peasants
and villagers lived virtually in separate worlds from the many systems
of elites, so much so that history was written (and rewritten) without them.[2] Today, not the remotest New Guinea hill tribe or Aus-
tralian aboriginal on walkabout can escape the reach of organized,

organizational society. One of the challenges of modern film-making, for example, is to shoot historical scripts in locations where the skies have no telltale jet streams. One of the tragedies of modern life is the global damage a single slip in environmental monitoring can cause. It isn't easy to escape the cares of the world. Those cares are catered to, constituted through, and often indirectly caused by a vast matrix of interrelated and embedded organizational structures.

What is an Organization?

Organizations come in every shape and size. They may consist of anything from a day-care center to a national government. In this study, we will be concerned with the dynamic properties of organizations in action, but it is worth noting that great attention has been given in the literature to isolating and characterizing a variety of forms of organizations into detailed typologies and schemata.[3] Typically these focus on elements such as size, goals, complexity, technology, environment, and social structure.[4]

What *is* an organization? Different things to different people, no doubt. In organizational research, one of the clearest articulations of organizations and their structure is offered by Stinchcombe: "a set of stable social relations deliberately created, with the explicit intention of continuously accomplishing some specific goals or purposes."[5] Interestingly, Stinchcombe's definition is remarkably close to the one for social structure discussed above (see p. 12). It has the solidity and fixity that social scientists attribute to presumed large-scale social phenomena. As a definition, it serves us well, but as a working description of organizations it is aloof from the battle, to say the least, as are many clear definitions of these complex human phenomena.[6] And it is a mistake, I believe, to simply assume that the study of organizations should be defined as the study of structure; the very dynamism of these pervasive social forms is lost in such an approach.

To get at the sort of organizational image I am emphasizing here, metaphors may provide more heuristic merit.[7] A favorite of mine is one of Herbert Simon's, which proposes that organizations are like Chinese boxes, systems within systems, nested, close-fitting, embedded in, and defined by, each other.[8] To be sure, organizations are rarely as elegant *or* as tidy, but the interdependence of both meaning and action has just the sort of reflexive equality that, I believe, is critical to a holistic understanding of organizational phenomena.[9]

Although definitions and metaphors of organizations abound, fundamental notions of what they "really" are remain largely taken-for-granted features of theory and research. From an ethnomethodological perspective, this is hardly surprising since organizational members themselves have flexible definitions of their own work, goals, alliances, commitments, appropriate technologies, actual boundaries, environment, competition, and so forth. Similarly, within the field of organizations, some researchers are interested in ecological effects,[10] others are focussed on interorganizational fields of dependence and collaboration,[11] while still others study vertical and horizontal features of a single organization. There are studies concerned with labor stratification within and across firms and with organizations as social networks,[12] as systems of power and control,[13] as information-processing systems[14] and as social organization across historical time.[15] And there are still further researchers who look at the so-called social construction of organizational myths and the creation of cultures within companies and corporate conglomerates.[16] This diversity has proceeded at the cost of theoretical progress, as noted above.[17] The overworked parable of the blind men examining the elephant comes to mind. Depending on orientation, organizations can be anything from Max Weber's rarified and idealized formal structures to Karl Weick's enacted entities.

Overall, Weber's legacy looms largest. Given his sweeping and enduring analysis of the rise of bureaucracy, this is hardly surprising in general terms. Yet Weber, never the optimist, would be surprised at the fervor with which he is quoted in organization circles today for, however many the caveats, most researchers seem to secretly cling to formal approaches in the face of the informality of all organizations, noted above.[18] Central to Weber's work are also important formulations of rationality and of social action. Since each are themes of this study, it will be useful to explore Weber's influence briefly.

Weber, Parsons, and Social Action

The debt owed and acknowledged by the field of study of organizations to Weber is, as noted, remarkable in many ways. Not the least is the continuing contemporary relevance of much of Weber's preoccupation with the nature of bureaucracies and organizations and their consequences for modernity.[19] At the other extreme is the frequent oversimplification of Weber's sophisticated views of organizations, rationality, and what Granovetter has rightly dubbed the embeddedness of economic mechanisms in social structural arrangements.[20] To be sure, Weber's essential formulations of both bureaucracies and hierarchies have served us well, and recent research has provided critical insights into both the form and function of modern organizations.[21] Critical readings have also been provided of the inherent dangers of reifying one or other view of organizations.[22] And Weberian scholarship itself has largely moved beyond earlier Parsonian blinkers into a more rounded understanding of Weber's overall project, and especially his approach to the problem of rationality.[23] Nevertheless, much routine writing in organizations falls into many of Parsons's rather programmatic pitfalls. In the process, the considerable concern in Weber's writings with action and the acting individual is either dismissed as "subjective" or viewed through the rather heavy filter provided by Parsons wherein action itself disappears into the theoretical thin air of the "unit act."

Throughout his writings on economy and society, Weber is quite clear about his concern for the essential social nature of action and for the distinctive ways in which actors orient their course of action to the actions of others. In this sense, he is highlighting *inter*subjectivity and the unfolding temporally located nature of action, rather than some "subjective" and thereby personal or individual understanding of events and their social structural relevance. In discussing, for instance, the practical operation of legal norms in contrast to the legal theory of such norms, he notes that "it is the 'orientation' of an action toward a norm, rather than the 'success' of that norm that is decisive for its validity."[24] Indeed, throughout *Economy and Society*,[25] Weber recurrently points to social actors' orientation to the actions of others during the *course of action*. So, for example, organizational actors attending to "policy" or "guidelines" in their daily activities are orienting to their fluid, local production *as they go along* rather than to any fixed, rule-governed quality. In Parsons, Weber's notion of "orientation" is largely lost[26] and we are asked to accept instead the internalized norms that guide conduct and the assumptions of rule-governed behavior that have so easily blinded researchers to empirical reality. Weber's notions of subjective orientation to action are equally easily turned into methodological issues and subsequently downplayed as less "objective." And, in stages, we are moved firmly away from Weber's interest in action taken to be understood "in its course" toward an abstract notion of action and a more diffuse understanding of the act. Human acts are thus transformed into social facts which can no longer be placed in a broader context of meaning involving facts which cannot be derived from immediate observation.[27]

I shall return to these themes in some detail in the next chapter, but it will first be useful to locate this rather specific view of social action within the study of organizations as a whole. As we shall see, agency and action play a very small part indeed in the contemporary sociology of organizations.

Organizations in Review

Rather obviously, a book on talk in organizational settings is not the best source for an overview of organizational approaches to the study of social order.[28] It is important, however, to examine some key themes in organizational analysis in order to frame my own concerns and the focus of this study. So the review offered here touches lightly and selectively on a field that spans several disciplinary areas and bridges not a few academic boundaries, as areas as diverse as sociology, political science, psychology, business, and communication all teach and do research on the pervasive modern organization. My purpose here is simply to review some central aspects of theory and research that are useful or contrastive to my goal of putting real moving people back into organizations.

The study of organizations as a systematic endeavour emerged after World War Two, first in the United States, later in Britain, France, Italy and elsewhere.[29] As founding fathers, organization theory acknowledges especially Max Weber and Chester Barnard, and the rather reified and simplified dichotomies that, Perrow notes, dominate the field all "stem from the contrast of the Weberian and the Barnardian models."[30] Barnard's *The Functions of the Executive* of 1938, a pathbreaking book on the cooperative and essentially moral basis of leadership and management, was among the first to isolate the organization as an entity. As such, it seems like rather naive reading, when viewed with the hindsight of over 50 years and with the emergence of the modern organization as so central a feature of modern life. The next 20 years were to see a range of now-classic case studies of organizations, among them Selznick's TVA study of 1949, Gouldner's studies of industrial strife of 1954 and 1955, and Blau's *The Dynamics of Bureaucracy* of 1955. By the early 1960s, several leading texts provided insightful indices of the "story so far," including those by March and Simon, Blau and Scott, and Cyert and March.[31] Organizational research was then also developing in Britain with the work of the Aston Group and, later on and in a more critical vein, with the work of Clegg,[32] Silverman,[33] and others. In France, Michel Crozier started the "Centre de Sociologie des Organisations" (CSO) in 1962 and published *Le phénomène bureaucratique* in 1963.[34] Interestingly for the topic of this book, neither British nor especially French research on organizations was to take the heavily quantitative turn seen in the US. To this day, French researchers primarily want to study human dynamics and to interpret them in the light of what the principal actors do and say.[35]

In the past 40 years, studies of organizations have been almost as varied as the phenomena. Despite the tremendous outpouring of work since the 1950s, a basic complaint made by Gouldner remains, namely that most accounts of organizations are "so completely stripped of people that the impression is unintentionally rendered that there are disembodied forces afoot, able to realize their ambitions apart from human action."[36] In most organizational studies, it is the bureaucracies and firms themselves that are characterized as autonomous units that "act," "think," "learn," and "decide," apparently without any need of an animating force other than their own internal combustion and propensity for "momentum," "inertia," and "entropy." These terms themselves give an important clue to the sort of latter-day Comtian social physics and systems theory that underlies the hopes and models of many organizational researchers.

Social actors are barely glimpsed in most of these analyses and are almost always presented as highly controlled by the collectivities and social structures of which they are seemingly an unwitting part. Alternatively, they are studied in the experimentally controlled settings favored by social psychologists. Moreover, although the absence of people in organizations has been modified somewhat lately,[37] social "actors" are usually treated as collective entities and individual action is viewed as messy and merely "processal." Overall, the assumption is that people themselves are pliable or, at worst, reluctant and unreliable.[38] This frustration of experts with the inhabitants of organizations has resulted in quite remarkable creativity in rationalizing and ultimately explaining away their behavior.[39] One of the earliest and most persistent of these explanatory tacks has been to contrast "formal" and "informal" structures, as noted earlier.[40] while the sort of direct observation of organizational behavior provided in this study rapidly reveals that organizations are operating in an informal mode virtually *all* of the time, the dominance of this formal/informal assumption merits our attention here.

In Dalton's classic work, he compares "managers on paper," which is to say formal organizational charts and their mapping of line and staff functions, with the interlocking of formal and informal rewards and activities, and even more cogently with formal and informal work practices, as well as with official and unofficial strategies and information channels.[41] Although some social psychological studies of management have had a thoughtful appreciation for the role of social action, sociologists, whose work is so dominated by the one-sided view of Weber's bureaucratic structures, have more often treated informal work practices as functional at best, frequently inconvenient, and sometimes downright deviant. This view is epitomized in the work of Blau where, despite an initial definition of "bureaucracies [as] complex systems of coordinated human activities,"[42] he then proceeds to explain away the collaborative and quite creative strategies of agents in the face of the functions, needs, goals, and overall agenda of the organization.[43] Since collaborative activities and local adaptations constitute the organization in action, a great deal of organizational insight is dismissed in this approach.

So for Blau and many other analysts the "dynamics" of organizations turn out to be the familiar disembodied and emergent properties of structure *over* agency.[44] This has the fascinating but not untypical result of studying social actors – peer relationships, informal networks, reciprocal practices, social exchange – with the express purpose of making them vanish into the walls of structure that surround and sequester them. Basic notions of structure persist in the writings of many of the most interesting contemporary practitioners,[45] and the predominant attention to structure *over* action is partly theoretical and partly methodological. In particular, systems theory underlies much of organizational analysis.[46] It comes in various guises, as Parsons's social system or a more general utilitarian model, as cybernetic systems and as broadly conceived set of system-based models.[47]

Within relatively recent writings, Scott's discussion of rational, natural, and open systems provides the most lucid overview of system perspectives on organizations.[48] Building on Thompson's earlier work,[49] Scott presents coherent, contrasting discussions of: (1) the rational model, based on the notion of organizational rationality providing the goals, formal structure, efficiency, and control of the system; (2) the natural model, which provides a more ironic view of organizations focussing on informal structures and an essentially structural-functionalist approach; and finally (3) the open systems model which is more tied to the classic general systems theory and cybernetic flow of information and control. Throughout there is a determinative core to these approaches and a decidedly unidirectional control of system over individual. Scott notes that practical research on organizations frequently demands a more holistic approach and that the very complexity of organizations and especially of their relative environments of operation has required researchers to adapt in various ways.[50]

The diversity of recent research on organizations resists facile summary, so I shall now quite selectively explore several strains of work that I take to capture interesting current approaches to the study of these assuredly complex modern collectivities. My aim is to highlight features that will inform the empirical analysis that follows and that will illuminate (or so I hope) my own contribution. In terms of this study, I shall focus on two relatively recent approaches, namely ecological and institutional analysis, and contrast them with my own.[51] In the process, I shall also provide a brief overview to ethnomethodological studies of organizations.[52]

To anticipate that discussion, let me stress here that ethnomethodologists never "study organizations" in the conventional sense. They are not interested in organization*s*, but in organization*n*,[53] which is to say that they are animated by a curiosity for the *organization of experience* and the "extraordinary organization of the ordinary," as noted earlier.[54] Activities in organizational and work settings are, for ethnomethodologists, simply a marvelous way of unravelling the fine detail of social organization. That organization may, indeed, be more or less hierarchically structured, resulting in more or less complexity of staffing, spatial divisions of labor, lines of communication, and so forth, but *how* these are achieved and occasionally subverted becomes the research question. The *why* of conventional social science is bracketed. If structure is not assumed to automatically constrain action then organization*s* become ideal prisms through which to observe organization*n* or *structure-in-action*.[55]

Organizations and Environments

The central concern of most organizations research is, however, to analyze structure. One way of extending this agenda has been to examine the way organizations may be shaped by their environments. The work of Thompson and the contingency approach to organizational analysis began to focus attention on the relation of organizations to their external environments.[56] This and later studies extended the systems approach noted above by proposing to view organizations as open systems, with units and subunits contributing to the formal structure but varying in their degree both of integration within the system and differentiation from each other.[57]

The general approach emerged as a solution to studying large complex organizations and their relationships and interdependencies with each other, as well as with the political and economic environments in which they operate. This focus allowed researchers to explore interests in the ways organizations create and compete for specific "niches" in a system. The past two decades have seen publication of a wide variety of articles, as well as numerous books with rather consistent titles like *Organization and Environment, Environments and Organizations, Organizations and Environments, Organizational Environments, Organizational Ecology,* and so on, each either propounding a "population ecology model" of organizational responses to the environment or providing alternative ways for tracking the critical relationship between organizations and their operative contexts.[58]

It is beyond the scope of my own topic to critique this work. Certainly much of the power of these rather diverse approaches to the study of organizational environments lies in their ability to deal with *groups* or "fields" of organizations. The population ecologists have been primarily concerned with how structural forces massively constrain organizations, while the institutionalists, such as Meyer and Scott, have concentrated on ways in which industries and professions legitimate practices through institutionalized norms. By studying organizational patterns "from after" these various supraorganizational approaches have been able to track organizations over impressive lengths of time with a high level of statistical sophistication,[59] and to identify the operation of distinct organizational fields.[60]

Clearly, organizational groupings or "fields" are an important aspect of how individual organizations operate, and organizational environments are surely important to our understanding of how particular people at particular points in time make the "decisions" and produce the "outcomes" we all take to be at the heart of the modern organization.[61] Yet, as I shall attempt to demonstrate, the ways in which organizational actors *realize* both the constraints and opportunities in their working environments is critical to what actually *constitutes* an "environment." Understanding the organization/environment equation must also include a close-up view of what people actually *do* in response to environmental pressures. When, how, and through whom a resource is "allocated" is a strikingly local matter, as are key actors' interpretations of their environment. My own position will be to suggest that the way environments are understood is central to what they "are" in any practical and thereby rational sense.

Obviously researchers interested in populations of organizations must, on methodological grounds, ignore this so-called micro level of analysis. But, in theoretical terms, lack of consideration of everyday actors' necessary sense-making can easily lead to assuming that it plays no role in the abstract fluctuations "observed" statistically. The result may thus have a certain elegance, in a scientific sense, but avoiding the messy real world will hardly advance organizational analysis very far.

With a greater appreciation of such matters, important studies of organizations and their environments have been conducted by Pfeffer and Salancik. Using a "resource dependency" perspective on power and control in and of organizations, they have added depth to the central debate over organizations and their environments.[62] At a more general level of analysis, Granovetter's considerable creativity has also focussed on the essential embeddedness of economy and society.[63] Most recently, the environmental theme has been taken up by the "institutional" school of organizational analysis.[64] Since the relation between interaction and institution is critical to much that follows, it will be useful to look at the institutional approach to organizations in some detail.

Organizations and Institutions

The institutional school of organizational analysis has been another of the more prolific and influential in recent years. In essence, it builds on the work of Phillip Selznick in arguing for the importance of the institutionalization of organizations and their structures over time. Hauntingly Durkheimian, institutional theory offers an odd blend of what might be called macrophenomenology and latter-day functionalism. The result is quite analytically powerful and is free of many of the methodological sleights of hand of population ecology approaches, sketched above. It is, moreover, solidly sociological in both theory and data analysis. The institutional approach to organizations, simply put, takes Selznick's distinction[65] between organizations and institutions seriously. It effectively extends the idea that institutionalization imparts permanence to an organization[66] by proposing to study the sustained and thus institutionalized structures that coordinate and control activities within an organization, or across an organizational field. This orientation is Durkheimian in that it tends to treat the organization organically, as a whole and as growing and changing in a kind of mimetic relation to other organizations.[67] Organizations are thus seen as diffuse cultural systems that imitate each other and conform to dominant functional forms. Through their institutionalization, organizations take on a life and direction all their own, but they are also seen to respond in creative (or not so creative) ways to their environment. This has led a number of researchers to examine firms in terms of their interorganizational networks and contexts.[68]

The notion of "context" is a core yet quite confused concept in the institutional approach (indeed in most social science research). Given an interest in how organizations persist across time and in the ways they connect to each other, John Meyer and his colleagues have given an interesting phenomenological spin to this basically functionalist orientation. To capture the ways organizations are themselves institutionalized, Meyer and Rowan suggest that organizational myths and ceremonies are created that sustain and shape the more concrete "products, services, techniques, policies, and programs" of firms.[69] Drawing rather loosely on phenomenology, they say that these myths are based on typifications of organizational practices which, over time, elaborate the formal structure of an organization and become the rationalized taken-for-granted and, of course, institutionalized rules of the organization. In the process – and it *is* apparently a "process" – these myths shape the ways in which organizations imitate each other and their environment to such an extent that "organizations structurally reflect socially constructed reality" in much the same way that (we are rather surprisingly told) Parsons's theory of organizations suggests.[70]

This synthetic blend of functionalism and phenomenology also reaches several other equally enterprising, empirically based conclusions. In the work of Meyer and his associates, for example, the entire structure of the educational system is presented as largely "symbolic" and ultimately mythical, although it is never clear *where* the symbols reside or how they work to become myths. In any case, this emphasis on symbol leads the authors to conclude, in a quite elegant analysis, that educational systems are "loosely coupled," an idea given considerable weight in the work of Karl Weick, discussed below. But, where Weick suggested that decentralized organizational systems such as education might well be characterized as loosely coupled, he intended this as a sensitizing device to help researchers "notice and question things that had previously been taken for granted" and was wary of overdrawing the idea.[71]

The institutional school of organizations has produced an impressive range of solid and informative studies. Yet the odd aspect of this approach remains the central notion of institutionalization itself, which is typically so divorced from anything like the actions of either social agents or the shifting dynamics of realtime contingencies as to be rather aloof and, occasionally, even cynical. Not only are everyday actors reduced to cultural dopes, but the organizations of which they are a central part seem adrift in a mythical sea. Unlike the genuine phenomenological concerns with typifications which are the practical realizations of social actors,[72] the institutional school seems to have finessed even language and meaning into universal generalizations in which "vocabularies of structure . . . are isomorphic with institutional rules."[73]

A central problem for institutional theorists is that in their eagerness to produce a neo-Durkheimian understanding of social organization they have tended to mis-specify that part of their emergent perspective that borrows from phenomenology and ethnomethodology. For institutionalists, the intersubjective and commonsense stock of knowledge shared by social actors is assumed to be non-problematic.[74] For phenomenologists and ethnomethodologists, in distinct contrast, the commonsense understandings of everyday life exist as background expectancies which constitute the *constant problematic* of social practices.[75] The intersubjective commonsense world, no matter how routine or apparently ritualized, is subject to constant dislocation and is irremediably and unavoidably local in its sensibility and instantiation. Contrary, for example, to Zucker's claim that "the meaning of [an] act . . . [is] increasingly objectified and made external to the interaction,"[76] ethnomethodology proposes the inevitability of a reflexively organized social world in which the meaning of objects and acts are *only* available through what is termed the indexicality of particulars. By indexical particulars is meant that meaning is constituted in the interplay of people and objects under the concrete conditions of a particular setting, thus quite the opposite to Zucker's discussion. For Garfinkel and like minds, *no* social act is "objective" or "exterior" to action but rather, through their locally produced intersubjective understandings, actors give to their actions that facticity and historicity so cherished by neofunctionalists and institutionalists alike.

All social conventions, however institutionalized they may seem, are, for phenomenologists and ethnomethodologists, reflexively embedded in particular social contexts. The taken-for-granted features of social order and social control are not, for Garfinkel and Schutz alike, invisible or even opaque to organizational actors as institutionalists assume.[77] Indeed, by using aggregate data produced through the very same institutionalized and ritualized practices they hope to study, institutionalists tend to confuse resource and topic.

For example, if organizations rationalize their personnel practices by perpetuating myths about affirmative action policies and statistics for public consumption, or organizations assign apparent importance to their advertising campaign even when there is no evidence that any particular advertising strategy actually increases sales, institutionalists would seem to treat these external accounts and legitimated vocabularies as "real" in that they are then taken to shape the behavior of other organizations. Ethnomethodologists, on the other hand, treat accounts in a far broader sense and understand their production to highlight the ongoing ways in which actors "bring off" their actions as accountable and reasonable to others and thereby breathe life into otherwise inert institutional conventions.[78] While these treatments are clearly complementary, much of the work of the neo-institutionalists tends to subsume the former in the latter. I am proposing an insistence on the bedrock quality of social interaction as a *primary* locus of social order. The *production* (and not just the reproduction) of social order is the *conscious* albeit subtle and certainly taken-for-granted accomplishment of knowledgeable human subjects who, in Wittgenstein's sense, know how to "go on" in social life.[79] that is to say that, far from simply reproducing institutionalized rituals and routines, social actors know how to produce specific next actions that, seen from afar, will look plausible.[80] Going on, in this sense, may also mean, and often does, that other organizations, whose membership is also knowledgeable, will *also*, for instance, engage in overt affirmative action compliance (however much internal labor market activities at variance with it are actually enacted) or will spend huge sums on advertising (despite the fact that a price cut is much more likely to stimulate sales). Thus institutional "isomorphism" is the local product of knowledgeable actors rather than an abstract mimetic process located in the structure of organizational fields.[81]

In the data to be presented in this study, for example, we will see that hospital accounting practices depend on a daily census of patients occupying hospital beds, all counted at a particular time and then billed as such to individuals and, more often, insurance providers and programs such as Medicare. The census is at the center of a complex and interlocking set of charges, all of which are based on daily occupancy and utilization of particular hospital sites such as operating room, recovery room, delivery room, and so forth. The "rationality" of such a policy demands precision and quite conventional notions of accountability. But, as we shall see, the "midnight census" is neither done at midnight – because the staff doesn't have time – nor is it a full "census" – since there is local error in the count. Nonetheless, in full knowledge of this lack of fit between the mythical tally and the local reality, hospitals routinely budget and bill on the basis of it. And everyone, nursing staff, auditors, and insurance providers, *know* what is going on. Seen from the outside, by the research sociologist, hospitals may well appear isomorphic along many dimensions and resistant to change, but such similarities are the conscious production of hospital staff and their environment. Thus the "certainty and predictability" of organizational life posited by institutional researchers[82] is also the conscious creation of social actors, rather than something that "happens" to them.[83]

Now, critiquing one theory with another, here using ethnomethodology to critique institutional theory, is only interesting up to a point (however psychically satisfying it may be!) The institutional approach to organizations is still growing and producing a striking range of research.[84] Ethnomethodology itself has much to gain from genuinely confronting a more institutional approach, and certain writers have explored the potential merger to considerable effect.[85] My purpose here is simply to highlight the frankly fundamental misreadings of phenomenological and ethnomethodological work upon which institutional theorists appear to base their understanding of such core concepts as intersubjectivity and the nature of taken-for-granted features of organizations. Those misreadings lead to rather odd tendencies to treat data produced *by* organizations as evidence *of* unwitting organizational practices, thus confounding research resources with research topics. While much social science research manifests this problem,[86] as I have stressed, my sense is that institutional research may be especially prone to this common confusion. Nonetheless, institutional theory and research has gone a long way, as DiMaggio suggests,[87] to redressing the rather impressive persistence of utilitarian theory and rational choice assumptions, and for that it has served us well indeed by reintroducing important institutional concerns into organizational studies.[88]

Moreover, while there is a tendency to explain away action by decoupling it from structure,[89] recent efforts have also been made to incorporate notions of "agency" and "interest" into institutional theory.[90] This is encouraging since institutional theory is a vital area in current organizational sociology. Just *how* coupling between organizational structure and practical action is articulated – whether loose or tight – is a critically important question for organizational theory and social theory more generally.

Both the work in institutional approaches to organizations and in the population ecology approach sketched above highlight the need to understand organizations as those Chinese boxes Simon suggested. Attempts to model the nested nature of organizations and their environments have compared "objective" versus "perceived" notions of the environment, available resources, interlinked dependencies, and so on. Most of the studies, however, side-step or fail to appreciate the inevitable and unavoidable contextual nature of all information and thus the fact that there really is *no* objective environment for organizations, *all* of whom are dependent on the perceptions of their members and, more centrally, on the ways local perceptions actually *constitute* the conditions of next actions and thereby outcomes. Even the births and deaths of organizations, so central to population ecology, are engendered by people's *perceptions* of when and where to start a business, how to attract business, where to raise capital, how to achieve cash flow, hire appropriate staff, build a reputation, and, on the other end of the cycle, of the timing and enactment of bankruptcy or management of a merger – these are far from being a neutral or objective series of decisions. Rather than see the slippage between formal structure and everyday practices as a kind of myth or as an informal strategy whose normative structure reproduces the organization in some reduced form, some researchers have recommended turning instead to the interrelated topics of information, decisions, and the *enactment of the organization* itself as central research areas.

Individuals, Information, and Institutions

There is an innovative intersection of organization theory and research critically located between these structural, institutional and functional approaches to organizations and a wide literature on social psychological and purely psychological aspects of motivation, leadership, and thus individual-level studies of organizational behavior. I am referring to the work of Herbert Simon and James G. March, and to the writings and research of Karl Weick. Interestingly, too, as noted at the outset, a recent book by Arthur Stinchcombe belongs in this discussion, as his essentially structural approach to the study of organizations has taken on a new "informational" emphasis. Each of these writers is distinctive in an ability to move freely between theory and empirical research and, most especially, between various levels of analysis. The result is a rich vein of insight which is often cited but much less frequently pursued by other researchers, although Stinchcombe has clearly been affected by March and his colleagues, so it remains to be seen just how his own new challenges will be taken up.

In some of his earliest work,[91] Simon shared the common assumptions of contemporary organizational pioneers; he tended to minimize the significance of oral communication and to locate the control of firms in the records and reports kept by them, in other words, in the files of Weberian tradition. The latter were assumed to provide the information base of organizations, while informal channels were taken to be peripheral: grapevines and gossip, and shoptalk more generally. Simon was interested in both cognitive levels of behavior and in the nature of economics and administration. With time, his project grew into a central interest in rationality and, especially, with rational action under conditions of choice and ambiguity.[92] In the process, his work became notably holistic: "A theory of individual behavior microscopic enough to concern itself with the internal organization (neurological or functional) of the central nervous system will have a significant organizational component. A theory of organizational behavior macroscopic enough to treat the organization as a monolith will be a theory of an 'individual.'"[93]

Both Simon and March became intrigued with the cognitive limits of decision-making, with the uses (and misuses) of information in organizations, as well as with the essential cognitive limits to rationality that give rise to what they call "satisficing" behavior on the part of organizational actors. This practical strategy arises, they propose, because rationality is "bounded" rather than singular, all-encompassing and balanced. Under conditions of varying choice and levels of ambiguity in the organizational environment, actors search iteratively through alternatives until a satisfactory (rather than necessarily optimal) option is encountered. Choice and ambiguity thus shape the "drift" of decisions and related actions that so characterizes all organizations.[94] Rather than being goal oriented and purposive, organizations and their environments lack the intentionality ascribed by many of the approaches outlined above.

James March and his many collaborators have extended the early March and Simon work of 1958, developing sophisticated, behaviorally based notions of firms and organizational decision-making. Classic notions of "preference" proposed by economists and proponents of rational models of organizations are redefined by March as *ambiguity*, so that organizations understand their past and present in terms of both ranges of uncertain actions and conditions of actions. This approach fundamentally questions the "purposive" model of organizations, as noted; actions within firms are taken to be far less tightly (and thus "rationally") coupled to each other and linkages between problems and solutions far more blurred and indeterminate.[95] March treats organizational actors as competent and knowledgeable but confused and easily distracted, as concerned about the outcomes of their actions for the organization, but also preoccupied with their own work careers both within and beyond the organization. There is much evidence, in the sort of talk-based data explored in this study, that he is correct. The result, according to March, is not so much that organizations are loosely or tightly coupled but that there is an essential tension between the logic of immediate moments and the organization "as a whole" so that it may at one point be closely connected and at a next moment quite distant. Again, the data of this study suggest that this elastic or flexible tension is indeed at the heart of organizations, and, moreover, that the unfolding *meaning* structures in which they are constituted guarantee just such a dialectic of action and structure.

March transforms theories of organizations into theories of organizational decision-making. This puts activity at the center of theorizing and results in a dynamic model and a flexible range of directions in which the researcher can move. March and Olsen, for example, in *Ambiguity and Choice in Organizations* (1976), one of the most original books in the whole field of organizational analysis, explore the connections between individual action and organizational outcome, noting the need for a theory that captures the "considerable impact of the temporal flow of autonomous actions" and the reflexive dimensions of the flow of those actions within a changing context.[96] This leads them to the conclusion that not only do problems seek solutions, but that within the temporal flow of organizational life there are often actors and solutions seeking problems to which they can fit their actions.

This alternative ordering of organizational action and reaction has much appeal in the sort of discussion which I shall develop. Dubbed the "garbage-can model" of decision-making, actors, problems, and solutions are connected more by their simultaneity in time and space than by their presumed causal connection.[97] Apparent disorder thus produces a local order that contains its own internal logic *and* that will, by the smoothing effect of organizational members' *own* accounts of their actions, be *seen* to be "rational" when viewed within the purportedly "larger" context of the overall organization. For March, and for Garfinkel as we shall explore below, social actors discover *from within* the logic and thus the "reason" for their emerging actions, and these produced in concert, readily shift between smooth and fuzzy outcomes. As they sift through locally relevant possibilities, however, social actors use their own agendas and understandings to produce "answers" that are then fitted to "questions." The result is oddly reasonable and is, in any case, imbued with rationality and purposiveness through the accounts provided by both the immediate agents and those who must, later, make sense of their actions. Rationality is thus, through and through, an enacted affair.

The notion of the "enacted" organization and environment was developed, with wit and to enduring effect, by Karl Weick. His central position on what he terms the *organizing* of organizations is stated from the outset: "assume that there are processes which create, maintain, and dissolve social collectivities, that these processes constitutes the work of organizing, and that the ways in which these processes are continuously executed *are* the organization."[98] Drawing on the work of social psychology and, especially, a combined phenomenological and ethnomethodological perspective, he goes on to speculate about how organizations are *produced* as a shared, and essentially *enacted*, set of coordinated actions. The process of organizing is thus critical to what organizations are, rather than some flux that disturbs otherwise rational systems, and the constitutive activities of organizational actors move to centerstage. The shared meaning actors attribute to their organizing within the firm is also used to enact the organizational environment. This enacted environment then shapes the ways actors react to it.

An important element of Weick's thinking, and in the position proposed in this study, is that the processes that constitute an organization – *any* organization – are similar. That is to say, there are, in Garfinkel's sense, local structures of action that are basic to all organizations, while, at the same time, they are tailored to the contingencies and activities of a particular organization. For Weick, a good way to learn something about an organization is to look for what he calls "interlocking behaviors that are embedded in conditionally related processes."[99] But he goes further, suggesting that we are to equate "the common term 'organizational structure' with the notion of interlocked behaviors."[100]

From the perspective of many so-called macro-organizational specialists this can easily be read as those institutionalized patterns discussed above, thus shifting the focus back to the institutional level. But this is a mistake, and even for institutionalists the notion of "reproduction" is a problematic of organizational life.[101] The interlocked behaviors of Weick's interest are central to this problematic just because all the rules and routines must be enacted by people. Rules,

however institutionalized they may appear from the outside, are codi-
fied only to a limited extent and even those limits are indistinct and
subject to interpretation.[102] This leads to quite a ethnomethodological
problematic, namely that how, where, and when particular rules or
routines get enacted is a matter of their *appropriateness* or *adequacy*
for a concrete moment in time and for a specific configuration of
actors, materials, tasks, and exigencies.[103] Organizations are enacted
because they have to be. What looks – from outside – like behavior
controlled by rules and norms is actually a delicate and dynamic
series of interactionally located adjustments to a *continual* unfolding
and working out of "just what" is going on and being made to go on,
which is to say, the organizing of action.[104] At the center of this
momentary yet historically embedded system of action is the fundamental problem of order, to which we will shortly return.

Also critical to both Weick's characterization of organizing and
March's various approaches to decision-making is a quite central
concern with cognition and, in particular, how cognitions blend to
produce organizational actions and outcomes. These cognitions, in
turn, depend on information about an uncertain and often ambiguous
arena for those same actions and results. In a major new study,
Stinchcombe has tackled these problems by studying common themes
and important differences in the work of Simon and March, on the
one hand, and a number of more conventional luminaries of organizational analysis, in particular Arthur Chandler and Oliver Williamson,
as well as Charles Sabel and Joseph Schumpeter.[105] In what amounts
to a significant new theoretical statement, Stinchcombe focusses on
the social structures in organizations that gather information and make
decisions. The structural orientation is quite consistent with his own
earlier work, but there are also important innovations that directly
inform my own interest in how individuals, information, and institutions connect.

In the light of a broad review of studies of organizations, markets, and economic structures, Stinchcombe takes seriously the notion of uncertainty, as developed across a range of theories, and adds
his own distinct temporal dimension. Information, he says, is critical
to organizations not simply in some principled manner that helps
reduce uncertainty and thus guide decisions generally, but because
information is unevenly and progressively available *in distinct social
locations* at different points in time and space. The key to effective
action thus becomes one of being "where the news breaks, wherever it
breaks" in order to have the *earliest available information*.[106] Organizations thus develop (or "grow" as he rather oddly puts it) "information-
processing and decision-making structures" geared to spot trends

and to filter solid information from the environmental noise that surrounds them. These structures, in turn, operate differently in different parts of an organization, according to "what uncertainty has to be dealt with to get a given subtask done," leading Stinchcombe to conclude that "many different rationalities" are in operation.[107] These structuring properties, in their turn, mean that organizations are more rational than individuals because they have more coordinated ways of finding and reacting to news. I will defer further discussion of this most stimulating work until later in these chapters, because a central and essentially a priori question remains. What is implicit and largely ignored in Stinchcombe's argument is *who*, *how*, and *what* is producing these social structures he values so highly. *Where*, in other words, do social structures "come" from? How *is* order produced such that its multiple and interlocked quality comes to a collective effect? *What* is social order?

Organizations As They Happen

Clearly, the ability to produce order out of apparent chaos is one of the most striking features of all human societies. The "problem of order" that Thomas Hobbes rather gloomily contemplated in *Leviathan* in 1651 was one of resolving issues of personal passions and systems of power, and his studies were "occasioned by the disorders of [his] time."[108] Midway through the most tumultuous century of human history, Talcott Parsons took up the problem of social order in a new key. He proposed, as we have seen, that social actors internalize common institutional norms and values, together with their attendant roles. In Parsons's grand scheme, the discrete motivations, actions, and accounts of mere mortals are epiphenomenal to the social system, as well as being largely opaque to the participants themselves.[109] With Durkheim, Parsons argues that social institutions all function independently of individuals, while human experience is assumed to be "confused and unorganized."[110] Despite his proposed "voluntaristic frame of action," there are no people in Parsons's pictures of society and there is no order but that imposed by an abstract societal force.[111] Notice that the basic assumptions of organizational analysis are identical, namely that the structure of organizations is imposed on rather hapless social actors.

While for Parsons conceptual abstraction was an essential element of scientific methodology, Garfinkel returned to the concrete conditions of social action.[112] In essence, he turned the problem of order

upside down. His "central recommendation is that the activities
whereby members produce and manage settings of organized everyday affairs are identical with members' procedures for making
those settings 'accountable.'"[113] Far from being the reductionist loop
some have assumed, Garfinkel is simply returning to society's members
the capacity to be knowledgeable agents noticeably and accountably
in charge of their affairs, a theme that I have stressed throughout
these opening chapters. The recommendation is a kind of sophisticated
version of "show and tell" or, more aptly, "telling it like it is." For
Garfinkel, the "observable-and-reportable" ongoing activities and
descriptions of daily life are accounts that "obstinately depend" on
the detailed work of their production. That detailed and detailing
quality of social life, so far removed from Parsons's lofty abstractions,
is proposed by Garfinkel as the central enterprise of sociology. In a
theme taken up in considerable measure by the conversation analysts,
Garfinkel effectively commends sociologists to study the *how* of
social life rather than the *why*, by proposing that in the details of
social action the social universe will be revealed.

The very word "ethnomethodology" presents something of a challenge to many readers, and, of course, this subfield of sociology *has*
been challenging to much of the social sciences in its stance and in its
research agenda. Yet the essence of ethnomethodological theorizing
and empirical work can be distilled into a number of interlocking
principles that are as remarkably simple as they are conceptually
challenging.[114] At its core, ethnomethodology insists on what Pollner
has recently dubbed "radical reflexivity,"[115] namely a fundamental
critique of the possibility of wholly objective "knowledge" or "truth"
due to the inherently and irremediably intersubjective nature of human experience. At this late date in the twentieth century, this view
is actually quite compatible with a wide range of perspectives in philosophy and the social sciences as more and more analysts reach the
limit of insight provided by scientific reasoning and mathematical
modelling of social phenomena.

Nonetheless, Garfinkel was one of the very earliest American social
thinkers to, as it were, pull the rug out from under positivism. He did
so by focussing on what he likes to call the ordinary life of the streets
and on the concreteness of action and, ultimately, of society. Reacting
to the kind of formal analytic theorizing of Parsons, Garfinkel proposed to look at what people are "really and actually" doing *as they
do* what they do and to discover in those actions the "structures of
practical action." These are, quite simply, the *self*-organizing local
structures that arise *within* interaction (or society), through which

and with which people collaborate to make the world and their actions sensible. That they *can* make sense (and virtually always do) is the reflexive property referred to above. It is also the remarkable achievement of "immortal ordinary society."[116]

In organizational terms, Garfinkel's emphasis on the practical and local, as opposed to the abstract and general, has the potential to explode long-standing myths about both the *how* and *why* of organizing and, ultimately, of organizations. Not surprisingly, and on solidly Kuhnian grounds, resistance has been high. Not the least of this reluctance has been the rather surprising assumption that if Garfinkel and like minds are correct, then "science" and sociology's role within it may be impossible. This assumption appears rooted in the commitment of sociologists to a dual task of developing generalizations and explaining particular cases, Weber's methodolological problematic.[117] If, as Garfinkel suggests, order (and organization) are unavoidably *local* phenomena then they must also be *particular* and thus resistant to generalization. In one sense, this is indeed Garfinkel's most radical and disturbing claim. He is, most assuredly, warning against sociologists entertaining *the dreams of positive science*, that is of being able to model the recurring features of social order with the precepts of positivism. The urge to create a *cumulative* science, according to Garfinkel, has driven sociologists to, as it were, miss the trees for the forest, that is to bypass the essence of a collectivity for the sake of a general view of the whole. They are, moreover, missing the delicate yet invisible ecology that supports both the trees and the forest and are thus missing the most fundamental of structures, This has led social scientists generally to search for theoretically important and "big" empirical problems that hold the apparent promise of advances in scientific knowledge. In the process, the basic benchwork practices of the natural sciences – of painfully detailed observation, description, experimentation, and repetition – have been ignored as social scientists rush toward the big prize: the Laws of Social Order.

Parsons, as the emblematic figure in American sociology, had set the tone of this enterprise for generations of sociologists. In *The Structure of Social Action* (1937), the prize was announced: by using the precepts of scientific rationality, sociologists could move from the encumbering details of daily life to a level of analytic theorizing and propositional abstraction whereby formal representations replaced what Garfinkel calls the "scenic features" of particular cases. Yet the current state of the social sciences would suggest that the escape has been neither successful nor felicitous. Within the "structure" of social action are finely, sequentially organized *structures* of action. Those structures are *both* utterly local and quite general. They are, moreover, *completely* within the command of competent members of society whose momentary and occasionally momentous competence depends on their "commonsense knowledge of social structures."[118] This knowledge of social structures is, however, by no means abstract and is, instead, constantly and unremittingly being discovered and detailed *in the course of action* that people take together. Thus Garfinkel's problematic is Weber's (and Mannheim's and Simmel's and so on), namely that the interpretive procedures social actors use to understand and act on the actions of others are *identical* with those actions.[119] Put more simply, actions and the interpretations of their meanings are *inseparable* and occur simultaneously *in the course of their production.*

For Garfinkel, and for all ethnomethodologists and conversation analysts, social order is organized *from within* and social structure is thus endogenous to action. This does not intend, however, to suggest that there *is* no larger social order of which some local action is a constitutive part. The central position of ethnomethodology is to insist that *how*, *where*, with *whom*, and even *why* particular aspects of social structure, biographical elements, or historical conditions are *made relevant* in concrete situations is a matter of members' methods. These "members' methods" are the subject-matter of ethno-method-ology, hence the name.[120] In the course of their actions together, social actors give to their actions and experiences a factual quality, thus treating the social world as a "determinate and independent object."[121] To conclude that this intersubjectively achieved facticity is Durkheimian[122] would completely miss the point of ethnomethodology and its twinned principles of reflexivity and indexicality. Working in concert, the social world created from within is reflexively organized through the intimate immediacy of indexical particulars. What this means is – quite simply – that the temporally unfolding details of social life both take and give meaning through their reflexive immersion in the whole setting and through their particular placement in a stream of experience unfolding at quite a specific time and place. Ethnomethodologists recommend for serious study what Garfinkel calls "fact production" in flight.[123]

Ethnomethodology and Organizations

To study organizational life "in flight" or "as it happens" has been a feature of ethnomethodological studies from the outset. From Egon

Bittner's much cited article[124] to many of the most recent studies of scientific work by Garfinkel and colleagues,[125] a variety of organizational settings have been a common location of ethnomethodological studies. Nonetheless, as noted above, the focus is *always* on the nature of organizing and on the temporal and sequential details of organizatio*n*, rather than on organization*s* as either theoretical or empirical objects.

Bittner's early conceptualization can serve to link my general discussion of ethnomethodological principles to the specifics of relevant organizational research. In his critique of Weber, Bittner highlights "a certain theoretical short circuit"[126] that has been reproduced by generations of organizational researchers; its limitations underline a key aspect of ethnomethodological thinking that will surface frequently in my own discussions of organization and organizational rationality. The short circuit is a common enough one. By isolating and making inventories of a set of elements that comprise a theory of bureaucracy, Weber and others who followed[127] ignored the fact that his theory takes for granted a far larger set of commonsense presuppositions or background information on which that theory rests. That is to say that he "failed to grasp that the meaning and warrant of the inventory of the properties of bureaucracy are inextricably embedded in what Alfred Schutz (1962) called the 'attitude of everyday life' and in socially sanctioned commonsense typifications."[128] This sort of theoretical short circuit results, routinely one may add, in the confusion of topic and resource discussed above, namely that in failing to explicate the commonsense meanings underlying a theory, those meanings become an unanalyzed resource for understanding the topics of research guided by the theory. Alternatively, a researcher can ignore the organizational members' perspective on their work world completely in favor of the idealized theoretical view of it. Either way, rather obviously, the research is confounded and theoretical insight is likely to be limited at best.

Ethnomethodological studies of organization, as will be readily apparent by now, treat members' competence in and local knowledge and understanding of a setting as a central topic of investigation, rather than as a resource for improving some social science view of that setting. This essential focus has been recommended by a veritable cavalcade of researchers.[129] Despite its considerable relevance to *all* social science research, the distinction remains, however, part of the taken-for-granted, seen-but-unnoticed grain of virtually all conventional research. With a dependence on outcome variables that are somehow presumed to be free from interpretation and local features of meaning, even sophisticated and sensitive quantitative research simply ignores problems of language and the language-mediated research instruments whose "data" is then assumed to be "objective."[130]

Some organizational specialists picked up these themes, most notably, of course, Karl Weick, and they figure as well in more recent explorations of language and meaning and the kinds of facticity highlighted by phenomenological approaches to the social world. Through the 1960s and 1970s, a variety of ethnomethodological studies of organizational and work settings were also conducted, starting even earlier with Garfinkel's own study of jury deliberations. The jury study, originally conducted in the 1950s, builds on yet earlier work by Felix Kaufman.[131] In the activities of jurors, Garfinkel proposes that "facts" and a "corpus of knowledge" are produced by sorting alternative claims by defendants, plaintiffs, witnesses, and so on, through the filter of commonsense models of action. What is meaningfully consistent is then treated as what "actually occurred," and the sorting through of claims "produces a set of accepted points of fact and accepted schemes" for constructing that "corpus of knowledge" which is then treated by the jurors as "the case."[132] Jurors use this retrospective-prospective mode of analysis to *reflexively* account for their own justifications of their decisions by fitting their process of decision-making to the outcome they have jointly produced.

In other words, "the outcome comes before the decision,"[133] and the course of the decision is then retrospectively routinized so as to *prospectively* shape the way the jury is then seen as an *adequate* and competent body of decision-makers. The reader will have noted the haunting familiarity of this local logic, since this kind of analysis is closely akin to the garbage-can model of March and his colleagues described above. We will explore these converging understandings of decision making in later chapters (especially chapters 6–8 below).

The emphasis of social actors' dependence on a retrospective-prospective method of reasoning should not be confused with "posterior" or "retrospective" rationality however. As I shall take up in some detail in the concluding sections of this study, organizational rationality is a local matter. The understandings and accounts of reasoned and reasonable activities develop for social agents over the course of action, not just as *ex post facto* rationalizations. This view of rationality is central to all ethnomethodological studies and highlights the way in which people are constantly and reflexively tying past to future through present orientations. Viewed as internal to action, both meaning and structure are constantly being updated so that *any situation* can "be retrospectively reread to find out in the light of present practical circumstances what [it] 'really' consisted of 'in the first place' and 'all along.' "[134]

In Sudnow's study of the social organization of dying, for instance, even the moment of death "occurs" in a social order and is both retrospectively and prospectively – as "dying" and later "death" – made to fit organizationally relevant categories.[135] Such apparently morbid topics have been of special interest to ethnomethodologists just because they are later treated as quite unremarkable and unequivocal "social facts" by the social science community. Both Garfinkel and Sacks studied suicide prevention centers, and Atkinson's later study of coroners' reports on sudden deaths enriched insights into the topic considerably by stressing the essential social link between categorization and demographic statistics.[136]

Even the written records maintained by organizations (and so often treated unambiguously by social researchers) contain and perpetuate the retrospective-prospective orientations of member of those organizations, imbuing the "official" record with the fine and fragmentary accounts of the immediate everyday world.[137] In his study of record-keeping in a public welfare agency, for example, Zimmerman found that the taken-for-granted features and use of documents operate such that "the record" does not "stand alone" but is invoked through just the sort of organizationally relevant procedures that meet the agency's moment-to-moment agenda. One bureaucracy's needs, moreover, of another's records are similarly identified and resolved not by some overarching set of policies or rules but by the "practical circumstances" of their use *together with* or reflexively tied to "the operational meaning and intent of organizational rules and procedures" as they unfold in the tasks and troubles of the work activity itself.[138]

More recent work on bureaucratic reports by Feldman stresses the distinct loose-coupling between actual decisions and the reports that record them, highlighting the need for a good deal of social science skepticism, on the one hand, and the merits of detailed descriptive studies of organizations, on the other.[139] A primary point in Zimmerman's analysis, and one that recurs in later ethnomethodological studies of organizational record keeping,[140] is that "not any piece of paper with any set of entries" will do since, no matter how official or accurate a record may appear, its occasioned use in particular circumstances may well be problematic.

The problematic quality of the everyday world is central to ethnomethodology. It is often seen to be at odds with the official view of organizational life, hence, as noted, the well-worn distinction between formal and informal rules and the general sense that organizational actors are somehow deviant and uncooperative. Ethnomethodological studies of organizations, even some of the best, have inadvertently contributed to the formal/informal distinction by emphasizing the subtle operation of "occasioned" activities in a variety of settings.[141] Moreover, their insistence on temporal and sequential enactment of social order has led some writers to assume that what is being proposed are the "emergent properties" of interaction, which is incorrect. The notion of emergent properties, quite a favorite for those who would account for process while studying structure, derives from that familiar Durkheimian idea of social properties that "lie outside the consciousness of individuals as such."[142] These properties are taken to be invisible and thus, in another familiar theme, to work essentially behind the backs of actors, who are then seen as simply reproducing an existing *and* emergent social structure.

In their studies of organizational settings, ethnomethodologists have instead been insistent upon the necessary intelligibility of actions that constitute the organization as a real and practical place. Throughout, ethnomethodological research is focussed, as indicated earlier, on the ways in which coparticipants recognize and accomplish their activities as a *self-organizing* system of relevancies, whether in the pristine and prestigious environments of scientists' laboratories[143] or in professional settings such as educational systems,[144] classrooms,[145] or courtrooms[146] or the half-worlds of skid-row[147] or a halfway house for narcotics offenders.[148] The work of Garfinkel himself and his recent students has tended to focus, as indicated earlier, on the *in situ* practices of workbench scientists. Researchers have also examined a variety of work settings ranging from a large bakery to the nuanced work of air traffic controllers at a major airport.[149]

Central to all these studies is the role of language and meaning, and, more specifically, *language and accountability*. In chapter 3, I shall expand more fully on the critical connection between language-in-action, meaning and accountability, focussing on ethnomethodological studies of language, conversation analysis, and the structures of practical organizational actions accomplished through everyday talk.

Organizations in Action

Much of the material to be presented in these chapters reflects, which is to say genuinely "mirrors," findings in Mintzberg's 1973 study of managers at work. In a rare organizational project, Mintzberg followed five chief executives as they criss-crossed their business day, took phone calls, attended scheduled meetings, scanned mail, received visitors, cruised corridors, placed more phone calls, and attended innumerable unscheduled meetings. His primary conclusions were that managerial work is highly fragmented, varied and brief, with remarkable emphasis on verbal interaction, the need for "instant communication," and "hot" information, on which to base still more verbal contacts and "live action."[150] Managerial work is, moreover, remarkably similar across types of organizations and industries. As with other comparable studies that report between 57 percent and 89 percent of time spent in verbal interaction, Mintzberg reports that verbal contacts, face-to-face and on the phone, accounted for 75 percent of his managers' time and 67 percent of their activities.[151]

In most organizations, most of the time, people mix work tasks with sociable interaction and they do so largely through talk. Since the organizing and structuring of organizations is also a primarily talk-based process, talk and task tend to intertwine in finely tuned ways. The casual talk that fills the air at the beginning of a meeting, or in a colleague's doorway, or around the high-tech work stations of the modern office deftly weaves sociable personal news and stories with organizational maxims, practical advice, direct queries about work in progress, tales of distant divisions, gossip about new accounting procedures, rumors of reorganization, and outright myths about organizational battles of old. In the process, talk at work is merged with talk *as* work.[152] The meetings, telephone calls, and "quick" consults that make up the organizational day are all talk and (mostly) work. Moreover, they build the relationships, alliances, and coalitions that blend individual into collective, discrete actions into collective efforts, people into collectivities. The "mystery" of individual *versus* collective is at least partly solved if we attend carefully to the ways in which various membership collectivities meet, merge and occasionally conflict at the level of talk. The notion of "collectivities" of individuals is, for both Parsons and Garfinkel, one of *membership* collectivities. How these work, as practical everyday matters, tells a great deal about how organizations are organized. For example, much of the boundary maintenance, spanning and buffering that preoccupies organizational theorists turns out to be "business as usual" for organizational actors, who daily confront these problems as practical matters and *together* must resolve them as such. The "togetherness" of organizational life is largely missed in the current literature which is so dominated by "economic man" and the rather unsociological assumptions of methodological individualism. As we explore "talk as work/work as talk," we will see that it is the concerted and coordinated actions of individuals that *dominate* organizations, rather than the self-interested, self-optimizing objects proposed by rational choice theory (and related versions thereof). People, as we shall see, *talk* their way to solutions, *talk* themselves into working agreements, *talk* their coalitions into existence, *talk* their organizational agendas, and, occasionally, talk *through* or *past* each other. Moreover, through their talk they not only reproduce the institutionalized arrangements of the organization and its environment, but significantly create and recreate fine distinctions that actually make the organization come alive.

3

Talk as Social Action

As far back as the Greeks and, no doubt, before, both the nature of language and the organization of experience into meaningful units has intrigued social thinkers. Language and the ability for abstract thought is fundamental to our humanness; each is intertwined with our essential need for social contact, a sociability on which our survival, development, existence, achievement, and ultimate contentment all depend. Our need for near-constant, proximate interaction with others engages us, from our earliest moments, in an urgent and reciprocal exchange with our human environment. The exchange quickly becomes a turn-taking rhythm with the world around us. Tiny infants suckle in a steady give-and-take rhythm with their mothers and their lip movements are synchronized with adult speech patterns around them. Within a month of birth, the babble of babies begins to select out the phonetic sounds of the local linguistic environment from the physiologically available range at birth. Tiny fingers reach out and grab bigger fingers in a game of basic solidarity; the grip is developmental, the rhythm social. Our social self emerges in an elaborate dance with the world, tentative and exploratory, to be sure, but with a growing rhythmic sense of belonging.

At the heart of these activities is turn-taking and the sequenced structuring of action. A turn-by-turn encounter with the world around us provides just the sort of cortical stimulation and essential feedback revered by behaviorists, but it involves something just as critical to being human. That is the discovery of our temporal and spatial location in a pre-existing social world. Turn-taking provides a central mechanism for pacing and placing each human actor in the ongoing stream of human events we call "society." Through sequential engagement of ourselves with other selves, we enter into the swift-flowing river of social life, and that engagement seduces us into the rhythms and routines of others, at first significant, in G. H. Mead's sense,[1] later more generalized. As we learn the routines of turn-taking, we take on that reciprocal moral code that guides human action, for it too is built into the rhythms of sociability. By taking turns, we find both our rights and our obligations, not simply as a normative and thereby external and imposed order, but built into the synchrony we ourselves create with others.

Without getting into any elaborate philosophical discussion or even Chomskian debate over the origins of language, we can observe that out of the fluid currents of daily intercourse, language and meaning emerge as collaborative and interactional creations. In a Meadian sense, meaning and the self are realized as thought becomes action through language, which is to say as language-in-action in *talk*. Language, in a genuinely *social* as opposed to linguistic sense, is an activity that engages human beings in the depths of their existence – as thinking, feeling, acting, *talking* social animals. When small children begin to talk, their intriguing one-word and two-word grammars are produced in a rhythmic exchange with caregivers. As they talk, the logic of their emerging linguistic and social competence is achieved across turns at talk,[2] as child and adult enact the communicative constitution of life.

Language, Agency, and Structure

Although a review of linguistics is hardly germane here, several central notions of language studies have direct bearing on how one might characterize the articulation of language and social action, and, indeed, on the nature of structure. Modern linguistics has in some measure been shaped by the work of the Swiss scholar Ferdinand de Saussure, developed in a posthumous publication of 1916 entitled *Course in General Linguistics*. Having a lifelong interest in the comparative study of Indo-European phonetic patterns, Saussure moved away from traditional philological concerns to develop the position that was to become the basis of European structural linguistics and, through Lévi-Strauss and others, much of structural anthropology for the majority of this century.

At the core of Saussure's work is the proposal to distinguish between *langue*, language as a general system, and *parole*, the spoken language produced by individual speakers. Not unlike Durkheim, Saussure suggested that whereas *parole* is located in the discrete speech acitivities of individuals, *langue* exists fully "only within a collectivity."[3] Language, as a system of interrelated parts, is thus a "social fact," as in the conventional reading of Durkheim, namely external, constraining, and so on. Interestingly, Saussure dismissed *parole* as largely uninteresting and concentrated on *langue*, developing the well-known system of signs that has so influenced structuralist thinking over the course of this century. Yet, as we shall see shortly, the possibility of audio tape-recordings of spoken language in the early 1960s and the emergence of conversation analysis and other sociolinguistic approaches to speech have revealed that talk, or *parole*, has its own remarkable structure. This structure does not work independently of human agency, yet it has much of the patterned and predictive properties of a grammar and the orderly "syntagmatic" qualities which Saussure ascribed to *langue*, namely that the ordered unfolding of the components are consequential to each other in a local yet generally systemic manner.

Both Saussure and Chomsky, however, emphasized structure at the expense of interpretation. This led linguists away from natural conversation toward abstract analysis of languages essentially divorced from their spoken usage. As recently as the 1960s, when Chomsky was urging highly formal models of language,[4] students of speech were inclined to treat ordinary discourse rather pathologically, as subject to faults, disfluencies, and a variety of departures from ideal exchange.[5] The notion of *systems* of signs, on the other hand, led generations of anthropologists and, later, semioticians to construct elaborate binary codes of meaning.

In practice, signs, symbols, and language all involve interpretive procedures through which agents ascribe meaning to them, collaboratively and interactionally.[6] What is central to *all* signs and the signalling process so casually invoked by Wall Street and the White House is that they are *not* stable or unambiguous. More complexly, signs "stand between" the object and the interpreter so that the object is known only "through the sign" *and not by any other means*.[7] Any individual makes sense of the world, then, through "signed" objects.[8] The "signing" process is achieved through language, itself so transparent as to be invisible and thus taken for granted.

Put far less abstractly, a junior executive in a firm takes her sense of corporate and work identity from the *signs* and *signals* put out by other organizational members; those signs "stand for" the organizational culture and are brought to life through language and in interaction. Even the material conditions of the firm and the industry of which it is part are "objectively" only available through language and other symbols used to interpret them. This is another way of considering the notion of indexical expressions, namely the essential embeddedness of meaning which is characteristic of all social activities. Far from being abstract and esoteric, it is fundamental to organizational life, language, and culture. To describe institutional relations, for example, as "symbolic" or an institutional process as "socially constructed" is analytically imprecise.

Nor are signs, signals and interpretations such as those just described a closed system, although some of the recent work of poststructuralists certainly falls easily into a kind of epistemological relativism.[9] When everyday actors use language, and draw on the signs and symbols of their environment to make sense of their actions, they do so *together*, taking account of each other's sense-making, however imperfectly. In the process, they constitute those meanings as active accounts of their shared biographies and commitments to each other. Signs are, as we shall see, profoundly *sequential* objects in a rapidly changing social milieu. Language and abstract symbols come alive in concert and in sequence, no longer the systems of discourse of poststructuralist parlance, but constituent elements of social order, an order, as I have indicated earlier, which is discovered and thereby structured *from within*. The structuring is done through talk, and through its recursive yet creative enactment as everyday human exchange.[10]

I have laid out these core linguistic considerations for a simple, if often ignored, reason. If we are to understand organizations and thereby, as suggested earlier, attempt a fuller understanding of modernity, we need to directly understand what organizations "do." But organizations do not *act* or *do* anything, people do, If we accept, at least as a working assumption, that organizations *are* the people who comprise them, then what we need is a far finer grasp of human action. Human activity is exclusively, and one may say irreducibly available through language. It may be the language of the social actors or even of the researcher; either way, the interpretations of the former shape the latter utterly. But this need not be either a methodological bind or any sort of linguistic black hole. Language is no more overpowering than "structure." It operates in a recursive yet quite clearly sequential manner and can be observed with considerable effect just because it is so readily manifest in behavior. If we look at language in use and that phenomenon over time, what starts as an apparently *linguistic* interest is rapidly transformed into a *sociological* analysis. Looking at language-in-action, we get a direct view of human agency.

Social actors categorize and segment their actions and understandings in important ways. Language thus acts as a filter through which the immensity of the world is screened, selected, and organized. People need categorization devices or typifications to make sense of the stream of life carrying them forward. Above all, they need "*membership* categorization devices"[11] – highly selective and interactionally variable mechanisms for "doing" *social* relations. Gender, age, race, occupation, education, religion, political affiliation, and so forth are all *members'* resources for achieving quite concrete social activities. It is members' categories and their invocation of those categories on social occasions that makes, for example, racial intolerance such a devastating force in all human societies. In organizations, the very "boundaries" that define them are permeable just because members' categorization of who is "in" and who is "out" is variable. A great deal of human energy goes into creating and *re*creating invisible bonds and boundaries. They are a fundamental locus of social change and these connections, commitments and constraints are located in the meanings social actors give to the world, a world that is simultaneously "there" yet constantly constituted through *new* human actions.

An essential part of this process is the way in which language provides a way of making sense of the past and planning for the future. Organizational actors, for example, are constantly looking back at past activities in a highly selective way and framing their current action, not to match or repeat past practice, but to *look* consistent. They use the same filtering process to look across the organizational terrain and adjust what they are doing to *look* like it is part of company policy. Routine questions are: "how did we do that last year?" or "what does New York say about that?" or "what are the finance boys going to make of this?" This is not so much mimetic behavior, in any strictly imitative sense, as a thoroughly reasonable and reasoned way of accounting for today's goals and agendas in terms of what will "look good" retrospectively.

Language-in-action as everyday talk thus provides the primary medium through which the past is incorporated into present action and each are projected into an evolving, never-to-be-arrived-at future. Through language, actors selectively attend to the past, in particular to the *relevant* aspects of the past that will make sense of the present, and to that version (account) of the present that will look credible in the future. This is, as I indicated in the last chapter, what ethnomethodologists call the retrospective-prospective nature of accounts and it is at the very heart of the organization of organiza-tions.[12] The present, too, is an intense, phenomenal experience un-folding all around, and actors selectively catch up relevant aspects of it, like threads to weave into their actions.

As we shall see, organizational actors are *acutely* aware of this as they enact their organization and its environment, both immediate and distant in time and space, and they reflect this awareness in their interactions. An important feature of talk is what Garfinkel terms its "inhabiting presence,"[13] which is to say the ways in which, through talk, we are constantly accountable for our actions but also hold others "unremittingly" so, producing from "within" the interaction its situated and also consequential character. The insistent features of all interaction demonstrate "how, over the temporal course of their actual engagements, and 'knowing' society only from within, members produce stable, accountable practical activities, i.e. social structures of everyday activities."[14] This "from within" feature of social order is, as I have tried to emphasize, important to an understanding of how structuration – or structure-in-action – occurs.

Language-in-Action

Lest the language of *this* discussion has become far too abstract, let us now look at a concrete example. The data and organizations in this study are discussed briefly below, together with details of the transcrip-tion techniques of conversation analysis (see also the appendix). The following example is an informal interdepartmental meeting between three hospital administrators who are, as an ongoing feature of their work, engaged in reducing costs in a large teaching hospital in the face of very real changes in their organizational environment. They are confronted with the introduction by the US federal government and many medical insurance companies of highly restrictive prepay-ment systems designed to "cap" potential (and rising) hospital costs.

I want to narrow attention here simply to the categorization de-vices in use by these experienced organizational actors, and, all too superficially, to the ways these conversational techniques serve to position their own negotiations within a quite complex matrix of organizational agendas and environments of action. In our example, Hal is the Chief of Physicians, Linda is a researcher/administrator working for him, and Paul is from the hospital finance department. Linda is explaining, primarily to Paul, a recent series of meetings conducted with medical staff and physicians on various wards of the hospital, designed to alert them to potential cost-reduction opportunities in their own units and to ways in which they could meet the larger hospital's goal while not reducing medical effectiveness:[15]

3.1 Hospital-2 (Ortho)
Simplified transcript

```
 1  Linda:   The- the point is that- that was the
 2           only area we talked about,
 3  Paul:    (Yeahm)
 4  Linda:   So far about whether or not (0.2)
 5           through what (.) we've
 6           accomplished which in this case?
 7           is- was getting the- (0.2) hearing what the
 8           physicians were willing? (.) and able- to
 9           give this up
10  Paul:    (Mm⌈hum)⌉
11  Linda:      ⌊This-⌋ this type of practise up if in
12           fact they were offered some organizational
13           help in getting these ⌈tests ⌉ do: ne.
14  Paul:                          ⌊Yeah⌋      And that
15           kinda astonishes me (it really does)
16                        (0.6)
17  Hal:     ⌈⌈What-
18  Linda:   ⌊⌊Well- ⌈shall we jus'⌉
19  Paul:          ⌊well, I mean⌋it's services that-
20                        (1.0)
21  Hal:     (right)
22  Paul:    I- we're talking r- U.H.H. (.) faculty
23  Hal:     Huh-huhn
24  Paul:             phys⌈i c i ans⌉
25  Linda:              ⌊(Hm-hmm)⌋
26  Paul:                           who are willing to
27           give up U.H.H. services? Give away business?
28                        (0.9)
29  Hal:     (Yehm) Oh ⌈t h e y don'- but I-⌉
30  Paul:             ⌊Yeah, for the hospi⌋tal
31           you're right. The hospital is basically
32           neutral.⌈Or re- or benefits for Medicare    ⌉
33  Hal:            ⌊Yeah, but you don't underSTAND⌋   ·
34           that THESE GUYS don't see any of that revenue
35                        (0.2)
36           that they understand
37                        (1.0)
```

38		see they- they only see the *reve* ⌈nue ⌉
39	**Paul:**	⌊Heh⌋
40		heh-heh-hun
41	**Hal:**	No, no, no, *you* understand
42		that it's- they don'- they only *see* it as
43		revenue, if it comes back to 'em that way.
44		But this relationship is with the U.H.H.
45	**Paul:**	(Right)
46	**Hal:**	*Not* with the ortho*ped*ic division
47		(0.7)
48		so that percentage is *so* far away from
49		their hands
50		(1.2)
51		arright?
52		(0.3)
53	**Paul:**	(Hm-hmm)
54	**Hal:**	that they don't say – Oh we're not gonna do
55		that, that's money in our *pockets*, I mean-
56		*you*'re assuming that ⌈they have uh⌉ *private*
57	**Paul:**	⌊*Oh*. I s e e.⌋
58	**Hal:**	physician mentality that they *see* the money,
59		they ⌈don't *SEE*⌉ the money!
60	**Paul:**	⌊Well th- ⌋ ((Khn-khn))
61		Yeah, but you're talking to uh- uh- you-
62		okay. The- the UHH physicians you're
63		*ta*lking to? then,
64	**Hal:**	Yeah.
65		(0.2)
64	**Paul:**	Are- uh are not the ones who would get
65		the pre-op- the pre-admission (0.2) money
66		any ⌈w a y, that's ⌉ whatcher
67	**Hal:**	⌊THAT'S RIGHT-⌋
68	**Paul:**	saying.
69	**Hal:**	*Tha*t's right.
70	**Paul:**	(right)
71	**Hal:**	*Now*, y'see- if *we* would say- if we'd go to
72		Meyerson and say what do you think about the
73		*i*dea of us ⌈sending these⌉
74	**Paul:**	⌊Heh-heh-heh⌋
75	**Hal:**	they'd say what the hell are you talking
76		about? That's our *money*!
77	**Paul:**	Yeah.
78	**Hal:**	We're not *ta*lking to them. We're not
79		talking to Radiology, we're talking to
80		Orthopedics, okay?
90		(0.7)

91	**Paul:**	⎡⎡Hah- huh- huh⎤
92	**Hal:**	⎣⎣And they don'⎦ And they don't *think* as a
93		(0.8)
94		*m*ega-organization that has lost *m*oney to
95		them as a *group*. They think of their
96		practice (0.4) in maintaining whatever
97		incentives . . .

Now, as a first observation, note the *inhabiting character* of this talk, that is to say that they "live" inside this strip of talk and are accountable – all the time – for what they say.[16] Reading slowly through, we can see the extraordinarily quick and immediate ways in which members demand "good reasons" from each other.[17] Talk creates and demands constant attention and continuous updating; there is no time out. Notice how each speaker tracks the other, correcting, agreeing, adjusting, and collaborating at each stage. Although this is a "routine" meeting, one of a series – as most meetings and virtually all interactions are – it would be hard to characterize the *talk* as "routinized" or "ritual." Nor can one imagine any ethnographic *description*, let alone some general discussion of organizational "culture," that could capture the detailed unravelling of this set of organizational issues, yet the issues are, as noted above, utterly critical to the survival of this hospital within the changing environment of US and world medical organizations. This is not "just" talk; it is the organization in action.

For now, I shall concentrate attention on the *organizational* categorization devices these participants are using collaboratively to track their understandings of the problem under discussion. To assist the reader's assessment of this small slice of interaction, let me also offer some further observations about this particular organization, gleaned from other parts of the same meeting. As indicated, Linda has been describing an earlier meeting with the physicians and nursing staff of the orthopedics ward and, in particular, certain surgical and pre-operative areas of potential cost-cutting in what has become a routine surgical procedure, namely the replacement of a hip joint, commonly and rather engagingly called a "total hip." We join the discussion as she explains that, so far, they have been concentrating on trying to persuade the surgeons to have routine pre-operative tests and X-rays done with patients *before* they enter, as it were, the organizational boundary of the hospital; this would cut out a set of costs that are otherwise incurred as soon as a potential hip replacement patient is admitted. These are the "tests" she is referring to at line 13 above, and the "organizational help" to be offered is that the hospital would, in future, instruct patients to have these tests done by their own physician, thus sliding the costs (and insurance liability) back to another organization.

The primary membership category in use here, and a rather obviously powerful one, is "the physicians," who, as it turns out later, are also "faculty" (lines 22–6) at this teaching hospital, as opposed to medical practitioners with what Hal (lines 55 and 58) characterizes as a "*private* physician mentality." Physicians *in* a teaching hospital are characterized as thinking differently from their colleagues in private practice, *and* this "thinking" has considerable organizational relevance. Paul, as an accountant, is surprised (lines 14–15); his framework is different, as he is oriented to the finances of the hospital as a whole, seeing it as "neutral" (line 32) from an accounting point of view as to where the tests are done (since, as they discuss later, there is revenue but little profit, given Medicare rates and the fact that most people having hip replacement surgery are over 65 years of age).

More importantly for our focus here, Paul sees the faculty as a *group*, a group of "co-members," namely as the faculty physicians that make up UHH services (University of Hartford Hospital).[18] The membership categorization device (MCD) "physician" thus is enlarged by Paul to make his own "surprise" into one that comments on a kind of accountant's "rational man" model.[19] But these are, in practical terms, Hal's team of physicians and he undercuts Paul's assumptions by providing a finer filter through which to understand "these guys" (line 34) as being none too sophisticated in fiscal matters. These are physicians in the orthopedics department who don't see revenue in another department (radiology) as revenue to them and so are willing to have the tests done outside the hospital, a point which is emphasized by Hal near the end of our extract (lines 78–80). What Paul, as a financial person, sees as funny (lines 39–40), Hal knows to be serious and consequential to any cost-cutting efforts on the hospital wards. He attempts to elaborate by explaining that the orthopedic physicians only *see* revenue "if it comes back to 'em that way" (line 43), although, from an overall hospital perspective, the accounting "relationship is with the UHH" (line 44) and not with the orthopedic division (line 46). These doctors do not, Hal goes on to try to explain, see revenue to Radiology as revenue to them, as a group of private physicians might, operating as a corporate unit (lines 48–59).

This example highlights the fine degree to which language-in-action makes available the *organizing* of organizations. These three administrators have to *work* to achieve conversational and organizational alignment on a set of critical issues; the alignment is managed *first* conversationally and *thereby* organizationally (and not the reverse). By segmenting both their conversation and their organization into meaningful units, organizational actors not only make sense to each other locally, they give to the world its practical structures of action.[20] That is to say, they give it its *structured* and thereby identifiable quality. When, in our example, Paul finally gets the point (lines 67–9), Hal can move on.

But he first provides a brief contrastive tale. The "story" he proposes is highly condensed (lines 71–6) and is even halted as soon as Paul laughs (line 74), as its elements are so familiar to these three meeting participants. Hal says that if he were to go to "Meyerson" (who is the head of Radiology) and offer to cut costs by having X-rays done outside the hospital, Meyerson and his doctors would protest, saying something like: "What the hell are you talking about? That's our *mon*ey!" (lines 75–6). But Hal goes on to stress this distinction in subunit boundaries: "We're not talking to them. We're not talking to Radiology, we're talking to Orthopedics, okay?" (lines 78–80). Notice that, at this point in the discussion, he wants no more ambiguity as to *who* the relevant co-membership is: "them" is spelled out quite explicitly, and he goes on to explain their inability to think of themselves as a "mega-oganization." This latter aspect of the ways organizational actors categorize the work environment in which they must make their decisions and assess their gains and losses is a core aspect of bounded rationality, to which we will return in the later sections of this study.

For now, it will be clear, or so I hope, that the ways organizational actors categorize and account for the world is not some woolly process of social construction, but a finely ordered and consequential alignment of differing perspectives, goals, and agendas. It will be seen, too, that the "signed" quality of the social world, discussed above, is deeply implicated in the constitution of that world. That is to say, *how* actors describe the organization is also how they orient to it; the two are, practically speaking, identical. This is admittedly a rather ethnomethodological way of defining organizations, but it is very much the position I wish to establish as we pursue these issues with conversational materials. It isn't "new," because March and Simon said it all long ago, but it is newly available to empirical analysis through the techniques of conversation analysis.

Examined under the social microscope I have just used, human intercourse turns out to be a finely tuned medium of meaning, tightly ordered yet flexibly organized. The central organizing feature in this verbal exchange is a quite specific and specifiable system of turn-taking, as fundamental as those early rhythmic exchanges of babies, described above, and just as universal. As the concept of conversational turn-taking, and the work of conversation analysts that developed it, is central to all that follows, it will be useful to look at this discovery in some detail.

Conversation Analysis

Conversation analysis began as and remains a centrally sociological enterprise. Harvey Sacks's initial and insightful idea was quite simple. He speculated that if sociologists were to look systematically at social activities that are terribly mundane, ordinary and local, instead of those "big issues" and "massive institutions" usually studied, they might discover extraordinarily detailed order.[21] As a student of Goffman and a young colleague of Garfinkel, he was inclined toward the domain of interaction and willing to suspend conventional sociological assumptions about the locus of social order. In his earliest writings, he proposed bracketing typical sociological (and social scientific, more generally) assumptions that large-scale, massive institutions are "the apparatus by which order is generated," and instead recommended giving serious credence to the possibility "that we may alternatively take it that there is order at all points" in the organization of society. He went on to propose something which, if treated seriously within sociology, could have extraordinary payoff, namely that rather than treat all this order as odd or as a mere resource for social research, we might begin to benefit from the fact that "given the possibility that there is overwhelming order, it would be extremely hard *not* to find it, no matter how or where we looked."[22]

Conversation analysis was thus born as an objective, empirical line of enquiry. Sacks was looking for a way of creating an observational science out of sociology, a way of directly observing the social world so as to provide a "natural history" of human activity. In much the same way as nineteenth-century natural scientists observed, noted, collected samples, categorized, and created taxonomies of phenomena in nature, he proposed that the same might be done with social phenomena, with the same insight, precision, and unmotivated delight in the orderliness of things in the world. The key, he felt, was to be able to systematically observe actual details of actual events, and to handle them formally with just the precision of description and detachment of observation of natural history.[23]

So, following our earlier discussion, both ethnomethodology and conversation analysis turn the traditional "problem of order" upside down. The question is not one of how people respond to normative constraints, but rather how it is that order is produced as a situated social matter, as activities organized in quite specific time and space. To understand the profound orderliness of social life requires not aggregation and abstraction but attention to the finegrained details of moment-to-moment existence, and to their temporal, spatial and profoundly sequential organization.

Sacks and his colleagues turned to audio (and later video) recordings of interactional activities. The idea was that tape-recorded conversations constituted, if not all, at least a "reasonable record" of what happened during a particular strip of social life. "Other things," as Sacks notes, "to be sure, happened, but at least what was on the tape happened," and it could be studied again and again.[24] It had the further advantage that anyone could listen to the tape or view the video and agree or disagree; in other words, a kind of grounded replicability is built into the raw data of conversation analysis. Talk can, moreover, be studied in a very finegrained manner and, in so doing, it is possible to get a quite direct grasp of how this most pervasive of social activities is organized.

The order that is produced is, in a very central sort of way, a member's order rather than an analyst's construct. In his earliest work,[25] using telephone calls to a suicide helpline, Sacks provides an innovative analysis of how and in what methodical detail members of society describe and connect each other. These are what we have been examining in the previous section of this chapter, namely membership categorization devices. Sacks evolved this grounded concept through analyzing the exhaustive, economical and methodic reasoning through which suicidal actors conclude that they have "no one to turn to." In their search for help, potential suicides analyze their situation and alternatives and converge on the conclusion that no one, neither family, spouse, room mate, pastor, nor friend, can help. Their reasoning is revealed in their responses to helpline personnel's "reasonable" questions and suggestions.

This early work led Sacks to focus on the organization of such simple conversational objects as questions and answers, offers and rejections, and other adjacently positioned talk. The "adjacent" pairing of conversational turns subsequently led to the emphasis on sequential organization, which is the hallmark of all conversation analysis.[26] Throughout his own work and until his untimely death in 1975, Sacks himself was simultaneously concerned with what he called the "apparatus" of talk[27] – its highly stable and intrinsically efficient turn-taking system – *and* with talk as a powerful index of the human condition.[28] While the pursuit of apparently fine details of everyday talk seems trivial to some, Sacks noted that the essential regularities of mundane interaction "need not imply banality . . . rather we need to see that with some such mundane recurrences we are picking up things which are so overwhelmingly true that if we are to understand that sector of the world, they are something we will have to come to terms with."[29] Many researchers are still coming to terms with the depth and insight of Sacks's legacy.

The Turn-taking Model for Conversation

Turn-taking is the central area of focus for all researchers in conversation analysis. As indicated in the opening of this chapter, taking turns is perhaps the most fundamental unit of social action. It provides a simple, economic and extraordinarily efficient way of allocating activities across any number of participants. In the process, it creates the rhythms of daily life, from the formal, public rituals and ceremonies of ancient religions and national states to the most intimate of human intercourse.

The most basic organization of turn-taking is that of ordinary, everyday, casual conversation. Early and most precise work by Sacks and his colleagues isolated the essential elements of conversational turn-taking.[30] By studying hours of audio tapes, they began to observe that underlying the ebb and flow of talk is a very simple yet highly specific system. Working from the data (that is, without a "theory" of talk), it became clear that the sort of concerted action involved in conversation demanded a local yet very general organizing scheme, one which would be recognizable and available to any speaker in any conversation in any setting anywhere.[31] They noticed that the economy of turn-taking worked like a kind of revolving gate, demanding and facilitating deft entry and exit, and effectively managing the flow of talk by spacing speakers and pacing topics. Turns, they observed, were valued, and as opportunities to talk they were distributed between participants and were, not infrequently, competed for, occasionally abandoned, and sometimes constructed so as to last as long as possible.[32] Each of these qualities, and others, were systematically accounted for, they noted, through a kind of analytic machinery.[33] There was, in other words, a deep structure to verbal exchange, a turn-taking model for conversation.

Since there is by now an excellent literature on conversational turn-taking,[34] my own discussion will be brief and fairly nontechnical. Yet the very simplicity of turn-taking makes it seem banal; even conversation analysts call it "mundane."[35] It is "in its methodic character that the simplicity of social life resides,"[36] a simplicity which we easily take for granted, as Garfinkel long since noted.

Because talk about talk can seem all too abstract, the discussion here will again be developed with small fragments from the larger study. Sacks and his colleagues developed their "simplest systematics" of conversational turn-taking as a basic model from which, they suggested, there would be many variants. The methodology has always been comparative, and everyday conversation is taken to be a kind of "bedrock" of all interaction, a primary, even primordial site of sociality. Its essential features are that:

1 one speaker speaks at a time;
2 number and order of speakers vary freely;
3 turn size varies;
4 turns are not allocated in advance but also vary;
5 turn transition is frequent and quick;
6 there are few gaps and few overlaps in turn transition.

The organization of turn-taking is endogenous to the interaction yet it is highly structured. Sacks and his colleagues also noted that the turn-taking system (or model) shows a bias toward short, economical turns, consisting of anything from a single word to a simple clausal sentence. Because of this bias, turn transition was possible at each completion of such a "unit type." So speaker change occurs either as a result of (1) the current speaker selecting the next; (2) a next speaker self-selecting; or (3) current speaker continuing. This system is, moreover, what the authors call "context-free" and "context-sensitive," which is to say that it operates without regard to particular speakers, topics or settings yet is sensitive to quite specific enactment, so that, as noted earlier, anyone can speak to anyone, anywhere, about anything, and do so nonproblematically.

Here, for example, are two sales representatives who have never met before, talking about a new sales manager they are about to work for:

3.2 Salesmen

1 **B:**   The *reps* report to him?
2 **A:**   Yeah.

3   (0.3)
4 **A:**   for *or*ders.
5 **B:**   Yeah, line stuff.
6 **A:**   Yeah 'sright. All the time.

In this simple, two-party exchange, only the first question by Speaker
B is a typical grammatical unit, though hardly a textbook question
since it is a declarative sentence in interrogative form. Note the slight
pause (three-tenths of a second) at line 3, where (in terms of the turn-
taking model's minimal unit-type) B could have spoken – in the absence
of which, current speaker (A) continues.

A feature of talk is its sequential form and, in particular, its "adjacent" organization. I will develop this issue in considerable detail
later, but for now it is worth noting some central aspects of the
notion of "adjacency" and of "adjacency pairs" in conversation. Examining naturally occurring talk, Sacks and Schegloff[37] noted that there
is a great number of "paired" exchanges "offhandedly present" –
objects like greetings, questions/answers, invitations/acceptances (or
rejections), summons/answers, requests/responses, and so forth. These
paired turns have an interesting technical quality: they are adjacent,
with the "first part" both projecting the second yet also only being
recognizably a "first" with the production of the "second part." For
instance, Speaker A's "Yeah" *makes* B's question a first to his second,
and the quick placement of "Yeah" completes this tiny micro-order.
Moreover, many adjacency pairs build in a kind of matching process:
greeting/greeting or question/answer and their absence is notable. A
first pair part can even be constructed so that the preferred response
is also built in. That preference is then likely to be honored in the
next available (that is, adjacent) moment, although it is subject to
revision:

3.3 Brokers

1 **Tammy:**   So you wanna come up and work on it now?
2 **George:** → *Sure.* Uhm- (.) that is- that- uhm- let's
3   say I'll be up within an hour?
4 **Tammy:**   Uh-huh, o*kay*!

The "preference" for adjacent agreement is built in here with Tammy's
assumption that George wants "to come up and work," and it gen-
erates an initial affirmative from him (line 2), which is then modified.

The same projection of agreement shapes Sid's opening line below, but fails twice (lines 1 and 3) for lack of sufficient detail:

3.4   Salesmen

```
1   Sid:      This must be a good one
2                        (0.4)
3             San Francisco-Chicago?
4  Linda:     Hm
5   Sid:      T'git bumped,
6  Linda:  → Oh yeah.
```

This example also displays rather well the retrospective-prospective quality discussed earlier. Speakers, moreover, commonly "pursue a response" until the issue is acknowledged, and hearers are under considerable constraint to attend to the unfolding meaning being produced.[38] Sid's explanation that getting "bumped" makes this route a "good one" is thus retrospectively *heard* by Linda for what it was all along, and gets an emphatic "Oh Yeah."

Adjacency pairs, and especially questions/answers, are very efficient mechanisms for moving forward task and topic, allowing listeners to pursue a topic for the information contained:

3.5   Bankers

```
1   C:      Unhuh? So for them, it's a case of turning
2          → it into a trust, rather than a custodial
3          → account?
4   A:      Probably the same thing is true for the
5             Goldman trust.
6   C:  → Really?
7   A:      Yep.
8   C:  → Why is that?
9   A:      Because of the same situation.
10  C:  → Which is?
11  A:      The assets in her account are her property.
```

Note that each question (arrowed) "drives" the talk forward in a quite specific and locally relevant, as well as locally managed, manner. Notice that each turn is "complete" but not all are grammatical sentences, yet the "syntax" builds across the turns into quite a clear picture of what Speaker C needs to know. What we have here is the highly interactive process of "gleaning" information. One question can thus be built off another most effectively. In the next example, an initial request for information (line 3) is bridged with a "can I ask you another" prequestion (lines 13–15) to produce a further information request (line 17):

3.6	Bankers

```
 1  A:    Records?
 2  B:    Yeah, hi, thissiz Rawlinson in L.A an'
 3     →  I wonder if you could give me the- thuh CCG
 4        rate for- for- uh lessee- uhm, December
 5        eighty-two
 6                        (0.4)
 7  A:    Jus'a sec (0.2) uh-
 8            ((keyboard in background))
 9                        (1.4)
10  A:    Uhm- that's- that's six point three five
11        (0.2) in (.) twelve eighty-two,
12                        (0.7)
13  B:  → Great. Than⌈ks        ⌉Uh, can I ask you=
14  A:             ⌊Mm-hmm⌋
15  B:  → =another quick question?
16  A:    Sure.
17  B:  → Whaddabout the- uhm the overseas rate
18        (0.3) for the same period?
19  A:    Right. Uh- nine point- nine-point-six?
20  B:    Uh-huh? Okay, thanks=
21  A:                      =Sure. ⌈Bye⌉
22  B:                            ⌊Bye⌋
```

This is, rather obviously, a typical internal exchange. Here B "self-identifies" by both name and office location to the person in "Records" and requests information. Tagged to his thanks (line 13), he "pre"announces "another quick question," which is to say, he doesn't just ask for the second figure, but conversationally cushions his second request, for the overseas rate (line 17).[39] The call closes with a quite rhythmic and typically synchronous "Bye/Bye," a paired terminal salutation.

At the heart of adjacency organization, conversational turn-taking, and its efficient interactional operation is the notion of "recipient design,"[40] namely the basic feature of conversation that gives it its "custom" or context-sensitive quality. Speakers create turns with recipients in mind, and listeners are motivated to "hear" a turn that is for them, and all participants closely and constantly track the trajectory of the talk to hear "their" turns.[41] This is, of course, most noticeable in multiparty talk, for which the turn-taking model's many provisions operate best, as we shall see in settings such as business meetings to be discussed shortly.

The close-ordered quality of conversational turn-taking and its recipient design allow for a high degree of "projectability" in interaction. This in turn gives to talk its rather syncopated and agreeably collaborative quality. Even total strangers can readily achieve this degree of intimacy, as in the next travel agency call:

3.7 Travel Agency/1

    A: Okay. And you want to rebook?
                (0.3)
    C: Yeah, *no*. I want to actually- want to *cancel* the booking,
                (0.2)
    so I *don*'t have
                (0.1)
    A: → A cancel*l*ation charge. ⌈Okay,⌉ what's your n*a*me?
    C: ⌊(yeh)⌋
    Uhm, Sim- *Sim*pson.
        ((sound of keyboard))

The collaborative sentence thus becomes: "So I don't have a cancellation charge." This useful projectability can be seen more extensively in this snatch of conversation between two financial services colleagues:

3.8 Brokers

    C: Is- if that's the thing for them to do?
    A: It *is* because when they need to- uh- cut a check for a grand for expenses or whatever
    C: → They can do it.
    A: We simply sell a hunk of the fund.
    C: Right.
    A: And the fund, as you can see, is so incredibly stable,
    C: → That there's no problem.

But projectability is, of course, not guaranteed and the candidate completion may require correction:

3.9   University Prov

```
 6   Prov:    I think I'd like to uh-
 7   Dean:    Cancel out?
 8   Prov:  → focus on tomorrow=
 9   Dean:                         =(arright)
10   Prov:    s'far as I can
```

Given the collaborative nature of talk, such corrections are common and quick. But, due to the turn-taking system's bias toward single sentence turns, there is a preference for self-correction.[42] Self-corrections or recycling of sections of a turn also provide an inbuilt way of extending a turn:

3.10   Research Group

```
1   Dan:    We may be able to p- be able to pry enough
2           loose- uh- uh enough money loose out of
3           Jet Propulsion Lab'rato : ry?⌈hhhh      ⌉ t'have=
4   Jeff:                               ⌊mm-hmm⌋
5   Dan:    =him work exclusively on the SAM research
6           projects
7   Jeff:   Uh-huh (0.2) That's great!
```

Notice that although Dan is left to his multiple, back-tracing corrections, he is also overlapped at the earliest syntactic point of a full sentence.

From the basic elements of conversational turn-taking, what Sacks and his collaborators proposed was that other speech exchange systems such as meetings, classrooms, interviews, debates, and even the most ritual of ceremonies would span a kind of continuum. The central differences between casual, freely occurring conversation and the sorts of exchanges listed depend primarily upon such issues as: allocation and duration of turns, selection and order of potential speakers, and designation and order of topic, as well as a specific method for ensuring that each speaker is heard and that discussion does not break down into many miniconversations. In meetings and on conference calls, the structuring mechanisms of turn-taking are indeed modified, as we shall see, but the core of organizational communication remains this simple, reciprocal and self-organizing system.

Turn-taking and Turn-making

The turn-taking model isolated and analyzed by Sacks, Schegloff and Jefferson is thus a very general yet specific system for handling turns, topics, and speakers in the most pervasive of all social activities: talking. Although the original work led to the name *conversation* analysis, it is clear that what is at stake is *talk-in-interaction*, or, more simply, *interaction* analysis.[43] It is equally evident that whereas a great deal of human interaction takes place in the casual or generally unstructured environments of family, friendship and leisure, a feature of modernity is that most human activities occur within organizations that create the context for work, public life, and any number of commercial, professional, or, most generally, institutional activities. The interactional and institutional linkages between talk and its many settings therefore need to be considered briefly.[44]

The question is one of how the *autonomous* domain of interaction supports and shapes the interests, issues, goals, and agendas that social actors bring to their shared activities. *That* they bring them is what we need to attend to here. Talk acts like a sharply focussed prism that narrows yet illuminates that fine line between individual and collective. The turn-*taking* system is also a turn-*making* opportunity for asking questions, soliciting advice, clarifying issues, expounding opinions, developing projects, negotiating agreements, resolving conflicts (and even creating them) and, in the broadest sense, achieving the *essential*, ongoing understandings that make social life work.

I want to be quite clear in this distinction between turn-*taking* and turn-*making* because from it flow important theoretical and practical implications. The turn-*taking* system for talk is a flexible yet formal framework located at a very subtle level of human action, but not, it must be stressed, operating "behind the backs" of its users. It is *structural* in the sense that it provides a stable, patterned and predictive scaffolding for talk, but it is also *interactional* in that anyone can create any variety of conversational collaborations through it, *all* of which are locally managed, that is, from within the interaction.

At the same time, however, people do not sit around taking turns; they *talk*. That is, social agents take the very general framework of conversational turn-taking and *make* it work for them as talk – for their immediate needs, topics and tasks, as well as operating in terms of their relevant identities and shared goals. Asking questions and answering (or dodging) them, for instance, reflexively embeds turn-making in turn-taking. In this way, the structuring properties of turn-taking provide the fine, flexible interactional system out of which institutional relations and institutions themselves are conjured, turn by turn. By making turns work for them, social actors draw on the resources of the turn-taking system to achieve all manner of activities, from a parliamentary debate or presidential press conference to an informal staff meeting or a family squabble. The business of talk, in a technical sense, is thereby transformed into business that gets done *through* talk.

The theoretical and practical distinctions are as follows. Foundational work by Sacks and his early collaborators proceeded necessarily in a highly inductive manner, generating inferences from a wide range of conversational materials recorded in casual telephone calls between friends, emergency public service calls, teenage therapy sessions, informal work settings, and even radio talk shows. The work was done comparatively and without attention to the context of these interactions.[45] The results have justified this analytic strategy since the "obvious" *context* of these entirely talk-based activities was initially ignored in the essential interests of exploring the even more fundamental social organization of the talk. The discovery of the turn-taking system itself depended on an unmotivated examination of these early audio versions of the social world. The theoretical stance that guided this "indifference" is central to conversation analysis and ethnomethdology,[46] namely that the assumptive and thereby *pre*-sumptive role of "outside factors" or social structure (or theories thereof) is to be *bracketed* in the interests of examining actual activities occurring in their actual sequence and thereby to understand and describe them. By giving back to social agents their knowledgeability of their own actions, it was then possible to sit back and observe the structuring quality of the world as it happens.[47] In so doing, it became immediately apparent, as suggested above, that there was order everywhere, and in the finest detail. The turn-taking model was a first, significant step toward "capturing" that order. To do so meant bracketing out the issue of *who* was speaking to *whom*, *where* and *why*, in the interests of learning *how* they were doing so.

This strict stance has stimulated a high quality of research insights and, over the nearly 20 years since the original article of 1974, has resulted in the transformation of conversation analysis into the subject-matter of a large, interdisciplinary, and by now international group of researchers. A review of this diversity would distract from our discussion here, but it is useful to note that the original insight into adjacency pair organization has, for instance, led to some quite creative work on laughter,[48] on transitions between topics,[49] on the organization of teasing and jokes more generally,[50] on the delivery of bad news,[51] on children's constructive talk,[52] on the placement of clichés,[53] and on an impressive range of "repair" strategies whereby participants "fix" the interactional troubles that arise in talk.[54] The adjacency organization of turns, of all sorts, is a *pivotal* area of social order, and the turn-taking system for conversation represents a finely geared "machinery" for sliding through the many modes of human interaction.

In recent years this basic research foundation in conversation analysis has provided a remarkable resource for a more organizational or "institutional" analysis of talk in work settings. The focus on turn-taking mechanisms has remained central, leading to comparative analysis of modifications to the conversational model in settings such as classrooms,[55] courtrooms,[56] plea-bargaining negotiations,[57] congressional hearings,[58] mediation sessions,[59] and medical interviews.[60] A wide range of studies in technology-mediated organizational communications have also begun to develop, such as police emergency services,[61] paramedic exchanges,[62] air traffic operations,[63] coordination between railway personnel,[64] television news interviews and speechmaking,[65] and so on. Many of these latter projects are using video analysis to understand the relation between talk, task and coordinating centers of control, especially in technology-rich environments.[66] The scope of this new direction for the analysis of talk across a variety of organizational settings has also generated considerable debate within the field regarding the relation between talk and organization, and, more generally, between talk and social structure.[67] One goal of this study is to address that debate by treating the reflexive relationship of talk and organization as a central problematic.

My suggestion to those concerned with talk-based work activities will be that the *recursive* features of both talk and its organizational context *matter* – to the talk, as well as to how the organization is created and sustained through talk. To organizational analysts who typically treat language as simply given, on the other hand, I am proposing that the very constitution of organizations depends on the production of local knowledge through local language practices.

Talk as Data

One of the problems of studying a social phenomenon as pervasive as talk is that it occurs all the time and in every imaginable setting.

People in organizations talk everywhere, in large formal meetings planned weeks and months in advance or in emergency sessions of one kind or another. They talk in small informal meetings, crammed into one another's office, or at staff meetings and production meetings in large windowless rooms with coffee machines in the background. They talk in plush conference centers or in the back of noisy taxis. They talk on the phone – constantly, or so it would seem. They hang out in doorways, hovering on the boundaries of each other's territories, exchanging not just pleasantries and football scores but urgent news and stale stories, new jokes and hot gossip. In the process, they pick up the tips of the trade and the subtle undercurrents of their workplace. They talk not so much up and down the hierarchy in the strict steps suggested by organizational charts, but all over the place – up, down, and most creatively laterally – weaving news and information, sniffing for smoke, watching for trends, catching the quickness or monotony of the moment.

The organizations in this study had many of these settings, and more. Of these, the most common were casual "corridor" conversations, meetings of every sort, and telephone calls. In practical terms, the latter two were most amenable to audio recording. Highly portable Walkman-style tape-recorders also caught some excellent cameos of organizational conversations – caught *al volo* as the Italians say, "in flight,"[68] the hurried shorthand of familiar exchanges as people dive from one meeting to another or grab a cup of coffee. Some of the most synoptic yet informative conversations happen in the many transition zones of organizations, in elevators, around the departmental secretary's desk, at the copying machine, in the mail room, in the buzz at the beginnings and endings of meetings, and the like.

Organizations whose talk was recorded for this study include a travel agency with two branches in northern California and one in Tucson, an investment banking house and a television station in southern California, as well as a high-tech research company, two hospitals, and a university's administration; there are also audio recordings of meetings in the White House in 1962, during the Kennedy administration. Though these materials were used for comparative purposes, it was not for the diversity or similarity of the organizations but to capture the broadest possible range of talk-based work activities. Participants in these conversations ranged from the President of the United States and the provost of the university to part-time secretaries at the university and an El Salvadoran refugee who worked at the travel agency. Most of the speakers were white and middle class, but not all; some had advanced graduate degrees, many were well educated, but a few were not. Known ages ranged from 68 (the age of an agent in the travel agency whose birthday was mentioned) to early twenties for part-time students working in the university administration. Most of the talk recorded occurred *within* the organization and among its members;[69] *most* telephone calls used were internal to the worksite or the organization, as in example 3.6 above.

Having offered these descriptions of the talk data, I must add two important factors. First, in an ethnomethdological study of this kind, *typical* variables such as age, race, class, and gender are not "automatically" treated as relevant; nor did I assume that organizational size or structure would be a starting point for analysis or an inhibiting factor in conversational practices. By this I mean that this kind of study of talk in organizations is "indifferent" to more conventional concerns such as organizational size, complexity, geographical location, even purpose, as noted in chapter 2.[70] Nor is the status of the speaker assumed to dictate the talk, though discourse identities and institutional roles are surely instantiated *through* talk. Since, as noted above, the structure of conversational turn-taking applies to *any* conversation and is both context-free and context-sensitive, such a stance is essential. Moreover, because the interaction order is taken as a domain in its own right, what is of interest is how (and if and when) aspects of biography and social structure are made relevant in particular talk settings, as discussed in the section on relevance, rather than an overarching assumption that, for instance, organizational status will *ipso facto* affect the talk that occurs in organizational settings. This is not to deny organizational structure or the operation of power and authority in interactional settings. All I am suggesting is that their manifestation is an empirical matter.

The second important distinction I wish to make is that the "unit of analysis" in this study is neither the organization nor the individual. The recurring discovery of similarities between organizations – their so-called isomorphism – is, in my view, a local phenomenon. It is thus hardly surprising that "structure" is so readily observed in more "macro" studies. But organizations must "make sense" comparatively to the people living and breathing them, whether the consistency of religion, the patterned predictability of a fast-food chain, or the oddly independent yet conforming style of an academic institution. I am very much inclined to agree with Weick in the basic notion that there are remarkably stable qualities of action across *all* organizations.

Obviously, however, what organizations "do" internally and in relation to the larger environment varies enormously, from the activities of a nation-state to the local infighting of a union shop or school board. Variance, in turn, drives statistical analysis (or much of it). Moreover, as Walter Powell notes, "organizations vary in the extent to which their success is dependent on solving technical problems or coping with institutional constraints."[71] So directly observing problem-solving in the context of institutional contingencies should be illuminating. The organizations in this study, while not the unit of analysis, are seen tinkering with technical fine-tuning in order to "bring off" an accountable institutional response.

All of the organizations studied here are service industry participants. They are caught in a web of institutional relations that link them to other organizations – investment house to investment house, broadcasting company to broadcasting company, university to university, hospital to hospital – and thence to the worlds of finance, media, education, and medicine. The linkages *between* these broader institutional environments are, in turn, interconnected and embedded in still more diffuse aspects of a complex, modern society. Merging a number of the themes developed so far, we may say that "the modern world is a world of organizations,"[72] whose embedded and interconnected accomplishment is the local achievement of its constituent members. Language and meaning articulate those connections, and it is within interaction that the constitution of organizations and of society is located.

4

The Interaction Order of Organizations

For those who would study organizations and, more generally, social organization, there is a maddening fact – described with characteristic offhandedness by Goffman – "that there are people out there moving about."[1] From his earliest writings to his presidential address,[2] Goffman was insistent on the central locus of face-to-face, co-present activities of people "doing things together,"[3] in concert, as a domain of sociological analysis in its own right.[4] But the activities of people commingling, collaborating, and even conspiring are often introduced into the works and words of organizational specialists as "anecdotal" evidence of some more solidly statistical finding. These "interactional vignettes" of everyday life are thus, as Goffman later notes, used to illuminate analysis and as a resource rather than a topic of inquiry.

Yet, as most of us spend most of our time "in the immediate presence of others,"[5] the consequences of this rather mundane fact are considerable, if taken seriously. And, as we shall see, direct observation of organizational behaviour and work practices *in site* provides quite distinctive insights into such issues as rationality, effective management, decision-making, resource allocation, and the like. For managers, talk *is* the work,[6] and upwards of 70 per cent of executive time is spent in verbal interaction.[7] It is tempting to think of talk in organizations as brief and episodic, and indeed Mintzberg's work discussed earlier would suggest that,[8] but it is also patterned and recurrent across time.

The patterning is not so much "ritual," as many assume, but has enormous consequences for the production and reproduction of the organization. Moreover, because of the embodied quality sketched above, the actions of human agents in situations of co-presence, and in the mediated co-presence of telephone calls, teleconferencing, conference calling, and so forth, also have consequences for the spatial and temporal organization of any firm.[9] And, despite advances in telecommunications technology, many levels of organizational activities require situations of mutual physical availability for a wide range of workers; this is so especially for management. High-tech firms and other settings that demand rapid innovation and the kind of spontaneity that is essential to creative activities are, in fact, increasingly designing their work environments with readily available and frequently spaced lounges and meeting rooms to provide for just such face-to-face encounters.

Goffman's interaction order is thus a tangible and consequential place located in real time and space, and organizational members expend an extraordinary amount of effort juggling schedules, shifting deadlines, and even bending regulations to bring off a smooth and near-constant flow of people, events and agendas realized together. The interaction order, moreover, *encapsulates* time and space within its own logic, bracketing out other activities and other actors while it focusses the attention and activities of present people and present topics. These are Goffman's "focussed encounters" and, if you track any organizational actor through their day, you find an almost unending series of such encounters, for some repetitive and routine, for others varied and occasionally intense.

Each, however, involves a great deal of seen-but-unnoticed coordination of time and space in order to achieve the focussed stretches of presence and managed periods of absence.[10] Interaction involves *and commits us* to specified times and spaces that we dedicate to each other and to the organizational relationships that are critical to our extended coordination of activities and agendas. In a veritable blizzard of facsimile mail, electronic messages, teleconferencing, conference calls, and old-fashioned telephone calls, organizational actors *still* seek each other out – all the time.[11] Across a cluttered desk, the broad expanse of a conference table, or the odd thickness of restaurant linen, people routinely get together and *talk*.

Since one such ubiquitous setting of talk is meetings, these will be the focus of this chapter, as well as a major feature of those to follow. While the meetings described here are mainly those of middle management, it is worth noting that, up and down the organizational hierarchy, in addition to scheduled meetings, many *micro*meetings take place. Any effective organization, whether large and standardized or small and personal, soon discovers the need for those ubiquitous face-to-face encounters. Even settings involving shift work, such as nursing environments or fast-food concerns, allow for quick meetings in order to transmit information and sort out misunderstandings. High-tech settings, including hospitals, are now increasingly having to schedule weekend and evening sessions of information and training. The dependence, again in virtually all organizations, on verbal settings to transmit and gather information is quite considerable, despite apparent use of memoranda and instruction manuals. This is all the more the case as one moves up the organizational hierarchy. Blending talk and task, meetings also tie up innumerable organizational hours and thus resources, a further reason why they merit careful attention.

The Interaction Order of Meetings

Meetings are where organizations come together.[12] They may be preceded, arranged, complemented, augmented and cancelled by other forms of organizational communication such as telephone calls, memoranda and reports, but meetings remain the essential mechanism through which organizations create and maintain the practical activity of organizing. They are, in other words, *the* interaction order of management, the occasioned expression of management-in-action, that very social action through which institutions produce and reproduce themselves. This chapter introduces a general discussion of meetings, designed to provide a descriptive framework for the analysis of the interaction order of organizations and to introduce the reader to "the way meetings are" in terms of the organization of interaction.

Meetings are also ritual affairs, tribal gatherings in which the faithful reaffirm solidarity and warring factions engage in verbal battles. They are, to borrow from Dalton's classic study, "a stage for exploratory skirmishes."[13] When in doubt, call a meeting. When one meeting isn't enough, schedule another. Agendas, actors, times and places may vary, but meetings are the proper, arena of organizational activity for management, locating and legitimating both individual and institutional roles. Indeed, the world of work may appropriately be divided into those organizational members who routinely attend meetings and those lower-echelon members whose duties tie them to clerical desk or factory floor. Clerks and functionaries may remain anchored at work stations while the sales force pounds pavements, but middle and upper-level management spend innumerable hours in meetings, doing business at the level of talk and justifying their activities and salaries through a calendar filled with meetings, both scheduled and *ad hoc*.

Meetings are the places where the many coalitions and agendas of the organization converge, "where aimless, deviant, and central currents of action merge for a moment...[and] all depart with new knowledge to pursue variously altered, but rarely agreed, courses."[14] Meetings, therefore, are the very stuff of management and, as such, play an oddly central role in the accomplishment of the organization. There is safety in numbers, so the saying goes, and so it is with meetings. The attendance of members of various ranks from various departments can be a measure of the status, significance, and eventual consequentiality of the actual occasion. And organizational members go to some lengths to guarantee certain attendance, both in terms of ranks, minimum numbers of participants, and so forth (see example 4. 1 below). The drums beat and from far and near the chosen foregather, face-to-face across the shiny table.

Meeting Talk

Meetings are, by their very nature, talk. Talk, talk, talk and more talk. But who talks when, to whom, and for how long is no casual matter. Talk revolves round the table on a turn-by-turn basis, one speaker at a time, but meeting talk is not simply conversation, however naturally it may occur. Turn-taking, turn allocation, turn transition, speaker selection, indeed the whole gamut of the Sacks et al. turn-taking model, take specific shape and direction in meeting settings. Sacks and his colleagues have, as we have seen,[15] insisted that theirs is a "simplest systematics" of a turn-taking system, and different types of meetings expose member and analyst alike to modifications of their basic model for everyday conversation, just as medical encounters or courtroom exchanges or interview settings diversely invoke their own turn-taking rhythms. Talk and its turn-by-turn sequential accomplishment are what meetings are about, however many memos, minutes or reports may be written before, after or in reference to the event.

Meeting talk takes specific form in that it is both occasioned by and constitutive of the self-same setting which it accomplishes. It is both situation specific and transsituational, operating within the enforced priorities of the organization and its environment, while at the same time contributing incrementally but significantly to the ongoing accomplishment of that social system. Meetings are, colloquially, where the action is, although, as we shall see, the "action" is talk and is very much embedded in the practical conversational activities of members rather than in an observably productive series of tangible decisions taken or actions precipitated. In fact, "action" should not here be confused with "decision," since, as will be proposed throughout this study, decision-making is a diffuse and incremental process which occurs in all organizational settings.[16]

Meetings also organize time and space in several senses. They derive their very existence from a perceived need to hold a specific gathering at a specific time in direct relation to the unfolding activities of an organization and its complex environment. Meetings may be scheduled months, weeks, days or bare minutes ahead of their actual occurrence. They are fitted into the rhythm of the organization and have slots within the ongoing temporal patterning of work, too early and the meeting is in some way ill-timed or incomplete, too late and it is without organizational purpose, and so on. They also have their own place in clock time and organizational space, a duration and location which can be, but is not always, related to their relative importance in the overall life of the organization. They can be "too short" to cover a given agenda, "too long" for their subject-matter or the patience of their participants. Meetings are, in effect, in finitely variable but, like talk itself, routinely structured.

It is just such structure and its relation to the structure of talk that guides this examination of the relation between the occasion of talk, in this case the meeting, and the ways in which talk occasions and encapsules the organization itself. As both turn-taking and turn-making are the basic modes that transmit and transform organizational agendas, decisions, and projected goals, the structure of meetings matters far beyond the four walls of these transitory events.[17]

The Structure of Meetings

In the simplest sense, meetings, like many activities within organizations, can roughly be divided into two general types: *formal* and *informal*. This, I should stress, is quite distinct from the frequent formal/informal dichotomy imposed by organizational specialists, as it is an interactional rather than theoretical construct. Schwartzman makes a related but not identical distinction between scheduled and unscheduled meetings, drawing on Mintzberg's earlier work.[18] My proposed distinction is slightly more elaborate as well as being more of a member's categorization; it is based on a combination of the kind of meeting and setting *and* on differences in the turn-taking procedures of these meetings. In Schwartzman's sense, "scheduled" meetings include both *formal* and *informal* gatherings, the difference depending on the level of formal procedures used for the allocation of turns, turn order, length, and so forth. "Unscheduled" meetings, on the other hand, typically involve turn-taking nearer to the model for mundane conversation, but nevertheless retain certain "formal" properties in terms of who opens, closes and directs the meeting, as we shall see.

Some working definitions may be useful at this point. I define a "meeting" as a planned gathering, whether internal or external to an organization, in which the participants have some perceived (if not guaranteed) role, have some forewarning (either longstanding or quite improvisatorial) of the event, which has itself some purpose or "reason," a time, place, and, in some general sense, an organizational function. Meetings, as I am defining them, are therefore not the casual encounters in a colleague's doorway, the shared cups of coffee or passing exchanges at the water fountain or the insights of the executive washroom. But they *may* be telephone conference calls, which involve similar structured turn-taking due to the multiparty setting.[19] The "quickie" calls and extended telephone consultations of organizational life are also of paramount importance in setting up major and minor agendas, drifting toward decisions, checking local trends and moods, and even for setting up meetings themselves, as I hope to demonstrate in these discussions. This chapter is, however, focussed on the interaction order of meetings.

Many of the large meetings studied here are primarily information oriented, whereas smaller, informal meetings are, at least in spirit, decision focussed. This is not to say that many decisions are actually *made* in most meetings, but they are often nevertheless the focal point. In fact, "decisions" – in the typical sense discussed in business and academic settings, indeed often with many diagrams and much hand-waving – are frequently invisible. It is instead the *incremental process* of decision-making that is the observable feature of so many organizational settings. Given the "drift of decisions" discussed by March and Romelaer,[20] this is perhaps "not news." But it should be, since most training in business schools and elsewhere is focussed on decisions rather than process, and most experienced decision-makers talk of nothing but process.[21] Indeed, as March and Olsen disarmingly say "ideas [about] 'decision' (as an outcome) and 'decision-making' (as a process) are already confused by a semantic presumption that the latter is connected to the former is some self-evident fashion."[22] Another problem with much of the literature on decision "making," indeed some of the best, is that it depends on cognitive models of individuals, whereas what seems to be needed are interactional models of people "thinking out loud" – *together*. This interactional process of thinking through talk is at the heart of organizational dynamics and decision-making.

An extended discussion of rationality and decision-making will be offered later (in chapter 8), but for now further definitions of meetings themselves are in order. Meetings may, as noted, be *formal*. That is to say, they may be officially convened by written summonses or fixed arrangements, have an organizationally defined composition of members, follow a prepublished or relatively fixed agenda, and be chaired by a designated official. They often occur at regular time intervals, and at regular preset times in the day and week. They may meet daily, weekly, monthly, annually, and so forth, and may also be convened in special sessions, also subject to special arrangements. In this study, the formal meeting format includes such settings as university councils, administrative staff meetings, an annual public meeting, a weekly production meeting, and an early morning brokers' sales meeting, but they could also include board meetings, committee sessions, faculty meetings, and so on.

Formal meetings are frequently a "matter of record," whether in the form of official minutes, inhouse memos or audio-recordings made available to absent members. For our purposes, a primary feature of formal meetings is the directed and restricted nature of turn-taking, channeled as it is by and through the chairperson, but the other features outlined above are also matters of members' descriptions and practices.[23] Members will, for example, note the fact that they were not advised of a meeting; will mark their speech as for or off the record; will examine, correct, and approve the minutes of previous meetings; will ask that certain documents, summaries or remarks be explicitly included in or deleted from the record; and will, overwhelmingly, mark verbal departures from the written agenda.

Responsibilities for channeling turn transition and allocation, and on occasion the actual topic content of a given turn, devolve on the chairperson, whether appointed, as in a board, council or committee, or as explicit convener of the meeting such as the sales manager at a brokers' sales meeting or senior administrative person in an internal meeting. Depending on the level of formality and the overall purpose of the meeting, turns may revolve regularly back to the Chair, may be taken in order and merely monitored by the Chair, may revolve round the room as members make reports in a staff meeting, or may involve the Chair taking questions and leading discussion, as in a sales meeting. Speaker selection depends on the chairperson, who has both rights and obligations in relation to the assembled members and the purpose of the meeting. The Chair attends to the agenda, taking points of order and information, guiding both discussion and speaker order, and generally maintaining order and temporal pacing.

Formal meetings are typically large, and it is not surprising that these extended verbal gatherings demand modifications to the basic turn-taking model for casual conversation, as size alone becomes a central factor in allocating turns.[24] Formal meetings provide a verbal, face-to-face forum in which organizational information can be introduced, discussed, updated, corrected, and, through representative membership, interdepartmentally transmitted.[25] The flow of that information depends, in turn, on a smooth meeting flow, which depends on a well-anchored turn-taking system. Large meetings are also major settings in which much organizational signalling occurs, and, as we shall see throughout these discussions, such semiotic activities are highly interactive affairs.

"Decisions" may also be made in formal meetings, at least in some rather final sense, but careful examination of these data strongly suggests that decisions either take the form of a proverbial "rubber-stamping" of matters negotiated and resolved elsewhere, or the "decision" of the meeting is to defer the matter at hand to another time and place, generally to a smaller more specialized gathering. Alternatively, a large gathering may address a prepackaged "decision" managed by some group, thereby merging the politics of information and decisions.[26] Generally, while formal meetings have the appearance and, no doubt, shared sense of democratic decision-making in action, the actual day-to-day decisions in organizations are not typically accomplished in large formal settings, however much they may be recorded in official documents or the power-packed boardrooms of media portrayal.

Informal meetings, on the other hand, are smaller and generally more *task* and *decision oriented*, at least to the extent that members are gathered together for discussion and advancement of a generally singular or narrow organizational goal. In the discussions that follow, monofocal decisional meetings include a television station meeting convened to discuss a program's budget, a hospital administrators' meeting focussed on cost-cutting measures, a university interdepartmental meeting called to discuss and advance problems in funding graduate fellowships, an economic planning session of the Kennedy administration focussed on eventual tax-cut decisions, and so forth. Even these gatherings, as we shall see, tend to be primarily organized around position-taking, which, rather than being some side-show to the "big decision," turns out to create the fine threads through which the web of opinions, options, angles, alternatives, and occasional actions of "decision-making" are woven.

Informal meetings, in definitional terms, embody the essence of "big" meetings and are understood to do so, yet they are also streamlined and conversational in both conception and organization. They are, for example, typically convened verbally, by telephone, in passing, and face-to-face. They have no fixed membership, though participation by particular organizational members is expectable and accountable, as we shall see. Informal meetings rarely have a designated Chair, although the highest ranked member of the assembled hierarchy usually opens and closes the meeting, as well as providing initial position statements, occasional summaries and topic refocussing. This "chairing" activity is often also territorial in that meetings frequently occur in the office or domain of the most senior person. Informal meetings are also generally unrecorded, in the sense of minutes or official report; indeed they may even be explicitly off-the-record, as in the Kennedy materials in this study. This is not to say that note-taking and later memos and reports do not occur, but these related written records are not part of the meeting *per se* but of the specific subject-matter, activities, discussions, plans or "decisions" taken during the meeting.[27] Finally, informal meetings rarely have a fixed or written agenda, although, most assuredly, there is a "reason" for the meeting and members orient to this in various observable ways.

All meetings are bounded in time and space. But, most of all, they are interactionally bounded. Both formal and informal meetings are, for example, self-contained in that they, as with most verbal interaction, have a beginning, a middle and an end, indeed distinctly so, as we shall see shortly. This "container" quality is managed in quite deliberate and organizationally consequential ways. Interruptions come as invasions of meeting space – whether late arrivals or telephone calls – and are discouraged. But meetings themselves are also often "sandwiched" into other activity streams and the transition zones are busy minimeetings. There is, for example, much premeeting talk, as well as frequent postmeeting exchanges. Nevertheless, formal and informal meetings alike have noticeable and analyzable openings and closings, even preclosing sequences; each frames segments of the interaction and the activities it embodies. Telephone conference calls, too, which are meetings-at-a-distance, similarly display these stable interactional properties, and they, in turn, shape what can and cannot be accomplished through these apparently efficient and time-saving arrangements.

Membership is a vital feature of all meetings, whether they are formal council or internal staff or sales meetings.[28] Meetings are, in and of themselves, membership categorization devices in the sense suggested by Sacks,[29] although admittedly transitory, and it is not uncommon to find people wandering the corridors of organizations looking for "their" meeting, scanning faces for suitable membership features. In some organizations, as Schwartzman elegantly discusses,[30] meetings *are* the organization, but even among professionals and personnel less inclined to pace their day through meetings, these ubiquitous gatherings are central to commitment, communication and continuity. As a result, particular people *make* a meeting, and making (or missing) a meeting is a noticeable affair.

Meetings cannot start, do not exist in some sense, without a perceived critical mass of members present, whether by mandated quorum or achieved understanding of requisite representation.[31] New members refer to veterans for the tacit procedures of a particular collectivity. Bureaucrats, whether in a university, television station, hospital, banking firm, or presidential administration, know and distinguish between kinds of meetings in terms of their membership. Indeed the very significance of the meeting derives much from which members of the organization are in attendance:

4.1 TV Station

```
1      Val:    And Carol is on the way.
2                          (0.9)
3  →   Ken:    My goodness! such a (.) heavy meeting!
4              with all this brass attending?
5              ⌈my God am I-         ⌉
6      Val:    ⌊Huh-huh-huh-huh⌋-huh
7      Ken:    =Am I ⌈impressed
8      Val:          ⌊(    ) invited for you
```

This example is from the television station program meeting. Valerie, the KKAY Station Manager, has convened a meeting of various executives of the station to meet with a producer whose show airs weekly on the station and is currently being reviewed for a new season and local sponsorship. The producer is Ken, who has just been introduced to Daniel Belson, Director of Public Information and a Senior Vice-President of the corporation, and John Peshkny, Director of Operations. Valerie indicates that a fifth member of the meeting, Carol Stevenson, Director of Development, "is on the way." Ken marks his assessment of attendance with exaggerated enthusiasm (lines 3–7). While this example demonstrates explicit evaluation of the relationship between members present and meeting status, it is a fairly rare case, at least within an actual meeting setting. Members, nevertheless, regularly and overtly engage in head-counts, and indeed plan for them along the lines of often diffuse organizational goals.

Typically, the essence of membership is marked by some kind of listing display (as in examples 4.3, 4.4 and 4.6 below) or by noting the presence of a quorum, as we shall see shortly. All meetings are key mechanisms for specifically transmitting and disseminating information and policies, enhancing communication flow, improving interdepartmental liaison, and, in subtle ways, effecting organizational control. So membership of meetings is quite a calculated affair; in effect, it *elaborates* the actual activity of the meeting by including and excluding various potential members or subunits of the organization. It also highlights the fluidity of organizational alliances and, although hardly surprising, the care with which members construct these interactional collaborations is a direct window on organizations in action.

The Social Organization of Meetings

To understand the organization of talk in meetings, we need to appreciate its situated character. At the same time, current research in the organization of conversation in general will allow us to better understand the organization of meetings *as* talk. Meetings are not, as noted earlier, naturally occurring conversation since they have a generally predetermined topic or topic agenda, a rather stable potential set of interactants, and some rather specific turn-taking modes. Turn-taking is, at times, "preallocated" but not in the strictly determined sense of, say, a television interview, courtroom, or tribunal.[32] Except in the most formal of meetings, and then only at certain points in the proceedings, turn order is not fixed, nor is length of turn. What is fairly fixed, however, is the chairperson's central role in monitoring turn allocation, although, even in the most formal stages of a meeting, points of order and information may result in quite a conversational "side" exchange between the questioner and the appropriate respondent. The interaction order of meetings is thus doubly "situated," first within the flow of talk, and, second, within the reflexive rhythm of the organization.

Openings to Meetings

Let us look then at the opening moments of meetings and examine how these structured sequences embody a variety of critical organizational issues. Openings bracket *out* the busy workday while bracketing *in* the local meeting membership – into the interaction order and the organizational tasks at hand. And, as noted above, the presence or absence of specific members is critical in the accomplishment of these openings:

4.2   Fellowship Meeting

```
 1  Matt:      Hi [: : : .]
 2  Dean:         [Tom ] co : ming?
 3  Matt:  →   (Sorry I'm late) I thought he was HERE!
 4                          (1.4)
 5             I told him I was gonna be late I
 6             (.) assumed he as uh=
 7  Jean:                        =I've been looking
 8             for two people coming along-
 9             no wonder I didn't see y[ou cuz I   ]
10  Matt:                              [No. I had ]da
11             two-o'clock and I knew I was gonna be running
12             late and I [as ] sumed he
13  Jean:                 [Oh.]
14  Matt:      =was gonna be here
15                          (0.7)
16  Dean:      Okay. (.) Ehm . . .
```

The sequence starts with a greeting, a fairly typical initial turn by arriving members drawn together from different departments, but predictably less common in staff or sales meetings, where departmental participants have potentially seen and greeted each other already that day. Matt is, it fact, arriving late to a meeting that has, for all practical purposes, been unable to start without him since he is the senior representative of the third of three departments in attendance at this meeting, namely the Financial Aid Office.[33] The Graduate Dean returns the greeting with a minimally overlapped question requesting information on the other Financial Aid Office member expected at the meeting.[34]

Even in informal meetings, there is a tacit understanding that a certain critical mass of members is necessary for the meeting to be organizationally and interactionally meaningful, so absences are accountable matters. In each case, the unofficial head-count also marks the opening of the meeting, because the agendas then proceed without further delay or further identifiable premeeting talk. In the example above, the Dean uses a typical conversational move to close down the topic of "excuses" and shift to his own agenda: okay + Ehm. He then offers a long description and assessment of an earlier meeting as a cushion on which to place his own proposal.

We will return to this laminated effect of meeting upon meeting in later sections of this study. It is worth noting that the layering effect that operates in these exchanges works to frame succeeding interactions and also builds toward decisions or organizational objects that, retrospectively, will look like decisions. Organizational decisions are *talked* into being in fine yet layered strips of interaction. That interaction depends for its organizational effectiveness and relevance on *who* was present during key encounters *and* on the unfolding local logic of turn-by-turn talk. This highlights a central problem for all organizations, namely that "individuals vary in the attention they provide to different decisions" and activities.[35] They have a tendency, in Jackall's evocative expression, to "look up and around"[36] when decisions are demanded of them, to compare their strategies with those of similar actors in related settings and to hope the moment will pass. Heavy commitments on other tasks and conflicting goals also fragment their attention. Thus they vary from one time to another and from one task to another, so that the constituent members attending to any set of issues at any given point in time (or space) lends great variability to assumptions about "who" decides or "who's" in charge. This fluctuation of attention, interest, presence, and time considerably undermines the purposive, goal-seeking assumptions of conventional organization theory.[37]

More formal meetings also have similar attention and interest gaps, but they benefit from a more clearly designed membership and a designated critical mass or "quorum" without which the meeting cannot function, which is to say that the proceedings are taken to be unrepresentative of the official membership and thereby nonbinding. Not unexpectedly, members attend to this factor overtly, particularly when numbers are noticeably low:

4.3a Council

1 **Dean:**   Do we have a *quorum*?
2 **Chair:**   No we haven't yet I'm waiting,

Immediately preceding multiparty talk has consisted of typical premeeting exchanges, interdepartmental updating and personal chatter about summer plans. This is the opening of a meeting of the University Graduate Council, a campus-wide body responsible for graduate affairs and advisory to the Graduate Dean, linked interorganizationally with similar bodies on each of the other campuses of the same university system. The Dean (line 1) has good organizational reason to be concerned about low turnout since lack of a quorum will mean a concomitant lack of the Council's approval on pending matters which affect the day-to-day affairs of the Graduate School (see also related discussion in chapter 5 below). The Chair provides a two-part reply and a double-edged account (line 2), and after some minutes returns to:

4.3b　Council

```
 3  Chair:   One two three four five? Frank is away,
 4           Jim Cannock is away, we have a new
 5           member? (0.3) who doesn't seem to have
 6           appeared?
 7                           (1.2)
 8           Uh-
 9                           (3.1)
10           Though,
11                           (2.6)
12  Dean:    Does five constitute a quorum? One
13           two (.) three four
14  Chair:   (five)
15  Dean:    ⌈Fi : : : v e          ⌉
16  Chair:   ⌊(I don't think) it does-⌋  I don't think it
17           does, let's see one two three four
18           five (1.1) six seven eight
19                           (1.6)
```

The head-count is aided and abetted by the Dean, while the Chair provides an account for absent members (lines 3–6), after which he continues his efforts at achieving a quorum as he scans the room for arriving members. The Dean persists with: "Does five constitute a *quorum?*" and he too counts, with the Chair chiming in (line 14), initially doubtful that five would constitute a quorum (line 16). His revised head-count, however, allows him to conclude:

4.3c   Council

```
19                       (1.6)
20   Chair:   Yes. We do have a quorum.
21                       (1.3)
22            So, let's call the meeting to order,
23            we do have a quorum,
24                       (1.7)
25            So, you all have had the minutes of
26            the last meeting? uh- any corrections
27            or additions,
28                       (2.1)
29            If not? I (.) would entertain a (.)
30            motion to approve the minutes?,
31                       (0.3)
32   Rock:    So moved,
```

The business of the meeting begins immediately, with approval of the minutes and the initiation of agenda items such as reports.

By contrast, internal staff meetings are typically relatively casual affairs, although they technically meet the criteria of a formal meeting outlined above. Members of these gatherings often orient to the mock formality of their meetings, as in the next example, in which Lana as the most senior person present is poised to chair the session:

4.4   Staff Meeting/1

```
1    Lana:  →  U : : : hm ⎡h : : : :⎤
2    Sandy:              ⎣Go!     ⎦
3    (   ):    ⎡Heh-heh⎤
4    Judy:     ⎣Okay   ⎦ ⎡go!  ⎤
5    Tina:               ⎣D'we⎦ have a quorum? ⎡would you say⎤
6    (   ):                              H⎣ u⎡ h   h⎤ uh⎦
7    Mary:                                    ⎣Heh- ⎦
8             heh-heh
9    Lana:    There is hope that we will move, the
10           uh- the uh student services people
11           have been told that . . .
```

Lana's long "U : : : hm" (line 1, with exhaled breath) marks a kind of transition or topic boundary, separating premeeting conversation from what is observably the opening of the meeting.[38] Sandy, orienting to the boundary quality of Lana's turn, jumps in with *"Go"* and is echoed by Judy's collaborative: "Okay *go!"* (lines 2–4). The laughter and Tina's mock severity demonstrate, I would suggest, their orientation both to the technically formal nature of the meeting and to its accountably casual atmosphere. These are administrative staff members who frequently attend and participate in meetings such as the university council cited above and their members' stock of knowledge provides them with ample resources to mock the "real" need for a quorum in the case of their internal meeting. Lana's turn (lines 9–11) marks the beginning of report activities, a primary feature of many meetings and a topic to which we shall return later. Note that both Sandy's *"Go!"* and Tina's quorum question elicit collaborative laughter, underlining the shared work of marking openings to meetings.

Openings to informal meetings can be either marked or unmarked. In the television station meeting introduced above (4.1) the meeting opening went on to be achieved as an announcement. In the next example, from a weekly travel agency meeting, the count and commencement are quite explicit:

4.5   Travel Agency/2

```
 1  Andy:    Let's- lessee John's out of town, and Helen's-
 2           Helen's in with Joan,
 3  Todd:    Yeah.
 4                          (1.9)
 5  Andy:    So I guess this is us!
 6  (   ):   ⌈Hmm    ⌉
 7  Chris:   ⌊Uh-uh⌋ Vicki's sup- s- supposed to bring those
 8           new co ⌈ntracts      ⌉
 9  Andy:           ⌊GOT 'em ⌋I got'em here 'case she doesn'
10           come,
11                          (2.5)
12        →  So, let's get started
```

Meetings, like telephone calls, also have "reasons" for their enactment.[39] Related to attendance assessment, participants to meetings often mark openings by clarifying its purpose, partly because certain people and documents give meaning and effectiveness to certain meetings. But more centrally because meetings "make sense" only in the recognizable temporal flow of the work they embody. Thus the head count may be quite summarily assessed and the reason for "why this

meeting now" more emphasized. These exchanges also mark the retrospective-prospective procedures outlined above, often summarizing
a kind of "how we got here/where we are going":

4.6 Sales Meeting

```
 1  SM:  →  I guess everybody's comin- 's gonna come- uhm
 2            I just don't want to have to repeat this?
 3                        (3.0)
 4            Okay! I think I'll just wade right in here
 5            and get this thing started,
 6                        (2.3)
 7            As you all know
 8                        (1.2)
 9            Uhm, there're strong rumors of a cut- cut in
10            the discount rate . . .
```

Or, instead, larger interdepartmental meetings may require explicit
introductions as a means of assessing attendance:

4.7 Advisers' Meeting

```
 1  Dean:  →  Seems virtually everybody seems to be here
 2                 (0.4) uhm
 3                         (2.8)
 4             'Cept unfortunately for uhm- Fred Brent (0.2)
 5             who's the new Associate Dean in the Graduate
 6             School, he exercised his (0.2) academic
 7             prerogative in bringing the wrong materials
 8             heh-heh ⌈h e h-h e h⌉ so he's forgotten- he's gone
 9      (?)             ⌊Huh-huh⌋
10             back to get them (   ) he'll be here shortly
11                         (2.1)
12             Ehm
13                         (1.5)
14             I'd like to introduce
15                         (1.0)
16             the
17                         (1.1)
18             various people in the (0.4) Graduate School . . .
```

In 4.7, the extended account of the Associate Dean's absence (lines 4–
10) is provided because this is *his* meeting, attended by the Dean

himself as a matter of courtesy. The latter fulfills the departmental activity of getting the meeting started by introducing his staff to the larger interdepartmental group.

Large meetings whose activities are not a matter of record do not require an official quorum. They do, however, involve participants in that so-human need to know who is talking to whom, as well as a need to achieve a "consolidation of attentiveness,"[40] namely a transition to focussed, single-speaker talk. The next example is taken from the opening of an annual public meeting of the campus "Status of Women" committee:

4.8   Annual Meeting

```
                  ((general chatter – subdued and tapering off))
1   WS: →   Hello! I think we'll go ahead and get started?
2                         (0.9)
3             Uhm- if- I'd like to say from my own point of
4             view that when people want cheese an' crackers
5             and wine I hope you'll just feel free to get up
6             and help yourself? Cuz there's plenty of food
7             back there.
8             Uhm, I'm Wendy Stoll? and I'm- would like to
9             to welcome you all on behalf of the Committee . . .
```

The meeting's convener greets the group with a general "Hello" that is hearable as being addressed to anyone present and proposes to "go ahead and get started." The meeting is arranged as a lunchtime event to fit staff schedules, and the speaker inserts an invitation to the assembly to continue to avail themselves of provisions. She then introduces herself and, aligning with the committee rather than her own department, another membership categorization device, welcomes the group. There follows the request than all present self-identify and announce their own organizational subunit.

Note that a general orienting pattern, in the immediate opening section, is an assessment of attendance and/or a proposal to "get started," which is typically prefaced by a standard topic transition marker such as: so, okay, uh, ehm:

Dean: Okay. (.) Ehm-   (4.2, line 16)

Chair: So, let's call the meeting to order,   (4.3c, line 22)

Lana: U : : : hm h : : : :   (4.4, line 1)

Andy:	So, let's get started	(4.5, line 12)
SM:	Okay! I think I'll just wade right in here and get this thing started,	(4.6, lines 4–5)
Dean:	Ehm (1.5) I'd *like* to introd*u*ce	(4.7, lines 12–14)
WS:	*Hello*! I think we'll go ahead and get st*a*rted?	(4.8, line 1)
TT:	Okay I'll start off an- I think . . .	(4.10, below, line 1)

As un-business-like as it may seem, "uhm" or "ehm" frequently mark the introduction of first topic, which is also as often the "reason for the meeting."[41]

In many large meetings such as staff, committee, and sales gatherings, announcements and general information items mark the opening discussion. In the next example, taken from an internal teleconference "teach-in" in an investment banking firm, staff in New York are initiating a presentation to a regional sales meeting-of-the-air, with participants located in Boston, Atlanta, Houston, Chicago, and Los Angeles:

4.9 Teleconference UT: Panworld

```
 1  LK: →  Okay (0.2) to those uh- on the system thissiz
 2            Liz Kanter in marketing? in New York? and I'd
 3            like to go over the roadshow
 4            for uh-  [for Pan-world ]
 5  (?):            [This is Boston!]
 6  LK:      Pictures? Monday the 9th they'll be in Los
 7            Angeles at noon lunch?
 8  (?):      Tell her we wanna (   )
 9  LK:      Tuesday the 10th they'll be in Minneapolis for
10            breakfast? (0.3) and Chicago for noon lunch?
11            Wednesday in New York management is available
12            for private meetings ((continues))
                           .
                           .
                           .
13                          (2.1)
14            Thank you, Joel?
15  JR:      Arright ((cough)) (0.6) ((cough-cough))
16            Good afternoon! This is Joel Roeder, corporate
17            finance (.) department uhm (     ) the
18            initial public offering of Pan-World Pictures?
```

19   (0.5) It's a simultaneous offering of *one*
20   million five hundred thousand shares . . .

Liz, opening with an explicit identification segment for those "on the system" (the teleconferencing technology used by the brokerage house), makes a general announcement about the scheduled "road-show" to promote the offering of shares by "Pan-World Pictures" and its management. In the premeeting moments of this teleconference, the Boston office was having difficulty linking to the system, hence the announcement (line 5): "This is Boston!" Rather like someone bursting into a meeting in progress, this interruption is ignored as a long list of locations, times, and activities are announced, after which the speaker hands over to the "chair" of the meeting who self-identifies and initiates an opening statement (note again the "uhm" at line 17 that marks the actual onset of the main meeting topic, and thus the reason for this long-distance meeting).

Finally, meetings often distribute documents, both before and at the onset of the occasion, and these are often noted – as in the next example, from the opening of another university meeting:

4.10 Staff Meeting/2

```
1  TT: →  Okay I'll start off an- I think most of you- or
2          all of you should have a copy of this and I'll
3          kinda give you a brief idea of some of the
4          things ⌈that        ⌉ has been happening (0.3)
5  (?):          ⌊((cough))⌋
6          and the new initiatives, THING I wanna touch on
7          first of all is the outreach because . . .
```

Yet, despite circulation of documents, organizational members rarely depend on the written medium to convey information. The speaker thus proposes to give participants "a brief idea" of a number of things – the formulation of "*some* of the things" serving as an important mechanism for anchoring her start to a long turn, as it cues listeners to track a multiplicity of conversational objects. This is underlined by her further noting (lines 6–7) that her discussion of outreach is the "first" among these.

It is in this way that extended turns are produced in ordinary conversation and, in meetings, they are further a resource for anchoring reports or staging position statements, in that doubly contextual way discussed below. Even the most informal of meetings displays this "report" or "position statement" orientation[42] as participants settle in to listen, doodle, daydream or engage whatever other silent device appeals to them. Meetings take on an internal rhythm of their own and even those who protest loudly are loathe to miss these oddly compelling settings. There is a way, as Schwartzman suggests, that the local life of meetings becomes so seductive (much as all interaction is) that the information conveyed in meetings or the decisions attempted are not the point, the *meeting itself* is: "There's dynamic of the meeting that leads you to a certain decision, and people on the outside wonder, 'How in the hell did you decide that,' and if you weren't at the meeting, you really can't appreciate how it was done."[43] At issue is not so much the "fact" of the meetings as its phenomenal quality. The intense and intimate realtime involvement of the interaction order, throughout so much of social life, leaves people saying: "You had to be there."[44]

Turn-taking in Meetings

Whether formal or informal, meetings and their agendas are achieved incrementally on a turn-by-turn basis, in various adjustments to the basic model for mundane conversation. In informal meetings, talk most approximates the conversational turn-taking model, with the general exception that long turns are expectable. This technical departure from the model is warranted as members construct and provide reports, accounts and position statements, as we shall see in detail in the next chapter.[45] In casual conversations, long turns are frequently projected and hearable as "stories," while meetings appear to provide a specific speech environment for expectably long turns that are less overtly marked.[46] These relatively long turns are routine and are typically unmonitored, which is to say that the typical interjection of "continuers" common in casual conversation is notably absent in meetings.[47] As in courtroom or plea-bargaining settings, speakers accomplish and are heard to accomplish legitimately long organizational stories, using these accounts to construct positions and realize agendas.

In formal meetings, on the other hand, turn-taking may be characterized as a rather distinct departure from the interactional dictates of the basic model, since, as noted earlier, turn allocation, transition, and even duration are overtly managed by the chairperson functioning as a kind of central switching station for the meeting. Indeed, the relative formality of the agenda and its turn-by-turn management is what *marks* these meetings as formal, rather than some factor external to the interaction. Formal, meetings, in part due to their size in terms of membership, have the notable feature of needing to manage many participants in terms of time and space, as well as keeping them focussed on a delimited number and order of topics. As we have seen, openings to meetings display a routine feature of moving from the multiple conversations of premeeting encounters into a single interactional stream.[48] This has been characterized as the transition "to the shared monitoring of a *single* sequence of utterances."[49] Highly formalized settings such as courtrooms or hearings or political forums typically use some noise-maker such as a gavel or official utterances such as "Be upstanding in Court."[50] The flow of talk that follows is also more constrained. Turns are "preallocated" rather than occurring in an unspecified order.[51] This modified turn-taking system is then a resource for maintaining orderly transition of topic and speakers, while simultaneously focussing the attention of all present on to a single stream of talk and task.

To propose that turns are "preallocated" does not, however, mean that they are "fixed" or "guaranteed" to work, as meetings vary in their level of formality *through just* the ways participants draw on the norms, say, of *Robert's Rules of Order*. Central to this is the fact that the *relative* formality of a given meeting is an unavoidably local affair. Meetings do not all proceed at the same level of formality and, therefore, turn-taking procedures vary; the courtroom or congressional hearing or annual board meeting is at one end of the range, a staff meeting or meeting of the board of a small company somewhere in the middle range and a variety of informal gatherings at the other end. In a sales meeting, for example, the sales manager dominates the talk, or, as in one case studied, introduces a market specialist as guest speaker, and that person then controls the meeting. Sales meeting members are essentially an audience whose speaker rights are restricted primarily to requests for information and clarification, since the purpose of these meetings is overwhelmingly informational.[52]

But, in general, organizational members clearly orient to the procedural possibilities of restricted turn-taking procedures and mark their departures with care. Here, to recap the university council meeting in example 1.1 above, Rock marks his interruption of the Chair's opening report explicitly, with a formal prequestion (see 4.11, line 1), which as a "preliminary to a preliminary" produces a question in the next available turn slot[53] and does so as a kind of "backing up" clarification request.[54]

4.11   Council

```
1  Rock:    Question?
2                         (0.6)
3  Chair:   Yeah?
4  Rock:    What is the (0.3) C-PEC (0.1) stand
5           for?
```

The responsibility of the chairperson in a formal meeting also includes close attention if not adherence to the published agenda, which subsumes speaker selection and turn order in that only speakers who are on-topic may appropriately speak, and departures from the agenda item under discussion are marked. The reports of various responsible officers, subcommittees and so forth typically initiate the meeting's agenda, and the membership are expected to confine their remarks during that period to clarification, comment or discussion on that particular report. Even turns by the chairperson must be warranted, since the role of the chair is that of facilitator of the meeting and not discussant:

4.12   Council

```
1  Chair:   Le : t me interrupt with a ⌈foot⌉ note
2  Dean:                               ⌊Yes ⌋
3  Chair:   (0.4) the most recent (.) uh- (0.2)
4           edition of the Bulletin . . .
```

Here the Chair marks the interruptive nature of his turn explicitly and is granted the turn space by the current speaker at line 2.[55] Even the use of the lexical expression "footnote" references the shared commitment to the official agenda. In academic circles particularly, a footnote may be seen as a way of legitimating a tangent, or even a way of tacking a considerable topic shift on to an ongoing discussion while at the same time achieving its relevance and "sequential implicativeness."[56]

The role of the Chair in any meeting further involves a commitment to move the meeting along in terms of both turns and time, though that "role" is also an achieved phenomenon, rather than being simply given by the organizational hierarchy.[57] In the next example, taken from the internal staff meeting cited earlier, Lana as acting chairperson moves members through their report turns:

4.13　Staff Meeting/1

```
1  Lana:    Ro : sa? it's your turn again?
2  ( ):     Heh- ⌈heh-heh            ⌉
3  ( ):          ⌊. h : : HUH-⌋⌈HUH⌉
4  ( ):                       ⌊Heh- ⌋⌈heh-heh⌉
5  Rosa:                              ⌊I  HAR⌋Dly wanted
6            a first turn?
```

Rosa has earlier in the meeting supplied information ancillary to another person's actual turn, and the round-the-table, report-making cycle has now officially arrived at her. Note, too, that Lana invokes a specific turn-taking option by selectively naming Rosa as next speaker, although this fact is available to all present by virtue of the fact that reports are being produced around the table, anticlockwise, person by person, another sequentially organized feature of formal and semiformal meeting settings.

Meetings further embody a kind of interactional division of labor that sustains and carries forward the immediate agenda and, through its sequential structure, an orderliness that internally creates both discourse identities and emerging work tasks. Moreover, the organization's flow of both work and information in many of these examples is simultaneously horizontal and vertical. Mirrored across the busy surface of many meetings are the alliances, coalitions, working parties and occasional ambushes that make the organization.

Closing the Meeting

So meetings are structurally organized as a single albeit extended conversational unit of organizational talk. As with openings, formal and informal meetings also have closings, coordinated exits from the enclosed boundary of the meeting such that, though general talk may, and overwhelmingly does, continue after the closing marker, it is no longer an accomplished part of the meeting. It is, in fact, postmeeting talk; like its complement, premeeting talk, it frequently involves two-party interdepartmental and interim exchanges and updates about specific tasks, recent gossip, and overall organizational mood.

Informal meetings tend to get closed down as key members leave, as in the next example from the interdepartmental meeting convened in the Graduate Dean's office, which figured in example 4.2 above:

4.14   Fellowship Meeting

```
1  Dean:    I've got- I've gotta run- I've got to run
2           to (.) Biology which has a (.) prior
3           commitment- I got about five balls in the
4           air on that one too) Jean? Why don't
5           you talk with Robert about some of these-
6           I- my suspicion is that we will not be
7           able to get together ⌈and wh ⌉ at I'M-
8  Jean:                        ⌊Hmhmm⌋
9  Dean:    Matt, in your absence . . .
```

In a single rather complex turn, the Dean accomplishes his own exit, the closure of the meeting, and thereby the status of any further talk. He also sets up the next decision or action points of this particular organizational problem which, notably, will not occur in another meeting but in two-party exchanges. While this is a single example, it appears typical of informal meeting closures and is oriented to as such by participants.

Interactional closings typically have a series of stages that operate to mutually coordinate the suspension of talk and, in the case of much work-based talk, the suspension of the activity. Closings have been studied for telephone calls by Schegloff and Sacks, in particular for the detailed ways in which members both achieve and sometimes delay a necessarily coordinated exit from an interaction.[58] Put simply, phone calls do not simply end when both (or all) parties hang up; hanging up is a highly collaborative event which, given the lack of visual contact, must be "talked" along.

Similarly, *any* bounded encounter requires the sort of deft and detailed actions that have fascinated both Garfinkel and Goffman. Even an attempt at a unilateral exit from a conversation in progress, as Goodwin has shown,[59] requires the departee to demonstrate the reason for the departure, verbally or nonverbally – in most cases, both. Hence the elaborate displays that delighted Goffman that bring off an escape as a graceful and delicately unobtrusive activity, with glances at watches, the almost imperceptible easing back of chairs, the sliding of tops on pens, papers one on another. Typically, people who work together, live in the same family, share personal or professional activities or, most generally, expect to see each other or speak to each other on the phone again, organize their mutual closings with the sequenced production of topical objects that stand as reasonable "preclosing" sorts of things: arrangements to get together soon, recaps of earlier parts of the conversation or meeting that offer a closing account, solicitudes of "good health" or of "not working too hard" or "taking care of oneself" are all among these, together with appreciations of current and past efforts, and so on.[60] In the above example, the Dean offers a variety of arrangement-like remarks. As he is exiting his *own* meeting being held in his own office, his apologies and arrangements inform his activity of leaving, while the talk further elaborates his efforts to project and thus control future events even as he exits.[61]

Meetings with larger groups, by contrast, have more structured closings, again achieving that shared attentiveness needed. They have, moreover, closings that mark "preclosing" sequences quite explicitly. The next example is taken from the internal staff meeting whose opening was explored above:

4.15   Staff Meeting/1

```
1  Lana:    Okay, anybody e : lse? got anything
2           else?
3                        (0.3)
4           Then let's adjourn?
```

Again, the conversational style is casual but clearly marked as a preclosing opportunity to reopen discussion; note for example the stressed and similarly inflected: "*e : lse?*" and "else?", and even the lexical use of the fairly formal term "adjourn?" and the very brief (0.3 second) pause at line 3. This very pattern is mirrored in our next example, from the relatively high-level, formal gathering of the University Council:

4.16a   Council

```
1  Jim:     Monday May fourteenth? (0.5) from
2           three thirty to five
3                        (2.4)
4  Chair:   That's it,
5                        (1.0)
6           Do we have any (.) other business?
7           any new business? Mel speak ⌈up   ⌉
8  Mel:                                ⌊C'd-⌋ could
9           I make sure that something
```

10		happened on item five along the
11		lines that
12		(0.6)
13	**Chair:**	Yeah
14	**Mel:**	that I was inquiring about- I-
15		(0.4) I know that one time Laura said
16		she was going to transmit a letter to
17		University Microfilms (0.6) on the
18		subject of uh-

Jim is in the process (lines 1–2) of providing information on the final agenda item, in response to one member's clarification request. The Chair waits approximately two-and-a-half seconds (line 3), and begins the closing of the meeting as is his prerogative and duty (line 4). But, given the multiparty focus, he also effectively invites preclosing items in a near-identical turn to Lana's in 4.15 above. Lana's utterance is casual, in that "anybody" who has anything else to say is invited to speak, whereas the Chair's turn reflects the formality of the meeting, it has reached the agenda item typically labelled "new business" and his invitation addresses that explicitly. A brief discussion ensues, and then he reinitiates the closing:

4.16b   Council (continued)

35	**Chair:**	Yeah yeah,
36		(0.7)
37		I think that's uh- uh very good sugg*estion*
38		to make
39		(0.9)
40		Any other?
41		(0.7)
42		new business?
43		(1.2)
44		Well then I'm
45		(0.5)
46		sure none of us will mind?
47		(1.3)
48		going out on the beach?

This time, he effectively closes the meeting, which breaks up into multiparty informal exchanges immediately, and the many pauses of this operation are typical of topic transitions and closings in all conversations. Meetings are thus *accomplishments*, as are all social interactions viewed from an ethnomethodological perspective. Their achieved interactional ordering, in turn, *structures* the organization from within.

Tracking the Organization

Meetings must, at least in part, be seen as symbolic affairs, not only because they are ritualized and patterned but because they function as routine yet vital, face-to-face encounters in a bureaucratic and technocratic society that has long since surpassed the practical need to gather actual people into physical proximity. But both the words "ritual" and "routine" need to be observed in action, where it immediately becomes clear that they take a considerable amount of work just to continue to *look* routine and run as smoothly as the term ritual would suggest. The central goal of Garfinkel's "incongruity procedures," or in popular parlance "breaching" experiments, was to discover and demonstrate *just* how fragile yet resilient are the routines of daily life and just how much people will do to keep them intact. Despite a high-technology society, the everyday affairs of corporations, public bodies and presidential administrations are still constructed in terms of immediate and proximate behavior.[62]

Goffman's interaction order, and the more technical one proposed here, constitute the essence of this proximity. The immediacy of interaction, especially in the encapsulated setting of a face-to-face meeting or the intense intimacy of a telephone call catches everyone up in its structuring rhythm. Meetings, whether interactionally defined as formal or informal, information or decision oriented, are matters of accomplishment, turn by turn and topic by topic, and organizational actors display considerable fluency in utilizing everyday conversational procedures toward multiple goals, and frequently, as we shall see, along several simultaneous agendas.

The structuring properties of the interaction order in realtime settings such as meetings have enormous (and as yet largely ignored) consequences for the overall structuring of organizations. Caught in a meeting and connected through a series of interactions across time and space are the people, ideas, decisions, and outcomes that *make* the organization. It is in the closed internal times and spaces of meetings, as well as in the many phone calls that link people, topics and tasks, that the actual structure of the organization is created and recreated. The interaction order contains its own autonomous logic and, reflexively, encapsulates the organizational domain.

This, then, *is* the business of talk. In the next few chapters, it will be my goal to apply these preliminary observations about meeting talk and related telephone and conference calls in two quite different yet, I hope, complementary ways: (1) to examine a range of more specific aspects of the organization of talk in the work settings that make up the business day; and (2) to discover *through* those materials how an apparently fragmentary process of information gathering, transmission, and very local assimilation is transformed into the goals, agendas and decisions of organizations.

5

Conversational Procedures and Organizational Practices

It is often said that we are the pawns of organizations. From government bureaucracies and faceless firms such as oil companies and financial conglomerates to the quite local tyranny of traffic conditions and slow-moving queues at the supermarket, organizational society dominates every horizon. The logic of these external forces is sometimes opaque, and certainly, we assure ourselves, not the product of anything *we* would do if put in charge of these operations. Yet most of us are, as noted earlier, as much *part* of some organizations as we are more passive participants in others. The former, of course, are transparent to us and largely benign, while the latter seem poised to confound our daily routines with forms, deadlines, regulations, price structures, complex clauses, and outright rejections, as well as confronting us with the blandly impenetrable loops in which our computer, video cassette recorder, car tape-deck, or once-simple telephone entrap us.

Faced with the multiple demands of organizations, it is even more tempting to think of the everyday world and its kaleidoscopic effect on our consciousness as fragmentary, fleeting and even shallow. Modern organizations are themselves highly charged with information, swamped in detail, linked to multiple channels of communication, and spinning at an extraordinary pace. Looking back to Mintzberg's study of managers of almost 20 years ago, those daily patterns were described as "fragmented, varied and brief," and we can only wonder at the intensity of current managerial experience. Yet, fundamental notions of bounded rationality remain – we can only attend to so much, just so much, in any 24-hour period. The "just-so" ness of it all is very much Garfinkel's preoccupation in his studies of the organization of experience. Each social actor in every situation comes together with others to do things with *just* what is available at that moment. The concrete conditions of real life demand such particularity, however much social researchers want the soothing effect of generality. At any moment, there are just so many resources, just so much information, just so much time. The sequential unfolding of events produces just that. Unlike economists, we cannot hold the world constant. It slips forward in time and across space. As social actors, we must act with just *these* conditions, and no others. We may choose *not* to act, but then under conditions that are not of our making (but that *are* being made by others). We are caught in the *durée* of lived experience and in the multiple realities described by Schutz.[1]

To organizational specialists this may suggest a metaphor like "collage," the hurriedly stuck-together bits and pieces of everyday experience, what Goffman called the flotsam of daily life. Certainly, as the phones ring, and the facsimile machine spews out more documents, and computers hum data down fibre-optic networks, life *can* seem a collage. But this is, I think, a superficial image.

Our lives and the organizations of which we are a part are more like a montage, the edited narrative of many, many moments which we join together to form a whole piece, a story that makes sense, the story "so far." Organizations and the people who fill them are the very essence of modern life. Their accounts are the running record of society. Their stories are the narratives of modernity. It is organizational actors who weave (and reweave) the stories and myths of the organization into those institutionalized practices described by Meyer and Rowan[2] and others.

In discussing language in chapter 3, I tried to stress the central role of interactionally accomplished meanings in the constitution of everyday experience. Sequentiality and temporal order, I suggested, play a fundamental part in that constitutive process. By looking at *sequence* we find the recursive structuring that turns individual actions into collective effects. Sequence turns action into the narratives alluded to above. Sequences of action, in turn, need to take into account the positioning of adjacent actions and their serial consequences. The reason-ableness of organizations that seems clear from within and considerably less so from outside is located in the sequenced unfolding of events. This is that familiar "you had to be there" claim, lending such particularity to these large domains we call organizations. It also highlights the essential intimacy and intensity of the interaction order stressed in the last chapter. Indeed, a major point of this study is also to propose that within the *details of action* we can learn a great deal about the structuring of social life. If we want, in other words, to learn about organization*s*, we must study organizatio*n* – close up.

This chapter looks at perhaps the smallest sort of organization: two turns at talk. In effect, I want to examine just how the montage of experience is constituted, moment to moment.

Adjacency Organization

The key to the practical efficiency of both information exchange and conversational turn-taking lies in the priority operation of *adjacently* organized turns at talk. While this finding may seem obvious at one level, extraordinarily microscopic at another, and superficially "reductionist," the social and social theoretic consequence are both remarkable and far-reaching. In terms of the analysis of interaction and often loosely conceived notions of "context," serious consideration of adjacency organization and sequentiality can dispel much of the usual preoccupation with "subjective analysis" and "interpretive" findings. Intersubjective understandings and shared interpretations are central to social life and to social research. And when we treat interactional context as the achieved and oriented-to accomplishment of actors, it becomes a clearly observable and quite empirical matter.[3] Close examination of talk, moreover, reveals just how the external constraints, internal politics and complex information base of organizations work. The inherent complexity of multiple tasks and flows of information is that they are located in and, most importantly, *channeled through* the dense interactional settings that comprise the working day.

At the core of the temporal, sequential, and conversational organization of *action* are adjacently organized units of *inter*action.[4] These efficient two-turn exchanges, discussed earlier, are organized in distinct and matching pairs: question/answer, summons/answer, request/response, invitation/acceptance, announcement/acknowledgment, compliment/response, complaint/response, and so on. They provide a kind of revolving door through which the complexity of organizational life can be channeled, assessed, and assimilated. In particular, questions and their answers provide the *primary* structure through which information is sought.

The organization of adjacency pairs is moreover a pervasive feature of all talk, whether casual conversation or formal occasion. As Harvey Sacks describes, "The basic sequence is a two-unit sequence; the two turns in which the parts of the sequence occur are placed adjacently to each other; and for all of them you can discriminate what we will call 'first pair parts' from what we will call 'second pair parts' so that the parts are relatively ordered."[5] Turns are built one upon another and in the organization of question and answers can be found the most basic yet most flexible "binding" or cohesion in interaction. It is a cohesion that is also deeply implicative of the topic under discussion and, across turns, of the direction and thereby the trajectory of the talk. It creates a kind of *conversational collusion*, tying topic, talk and task together. Adjacency pairs of all sorts function as a kind of driving mechanism urging forward turns and topic, insistent in both design and impact. The interactional and structural force of a question demands its answer. Answers derive their status and shape from their immediate placement after a question in the ongoing flow of talk, and from their reciprocal recipient design. The one shapes the other, in predictable, precise, and patterned ways.

Functioning as a local system, they are necessarily constraining on participants, yet also enabling. Indeed the enabling aspects of adjacently paired turns provide the locus for shifts in topic and agenda, as well as the reorientation of conversational trajectories and organizational goals, as, for instance, in this premeeting exchange:

5.1   University Prov

| 1 | **Prov:** | → D'we have a *meet*ing? |
| 2 | **Dean:** | *We* have a meeting. *You*, me and *Trev*or, |

Organizational actors use these pervasive and handy connections to constantly update their shared information base and to coordinate people, materials, and schedules with a view to moving along the business of the day, as in this phone call:

5.2   Research Group

3	**Jim:**	Uh there's a note on my desk? (0.4) that
4		says there's a meeting arranged for next
5		*Thurs*day? Three to three forty-five? (0.6)
6		→ Izzit the one *you* were trying t'set up?
7	**Simon:**	*Yes.*

Framed as statement + question, each segment of this extended inquiry has an interrogative inflection, locating a note both on a desk and in a stream of organizational liaisons, and reconfirming that *this* one, *this* Thursday, at *this* particular time, is *that* meeting which Simon had told him about before. "Uh" marks the "reason" for this telephone call that Jim has placed to Simon, in this highly indexical yet self-explicating strip of talk. The fine thread of talk links time, space, people, action, and organization in a seamless web – here elaborated in a single turn at talk.

Questions may briefly solicit a singular bit of information or, by contrast, initiate a protracted enquiry, negotiation, or planning session. Questioners, in other words, may simply and economically express a classic "need to know," directing their question to an organizational member "in the know" and receiving the requested, practical information. Conversely, a question can be both "loaded" and "leading," identifying in its thrust multiplex issues which are *interactionally* meaningful, in terms of the sorts of local identities and activities involved. They may also be *organizationally* relevant in that who is asking what question of whom is a matter of interactional hierarchies of individuals and information.

Inserting a quick question into a meeting may, for example, be quite a controlled way of interjecting oneself at a key point in the busy flow of topics and agendas. It also *creates*, by virtue of its placement in terms of those topics, an opportunity to position one's own agenda in a relevant context and thus catch the ear (and attention) of participants:

5.3   Council

```
1   Dean:  → Could I ask ⎡a question⎤ before we move
2   Chair:            ⎣Y  e  a  h⎦
3   Dean:    on?
4   Chair:   (yeah)
5   Dean:    D'you recall? (0.2) uhm- (0.6) the-
6            the table of . . .
```

Large formal meetings, as we saw in chapter 4, provide in their turn-taking for the importance and effect of questions by requiring speakers to, as it were, queue for their turn to pose a question or respond to current speaker's actual or implied question. In this example, the Dean defers to the Chair of the meeting by locating his question within the interaction order of the meeting. He justifies the location of his projected question in terms of local topical organization. Failure to so mark an unscheduled turn is noticeable to various degrees depending on the level of formality, the topic under discussion and, at times, the degree of potential disagreement among participants. The Dean produces "just enough" for the Chair to grant his request, just enough and no more, in a routine demonstration of both the projectability and pragmatic placement of talk.[6]

The Chair's quick affirmation and its recycled echo marks not only the Dean's projected request but also his situational and organizational obligation to request speakership and the Chair's reciprocal responsibility to monitor for such requests. When the Dean further marks his intrusion by providing a warrant: "before we move on?", he displays his orientation to the turn-taking conventions of a formal meeting setting and to who controls the official agenda. Formality is, as indicated earlier, produced as a collaborative matter. He also manages the "once through" quality of social organization, since slipping his question (and topic shift) in *here* in the temporal and topical flow insures joint attention, and anticipates an organizational agenda which, through this positioning, further frames unfolding issues.[7] Since the attention of organizational actors is fleeting, at best, a quick question, well placed, will gain far more "readability" than a memo or report on the same topic. A great deal of interactional "value" is thereby packed into a fleeting moment of talk, into a well-placed question or pointed answer.

In any interaction, the placement of questions and their answers is analyzable both in terms of their immediate environment, and in terms of their *location* in the talk so far and in *relation* to the talk still to come. Placement of a question may, as noted, be a way of achieving coordinated entry or reentry into a meeting.[8] Locating a question precisely may also provide for a conversational or interactional stance, one which may be significant in organizational terms as well.[9] A question, both in precision placement and interactional thrust, may serve the surface appearance of request for information or clarification while at the same time providing the speaker with a manufactured opportunity to shift topic, deflect argument, take a position, or accomplish disagreement. This is the joint action of turn-*taking* and turn-*making* noted in chapter 3.

Moreover, while questions demand answers, and do so in routinely patterned and predictable ways, careful examination of a range of questions in telephone calls and meetings suggests that their placement and purpose varies, and that placement is purposive along a variety of lines. Placement may be a matter of timing as much as interactional opportunity, as in this snatch of conversation recorded during the paper-shuffling, door-exiting activities at the end of a long meeting:

5.4　Council-2

```
1   Jim:  →  Hullo (.) Tom, (1.1) dja get my note
2            about the- (0.3) Signal Program?
3                      (0.7)
4   Tom:     Ah sure did, thank you.
```

Given that some members of different departments in a large organization meet relatively infrequently face-to-face, premeeting and postmeeting talk provides an opportunity to update information about shared, parallel or related activities.[10] This brief exchange, between members of different departments of a university, highlights some of the features of these miniature updates.[11]

In the following phone call, the status of a work project is tracked and its viability as a next activity assessed. This too is common feature of the organizational day:

5.5　Investments-3

```
1   Rhonda:   This is Rhonda.
2                        (0.2)
3   Bill:     . hh Hi, Rhonda! Bi ⌈ll here?⌉
4   Rhonda:                      ⌊Hi Bill?⌋
5   Bill:     Returning . . . not Marco's (0.2) but Ron's
6             call?
7   Rhonda:   Right. Just a minute.
                ((caller on hold: 6.5 secs))
8   Ron:      Hull ⌈o ?⌉
9   Bill:          ⌊Hi⌋ Ron. Sorry I didn't get back to you,
10  Ron:   →  OKay. Did you talk to . . . John?
11  Bill:  →  Yeah and I got the figures
12                       (0.3)
13  Ron:      Oh- already?
14  Bill:     Yeah,
15  Ron:      Okay. (0.2) ⌈You⌉ want to come up?
16  Bill:               ⌊. h ⌋              Ri : ght.
17  Ron:      Okay, I'm here?
18  Bill:     Right, bye.
                      ((click))
```

The question: "Did you talk to John?" seems straightforward enough, yet Bill rushes to elaborate (line 11). This might be categorized as an "indirect speech act" in that it solicits the underlying agenda of a set of figures needed for a task, but clearly it is, first and foremost, a question about talking to John. Extended in interactional time and space is the fact that John has papers needed for a work activity, and thus "talking to" him effectively tracks the papers and the status of the project, as well as timing the meeting of Bill and Ron. People in organizations "control" information, resources, benefits, and so forth, and that gatekeeping process is far from trivial. Their control is often decidedly spatio-temporal in that until, for example, John releases certain information to Bill and Ron, neither can proceed. John, as we all know, may not be highly ranked in this organization, indeed he might be quite lowly, but until Bill both talks to him and gets a particular set of figures, this particular work task is in organizational limbo. Moreover, Ron is surprised at the speed, as indicated by his "Oh" + "already?" (line 13). The *temporal* flow of information and objects is thus a central organizational problematic.

The obvious and practical need to keep track of people, paper, procedures and events in organizations is one which is routinely accomplished at the level of talk, indeed primarily so. These frequent exchanges are usually brief, economical and highly synoptic, but they move forward the multiple agendas of the organization. The following collection of questions/answers come from a variety of settings within the organizations studied:

5.6   Travel Agency/1

```
1  Helen:  → You haven't seen Sheila have you?
2  Mary:     No- Yes I have.
3  Helen:    Oh,
```

5.7   Research Group-2

```
1  George:  → Have ya talked t'thuh desi : : gners yet?
2  Sally:     Not yet
```

5.8   TV Show

```
1  C:  → We'll just take our cues from you, basically?
2  A:    Okay
```

5.9   TV Station

1   **F:**   →   Is that Harry W*o*rth?
2   **E:**   I believe so, yeah.

5.10   Staff Meeting/1

1   **Sylvia:**   →   What d*a*te iz this?
2   **Linda:**   Sherry's trying to set a date and they're
3   talking about the te*n*th ⌈'r something⌉
4   **Kate:**   ⌊Yeah I think⌋
5   it's a T*u*esday?

5.11   University Prov

1   **Prov:**   →   *You* appoint the graduate advisers
2   don't you,
3   (0.3)
4   **Dean:**   No *actually* what happens is *you*
5   appoint them

5.12   Investments-1

1   **B:**   →   Uh, what do you think of our *ma*rket?
2   **A:**   I think it's *hot* *r*ed hot and we should be
3   investing frankly,

5.13   Investments-2

1   **A:**   →   Oh, th*a*t's the book you're talkin about?
2   **M:**   Well, no this *i*sn't a b*o*ok, this is just
3   a- a *r*esearch report

5.14   Council

1   **Dean:**   →   Do we have a q*u*orum?
2   **Chair:**   No: we haven't yet I'm waiting

5.15   Kennedy

1   **Bell:**   →   What was that number?
2   ( ):   Four hundred fifty-sixty

5.16   Council

```
1   Rock: → Whe : n's the mee : ting coming up?
2   Ed:     U : H we're gonna try t'make it (.)
3           to : wards the e : nd uv next mo : : nth
4           uh-U : : ⌈: H   ⌉
5   Rock:             ⌊Next⌋ month
```

These "questions" also take many forms in interaction, only some of which look like grammatical varieties:

→   You haven't seen *Shei*la have you?   (5.6)

→   Have ya talked t'thuh desi : : gners yet?   (5.7)

→   We'll just take our cues from you, basically?   (5.8)

→   Is that Harry W*o*rth?   (5.9)

→   What d*a*te iz this?   (5.10)

→· *You* appoint the graduate advisers don't you,   (5.11)

→   Uh, what do you think of our *ma*rket?   (5.12)

→   Oh, th*a*t's the book you're talking about?   (5.13)

→   Do we have a q*u*orum?   (5.14)

→   What was that number?   (5.15)

→   Whe : n's the mee : ting coming up?   (5.16)

In these examples, several are accomplished with "tag" or end position markers (for instance, 5.6, 5.8 and 5.11) or inflection (5.13). Note, too, that almost all contain stresses on the key word in the question, adding a significant local "tilt" to the inquiry and further shaping the "second pair part" or answer. Only some of the questions are likely to turn up in a grammar book or phrase book for foreigners, yet each operates directly and immediately to produce a turn that retrospectively stands as an adequate answer to the projected inquiry.

Questioning approaches may also turn out to serve multiple interactional activities, such as requests for explanation or clarification, as in 5.13, and the following examples:

5.17   Investments-3

1 A: → What is the str*a*ngle?
2 D: A str*a*ngle is being in a long f*u*tures
3   contract and short in *o*ptions.
4 A: Ah, I *see*.

5.18   TV Station-4

11   Len: → Uh- who- who- who are they   the- they- they're
12   the ⎡pro*du*ction house⎤
13 Andy: ⎣*They're* called   ⎦ S.A.F.
14   (0.2)
15   *Sorry Artists Film* Productions

There are also multiple uses of straightforward "repeat" requests:

5.19   Investments-4

1 A: The one about the baby bells,
2 M: → Pardon me?
3 A: The one about baby bells?
4 M: Uh- uhm yes.

and requests for favors rendered or actions to be taken, posed as questions:

5.20   Investments-3

1 A: Would you handle margin for me?
2 C: Ok, that's fine.

5.21   Dean's Office

1 **Dean:**   Okay would you do me a favor
2   then (0.8) and uh-
3   (1.4)
4   and- uh- and attach both of them and see
5   they go (.) to Lara
6 **Helen:** Okay,

or questioning may involve a more extended and nested sort of clarification sequence, often marking an underlying set of issues that the
interactants are simultaneously tracking, as will be discussed below:

5.22   Investments-4

```
 1  A:  →  I'm confused here. Cable 9 is the (.) one
 2            with the splattering of little cable stations
 3            in the West Virginia hills, or some darn
 4            thing?
 5                                      (0.2)
 6  B:     Now, Cable 9 has uh, one
 7  A:  →  'R (.) Atlantic City?
 8  B:     West Virginia system. No, Atlantic City's
 9            separate- b- but- but it's got systems
10            contiguous t' Atlantic City? and it's got
11            other Jersey systems,
12  A:     Uhuh,
13  B:     It's- i- it's got a splattering of Jersey
14            systems
```

Note here how A's "linked" questions relating first to "the West
Virginia Hills" (lines 1–4) and, almost immediately, to "Atlantic City"
(line 7) constrain B to respond sequentially. Cable 9 has "one" West
Virginia system, it turns out, but – untangling both the talk and the
geography – it is revealed that Atlantic City (in New Jersey) is "separate" but the source of the possible confusion is that, *in* (New) Jersey,
Cable 9 also has (echoing A in line 2) "a splattering" of systems. Thus
information gathering is an embedded and sequential matter, and
can *most* effectively be handled through the "recipient-designed"
mechanisms of interaction. By this I mean that a written *report* on
Cable 9's corporate structure would not guarantee that Speaker A has
sufficiently understood the matter to be able to act (in the case of
5.22 above, in order to advise a client on a possible investment).[12]

Throughout these routine informational exchanges, the relevance
of a single question or request to a singular answer or compliance is
frequently not limited to the immediate environment of the adjacency
pair, as we shall see. Information and clarification requests may indeed solicit needed expansion or detail of a given point of focus. They
may also serve broader conversational and interactional activities and
thereby influence both the immediate setting and more diffuse organizational concerns well beyond the structural constraints of the
adjacency pair organization itself.

Questions and their answers are part of the topic, texture and tone of organizational interaction and typically provide for their *in situ* status at several levels. In other settings, such as casual conversation, questions may be pretopical or topic generating in operation,[13] but in organizational settings they are, more typically, topic-embedded and elaborative. As talk and task blend, work conversations display a *narrowing* as opposed to topic-generating tendency as members attend to the "quickie" contacts that connect the many fragments of a workday:[14]

5.23   University Prov

```
 1  Prov:  → Do we have a meeting?
 2  Dean:    We have a meeting (.) You, me and
 3           Trev ⌈or,    ⌉
 4  Prov:         ⌊Does⌋ it pertain to tomorrow at all?
 5  Dean:    Just a very little bit of it pertains
 6           to tomorrow
 7  Prov:    I think I'd like to uh-
 8  Dean:    Cancel out?
 9  Prov:    focus on tomorrow=
10  Dean:                    =(arright)
11  Prov:    so far as I can
12  Dean:    Well, in that case- ⌈the  A M O U N T⌉
13  Prov:  →                     ⌊Well the two things-⌋
14  Dean:    of time that have to spend with you
15           ⌈in-   ⌉ is a relatively small amount on
16  Prov:    ⌊Okay,⌋
17  Dean:    tomorrow but I- I do have to uh- if you want
18           to raise specific issues that I can get
19           down and get my- my staff cranking on (.)
20           fine.
21  Prov:  → There are a couple of things, that're backed
22           up. One is tomorrow, the OTHER is- this is
23           the last day on those new equipment
24           requests . . .
```

Example 5.23 is a recap and continuation of example 5.1 above. If we look at it again, it is clear that the Provost (line 1) was actually asking a "loaded" question. That is, information about a possible meeting was merely a first stage to a large set of issues. He follows his initial question with another, asking whether *this* meeting pertains to a large one scheduled for the next day (with a group of visiting administrators from the state university system). The second question also narrows the topic to "two things" (introduced at line 13, and recycled at line 21), which he uses to block a general meeting with the Dean in the interests of two pressing problems, related to tomorrow's meeting and a deadline of today. This is the satisficing and selectively narrowing strategy routinely used by organizational actors to get the practical matters of the day done. In terms of the temporal flow of events, *only* actions related to his two stated objectives interest the Provost and for good organizational reasons. Questions thus become transformed into quite pointed enquiries and, through their place-ment and sequential flow, are effective markers of unfolding agendas and of a kind of interactionally bounded rationality (see chapter 8 below).

Information is checked and verified as well as simply elicited through questions, and both interactional and organizational conse-quences flow from the answers provided (or avoided). Across the busy surface of the meetings and telephone calls of the workday, members are thereby constantly probing the retrospective-prospective accountability of action and its consequences. In a very practical sense, these sorts of verbal exchanges are the core of bounded rationality, satisficing, coalition building, and ultimately the overall rationality of the organization.

The next extract is from a previously cited internal staff meeting in a university administrative department. Katie has just concluded a fairly extensive report on increased applications to graduate school from US domestic students:

5.24   Staff Meeting/1

```
1   Susan:   → Is this in (.) things like Engineering
2                too for insta⌈nce
3     Katie:            ⌊Uhm. I haven't had a
4                chance to break it down into depart-
5                ments yet because I got the tally
6                yesterday . . .
```

Susan, a veteran of these internal meetings, poses a clarification re-quest: "Is this in (.) things like Engineering too." However, it is not just a clarification request nor does it address simply the immediate issue. It is a "query," in the sense that in addition to producing a question, Susan has also rekeyed the discussion by questioning the status of the increased student applications in Engineering. In a single turn, Susan moves from a local report to a decidedly global issue.

Here, then, I would propose a necessary distinction between "*questions*" that narrowly seek some limited and local range of information or related reaction, and "*queries*" that break frame or rekey the ongoing verbal interaction. Susan's query escalates a routine internal report to the level of state, and even federal, funding for higher education since both the state legislature and federal agencies treat the funding of engineering as a hot political and economic issue encompassing both a concern for increased levels of American technological superiority and an increasing reluctance to use taxpayers' money to train Third World populations in that same technology. Breaking frame and rekeying, then, are major operations of queries, addressing not only shifts in topic but changes in ways of treating the same topic.

Example 5.25 features another apparent informational request in a different university meeting:

5.25 Fellowship Meeting

```
1                         (1.3)
2    Matt:  →  What is the maximum amount you want to
3               gi- wha- what is the amount you want to
4               give each (.) of your fellowship
5               recipients,
6                         (0.4)
7               cuz I sense that's (.) the dragging=
8    Dean:     =Forty-eight hun ⌈ dred ⌉ dollars?
9    Matt:                      ⌊=point⌋
9    Dean:     PLUS? (0.7) fees, plus out of state
10              if they're eligible,
11                        (0.6)
12   Matt:    (Hm.)
```

In this example we gain further insight into the possible range of a given question, and with it the need for the proposed distinction between question and query.[15] The format here is that of query + reason for query. A more general formulation might be: question/ query + rationale, since a first query is often followed by a second query which glosses the rationale behind both and may, in fact, project further queries in a kind of chain effect.[16]

Questions may be one-off affairs, or a question may lead to a query, while queries are often issued in series. In the above extract, with a single adjacency pair, we are plunged into a major organizational controversy, namely the maximum ceiling of funding allowed for graduate students when combining all sources of funding, a ceiling negotiated at the level of the state university system's administration and a bone of considerable contention between the three departments at this particular meeting. Indeed, one may speculate that these interactants have been over this ground many times before, that the Director of Financial Aid may well know the answer to his own question and that the Dean may know that he knows and so on. Yet, recursively, these exchanges shape the drift of decisions and even outright reverses of decisions. Graduate fellowship funding, ceiling levels, fund sources and the like are recurrent features of the everyday interaction between these men and these two departments, as well as between members of this organization and other campuses of the university system. The practiced manifestation of these relations through talk is one mechanism by which organizational activities, and thereby the organization itself, are produced and reproduced across time and space.

Questions and Queries

Finer distinctions between questions as first pair parts will now be useful as we look more closely at the placement of a given first pair part with particular reference to the talk it projects, as well as the ways in which it is sequentially implicative. Questions and answers are systematically packaged as organizationally relevant and motivationally transparent activities, as well as being sequential phenomena.[17] And, as we have seen, questions take many forms, as do their answers.

Goffman provided students of talk with an important distinction, for example, between "replies" and "responses."[18] Replies are proposed as second pair parts that address the question posed by providing part or whole statements, directly and cogently. Responses, on the other hand, are presented as conversational objects which, while satisfying the constraints of conditional relevance and sequential implicativeness, do so by breaking frame.[19] If we extend such a distinction to demarcate "questions" from "queries," a question may be understood as a first pair part which is recipient designed along pragmatic lines to elicit a reply, in Goffman's sense. That is to say that a question is sequentially implicative of preceding talk in such a way that it interactionally projects a specific kind or range of answer, namely a reply that directly and unambiguously addresses the mode and manner of that question. Such a reply is addressed to meaningful elements of whole statements related to the question at hand. The one addresses the other and is pragmatically and purposively designed to do just that and, arguably, no more.

A query, on the other hand, breaks the conversational frame, addressing an aspect or issue beyond the frame of the current discussion and, in so doing, typically elicits a response which acknowledges the framebreak and seeks to provide an appropriate rejoinder, fitted to and fitting the organizational thrust of the query. This is to say that the query is oriented to by recipient *as a framebreak*.

I am suggesting then that *questions* have the surface quality and interactional consequences of being essentially straightforward, eliciting a typically factual, accountable reply. *Queries* are instead hearable and treatable as addressing or leading to alternate and diverse levels or frames of discourse. Responses to queries similarly display a sensitivity to their achieved rekeying and to their potential to address multiple levels of organizational concern, whether by providing collateral information, defensive deflections, further elaboration or anticipation of the line of enquiry, or even a declining of such a projected direction of discussion. Just as witnesses in court or lawyers in plea-bargaining sessions anticipate and attempt to deflect lines of causal or punitive queries, members of specific departments in specific organizations hear and orient to the organizationally grounded presuppositions and projections contained in co-participants' talk. Their responses may, for example, justify an action, or project a plan, or accelerate an anticipated line of enquiry, or elaborate a position recursively, indeed even accomplish a command.

Queries have the further feature, as indicated, that they are frequently used in sequence, chained together by same speaker to follow a particular line of reasoning or to lead to a particular position. A query breaks frame as the first stage of a series of same-speaker turns that may address broader organizational issues or selectively narrow a topic along relevant lines. It may be overt and thereby hearable for its intended rekeying of the talk at hand, or it may be disguised, marking a subtle shift but initially unclear in its intended direction. Recipients appear alert to the potential of direct or indirect queries and may themselves provide direct or indirect responses. In extract 5.26, for instance, President Kennedy and his economic advisors have been silently examining a newly compiled summary of budget figures that provides the primary focus of a meeting on possible tax cuts:

5.26   Kennedy

```
1                         (26.3)
2   JFK:    How many copies of this have you
3           made Dave?
4   Bell:   Well they're- they're all here . . .
5           in the room sir except uh (0.6)
6           for about three more that are in
7           our- (0.8) in Bob Turner's office.
8                         (2.9)
9           This is handled (.) the way
10  JFK:                          ⌈Yes⌉
11  Bell:                         ⌊Ea⌋ch
12          of these things has been handled over
13          the last number of years . . .
```

Kennedy's query (line 2) is notable in numerous ways, not the least of which is its placement early in the meeting, after a considerable silence during which it may be presumed (from earlier data of this meeting) that the gathering has been studying page 2 of the budget summary which details a discrepancy between the economic projections of the US Treasury and those of the President's Council of Economic Advisors (see further discussion in chapter 6 below). This preliminary document is currently internal to the Kennedy administration and therefore a matter of some security.

Clearly, Kennedy is not simply curious about Bell's photocopying habits. His query instead specifically addresses the number of copies in circulation, with an emphasis on both the noun "copies" and the verb "made" in an implicit assumption of responsibility with the formulation "have you *made* Dave?" Bell's response is fitted to just such responsibilities since it addresses first the locality rather than the totality of copies, claiming that they are "*all* here in the room" except for a number of others that he goes on to account for (lines 6–7). Note, nevertheless, the long pause of 2.9 seconds at line 8, followed by Bell's recourse to the way things are routinely handled, a claim of the recursive features of organizational procedure that earns him Kennedy's acknowledgment at line 10, while Bell persists in providing a fuller account (lines 11–13).[20]

Nor are such patterns a matter of idiosyncratic or personal style. In the many meetings studied here, in the Oval Office, university administration, travel agency, hospitals and elsewhere, talk is frequently woven along *parallel agendas*, employing such devices as chained queries, position statements, minimal responses, clarification requests, and so on.

The Power of Queries

We have seen, therefore, that while questions in meetings are a matter of relatively routine production, queries are distinct in their interactional and organizational significance. The former are fairly basic interactional moves, the latter quite accomplished procedures that follow their own, often specific agendas. The structural organization may be identical, but the organizationally relevant consequences differ considerably. Queries, chained across turns, readily provide what Goffman called "sequences at a higher level,"[21] where the thrust of the talk is sustained across several (or many) intermediate moves as one participant reveals a specific agenda (see chapter 7 below). The structural demands of adjacency pair organization therefore inform our understanding of turn-by-turn talk, but a careful explication of differences between questions and queries reveals one aspect of the business of talk and with it the business that is accomplished through talk in organizations.

Indeed, it may be argued that queries carry their own interactional and organizational force. Let us look at one final example of the operation of queries:

5.27   Hospital-2

```
 1  Steve:    Now look- (0.2) in this section's
 2             calculations we have seven hundred
 3             thousand. (0.7) This seven hundred
 4             thousand gonna go into these line ⌈items⌉
 5  Bob:                                        ⌊Have⌋
 6       →     have you seen the- uh- the budget (0.4)
 7             have you read the bud- on-
 8  Stave:    No.
 9  Bob:  →   The latest one?
10  Steve:    No
11  Bob:  →   Haven't you seen that?
12                        (1.0)
13  Bob:      Cuz I really think it's- it's- uh, relevant
14            here.
15  Steve:    Yeah
16  Bob:  →   In other words, what kind of allocation can
```

```
17          → that seven hundred thou- what- how is it
18            gonna work?
19                      (0.9)
20  Steve:    Well (.) I- uh-
21                      (0.6)
22   Bob:  → How can it work if it isn't included uh-
23            in the master budget?
24  Steve:    Yeah, well- uh-
25   Bob:  → I mean where's it gonna come from?
26                      (1.6)
27  Steve:    Uhuh. (1.0) Well, the point I was trying to
28            make is- was that the kind of allocation is
29            one that provides for radiology and- and
30            out-patients as well as to revise at
31            mid-year ...
```

Here, two hospital colleagues in the same department are trying to work out how to present a minibudget at a meeting later the same day. Steve, who has been preparing the rough figures on which the estimates are based, is taking Bob through each section of the document they will jointly present. But where Steve is admiring his own ingenuity in burying certain figures within standard line items, Bob has a different concern, that of how *this* set of figures will fit the logic of the master budget. Bob's insistence on the relevant fit is traced through a set of queries that incrementally build to a critique of the strategy Steve is so pleased with:

```
1  Bob:                                    Have
          → have you seen the- uh- the budget (0.4)
            have you read the bud- on-
2  Bob:  → The latest one?
3  Bob:  → Haven't you seen that?
                      (1.0)
   Bob:    Cuz I really think it's- it's- uh, relevant
            here.
4  Bob:  → In other words, what kind of allocation can
          → that seven hundred thou- what- how is it
            gonna work?
5  Bob:  → How can it work if it isn't included uh-
            in the master budget?
6  Bob:  → I mean where's it gonna come from?
```

Through a chained series of queries, Steve is forced into a verbal corner (lines 20, 24, 27–8) and Bob's own agenda moves to the center of their discussion. The *relevance* of one set of figures to another fits local action to larger structure *so that* the local goals are met while managing the master budget as a background to them.

But what is also critical is the sequential context in and through which this discussion emerges. Bob invokes the adjacently organized, sequential structure of talk to force to the surface a submerged organizational issue, namely that funds have to "come" from somewhere and be seen to "work." Talk and the actions it embodies and enacts are thus "doubly contextual" in just this sense.[22] The immediate context of action is turn-by-turn talk, here used to move an accounting practice (Steve's line items) into a broader organizational frame (the fit with the master budget), which through *just* such moves realizes both the environment of the talk and the project at hand. The question/answer organization of interaction is used to structure this minimeeting which, from within its unfolding sequence, creates the basis for the later meeting one the same topic. As Bob draws Steve's calculations into the larger arena of the master budget, they *together* constitute just what their morning's work is, but *also* how this subunit of this particular hospital fits into the long-term goals of the organization as a "whole," and, I would suggest, the organizational environment in which it operates.

Adjacent Actions

The sequential structure of talk is thus a *primary* locus of organizational action. Through questions and their answers, as well as through queries and their responses, organizational actors align local agendas with larger goals and do so in such a way as to significantly create or subvert those distant and abstract issues.

This chapter has looked at the ways adjacency pair organization in talk provides the linchpin of all interaction. Finegrained as they may seem, these fleeting moments of exchange anchor and articulate a remarkable range of organizational activities, from a small informal meeting to the tense courtrooms, tribunals and parliaments of modern democracies. Questions and answers, as well as queries and responses, provide a finely tuned local organization both to information exchange and the negotiated environment of multiple goals and agendas designed to meet them. Questions that appear utterly straightforward may be transformed – through chaining – into a powerful device that positions the speaker to pursue a topic and tack. Questions have, moreover, the ability to *push* against the flow of another's talk. And queries, as I have defined and discussed them, have the further interactional potential, again through their precise sequential placement, to carry forward both interactional and organizational agendas.

The idea of "question time," whether in parliament or in a presidential news conference, suggests an exchange of information of a highly one-sided kind, yet, as I have indicated, many questions are actually queries that set up speaker and respondent to pursue a quite specific and often loaded local agenda of talk. Questions and their answers are paired objects in conversational terms and, through their pervasive paired structure, move forward the work of the day in a sequential and adjacent manner. In organizations, these local exchanges of information, opinion, options and objections are critical to effective and efficient operations. In the next chapter, we look explicitly at this insistent form of organizational life and, in particular, at the interactional context of virtually *all* information exchange.

6

Information, Interaction, and Institution

In Dublin, where James Joyce grew up and sought his inspiration, there is a wonderfully Joycean sort of noun, a "clatter," which, when pronounced with the palatal "t" of the Dublin dialect, invokes both the sound of cartwheels on cobblestones and, somehow at the same time, the intimate indeterminacy of a collection of objects being shoved together for some purpose. A clatter is a collection of things that have, simultaneously, similarity and diversity. In the streets of Dublin, you could have a clatter of boxes or of fish, a clatter of children, of hats, of politicians, or of words. "Who was there?" you may ask, of a wedding or a wake; "Oh, a great clatter of people to be sure," comes the reply.

A clatter then is a collection, or, more precisely, a membership categorization device or way of typifying and grouping people, objects or activities (cf. chapter 3 above). Out of apparent chaos comes a convenient and local grouping that has a for-the-moment, just-here-and-now organization. The collection or collectivity is practical in that it solves some ongoing yet immediately relevant activity. It is a member's term in that it provides, through its construction, an inclusionary as well as exclusionary distinction which solves some local problem and, simultaneously, connects to a larger unit or set of events or people. As a categorization device, it groups the objects of the world for some relevant action or set of actions. Over time, some of these groupings or collectivities may become more stable and take on a kind of enduring quality. A few may become more formally organized and thus take on the guise of persistence and even permanence. They take on, for their members, an external and even historical importance. They become organizations and institutions. All too easily, as I have stressed, we wind up thinking they control us, rather than the other way around. Words and social conventions thus carry with them a considerable freight of meaning and an occasionally onerous aura of importance. As social scientists, we easily set out to study that importance rather than the social action that created it.

Yet the problem is a fascinating one: how does one, and then two or three activities or actors become a collectivity? Where *is* the fine line between individual and institution? How *do* people do things together? Once institutionalized, how do essentially single, momentary acts get done as a *constitutive* flow of actions that smoothes out to produce (and reproduce) the collective? Conversely, how does an abstract and amorphous social institution or a large yet faceless organization persist, prosper and occasionally fail? The nation-state seems a good example these days, but the New York Stock Exchange or the local school board will do just as well. The central question is: what sort of ordering device *is* an institution or an organization? And, finally: who or what is doing the ordering?

Information on the Move

In this chapter, I want to step back somewhat from the finegrained analysis of paired turns at talk to consider a number of broader issues in the role of verbal interaction in everyday work settings. The last few chapters have involved a close analysis of the interaction order as a local and endogenously organized activity. Meetings, telephone calls and organizational exchanges of all sorts, I have suggested, are small worlds of interactive order, ritualized to some extent but decidedly dynamic. They are purposive encounters, encapsulated and organized, yet significantly organizing as well. They are in some sense isolated from the ongoing flow of the organization as a whole and have their own organizational and conversational boundaries. Yet they are also a constitutive part of the organization: without it they lose their force and purpose; without *them*, the organization itself would grind to a halt. Few, if any, organizations can function without considerable daily hours devoted to time-consuming, face-to-face encounters or the innumerable telephone calls that are the interactional glue of all modern firms and bureaucracies. Even the stratified work settings of factory floors, clerical pools, and the many service delivery encounters of postindustrial economies depend on effective transmission of information for their efficiency as well as staff training and labor relations. Information, in turn, depends on *verbal* environments.

Through their exchanges, organizational members legitimate the day-to-day work plans, decisions, and accounts of the institution, even though in any one setting the actual activity of "planning," "deciding" or "reporting" is limited and often appears almost tangential to the topics and tasks at hand. Verbal communication and verbal categories also realize the "boundaries" of the organization as practical matters, designating the "edges" of responsibility, redefining realms of influence, and substantially guiding resource access and allocation. Much of resource allocation, even its perceived unevenness or scarcity, is a matter of being "in the know." For this, it is rarely sufficient to read company memos and reports of competitors, nor is it a matter, at other levels of the organization, of scanning the noticeboards in lunchrooms and locker rooms. What people need to know is what these disembodied pieces of information "mean" – for them, for their subunit, for their project, for their division, for their salary prospects, sales commission or dividend at particular moments in time. The practical "readings" of these materials and related (or unrelated) rumors, stories, and so forth *require* interactional settings. Organizational members "know" well enough what "downsizing," "restructuring," the "bottom line" and "rationalization" mean *in some general sense*; what they need to know – always – is its local and practical meaning and how that local aspect fits "back" into a global picture.

For this, they require and seek out verbal updates and interpretations, preferably face-to-face, but equally intensely via telephone calls and occasional more structured conference calls and teleconferencing. The information must be reliable and that reliability is tested in the intimacy of turn-by-turn interaction, with just the sort of questioning techniques examined in the last chapter. In the close-ordered intensity of verbal interaction, social actors discover "what's up" (and what is not). They can test news they have heard elsewhere. More importantly, they can interactionally construct a shared understanding:

6.1   Salesmen

1	**Dave:**	Let's compare stories. Let's see- let's *see*
2		if he's throwin' me a curve ball here?
3	**Rod:**	Uh- Dan supplies direct to that other company

4		and cont*rols* all orders,
5		(0.3)
6	**Ralph:**	It's a kind of ego thing (0.3) with him
7	**Dave:**	Yeah?
8	**Rod:**	What's- what about the other guy? Isn't- is
9		*he* in on th*is*?
10	**Ralph:**	Who?
11	**Rod:**	⌈⌈Uh-
12	**Dave:**	⌊⌊Bernard and uh- D*an*, yeah. Bernard Holmes
13		No- no-no that's not- Ren- Re*nard*
14	**Ralph:**	No, no, no. Bernard *Helm*=
15	**Dave:**	=Oh yeah cuz y'know
16		→ the- the bo- bottom*line* is jobs. They're
17		→ *cutting jobs*
18	**Rod:**	Yeah.
19	**Dave:**	→ That's the *real* story

By "comparing stories," in the above example, Dave is testing the reliability of some earlier information and also testing a hunch. Rod and Ralph are taken to be "in the know" about another sales representative, Dan, and the ways his arrangements control a certain flow of orders (and thereby commissions). Dan is identified as working with another sales agent, eventually pinned down (line 14) as Bernard Helm. With this information established, Dave then offers his assessment of what this side arrangement "means," namely that the "*real* story" (line 19) is about job cuts and profits. As this comparative discussion unfolds, Dan's understood control of all orders from a large customer is seen as based, in turn, on whom he knows, another commonsense characterization of the way individuals link to collectivities through information. In conversation analytic terms, it is also important to note that Dave's proposal to "compare stories" contains an interactional agenda which is *not* located in adjacent turns. The proposal/invitation projects Dave's own later conclusion about what the "real story" is, with the clarification of Dan's activities providing an insertion sequence in which Ralph and Rod collaborate in filling in missing information.[1]

Information, Reports and Positions

Interactional and organizational agendas thus converge to tease information out, transmit it to other key actors, and to build on the latest information to achieve local agendas. To this end, phone calls and

meetings are used as staging posts in the construction of both information and agenda. A key factor in the sequencing of these activities
is alerting relevant actors to the current state of earlier conversations,
informational items and agreements. In this way, plans and the decisions that shape them emerge as a layered series of minor moves,
rather than arriving on the scene full-blown and clear-cut. The next
few data extracts are taken from a single morning's phone calls, made
by a research project director to a variety of intraorganizational
participants:

6.2   Research Group

```
 1   Vic:     The primary reason I'm calling . h is-
 2     →      uhm- (0.3) . hh : You will recall that when we
 3            submitted our earlier budget? that we
 4            deliberately pulled out? (0.4) a series of
 5            three subheadings, and said we would bracket
 6            those- uhm, for the time being? But that we
 7            would bring 'em forward into c- the coming
 8            year?
 9   Alan:    Ri⌈ght.       ⌉
10   Vic:  →    ⌊Well,⌋ it's now ready for that?
11            Now- ((khnn)) there- there are several ways
12            we can go- go at it. And they're very
13            complicated an'tied in with the
14            nature of the accounting procedures, mm-
15   Alan:    Yeah.
16   Vic:     =on the one hand, and the computing
17            environment (0.2) on the other?
18   Alan:    Hmhmm?
19   Vic:     So what I want to suggest is . . .
```

Victor uses a common "collecting" device: you will recall? + recalled
item, to update Alan on his current agenda. The technique achieves
immediate conversational alignment, which in turn structures the
unfolding agreement Vic seeks. His effort involves helping Alan remember the arrangement *his* way by using the preferential structure
of agreement in conversation to bind both the cohesion of turns and
of earlier organizational arrangements over bracketed budget items.
Laying a conversational base, he sets up a contrast between potentially conflicting accounting and computing. These organizational
categories then constitute the context out of which he begins to develop his "suggestions," blending talk and task into a single flow.

After a long and detailed conversation with Alan, Vic then turns to a series of calls within his own subunit, aimed at reporting on his negotiations and setting up a subsidiary series of meetings:

6.3 Research Group

```
 1  Jack:    Uhuh.
 2  Vic:     They (0.2) say that we can make a
 3           request f- to cover you essentially
 4           effective immediately? . h by
 5           augmenting (0.1) uh- our present request,
 6           however as to how we handle the thing
 7           in our environment, we've gotta meet
 8           together, and I will get with Dick? an we'll
 9           have a meeting as quickly as possible if
10           necessary this afternoon to discuss the
11           issues that are involved . . .
```

6.4 Research Group

```
 1  Vic:     Uhm, we have uh- uh good opportunity
 2           and a problem now lemme tell you what
 3           the good opportunity is- I've been told
 4           by Anderson who's the Dean over there
 5           of uhm- the Research Center, that of course
 6           if we want to ahead we can do it? We can
 7           ask for a larger amount? We can get it as
 8           an augmentation to our d- (.) existing
 9           grant in uh- anticipation of the
10           summer revision,
11                         (0.4)
12  Ray:     Yes?
13                         (0.5)
14  Vic:     Okay tha's the good news?
15  Ray:     Hmhmm?
16  Vic:     Now the bad news is- is that we have
17           a- (0.2) a very large number of competing
18           objectives. Uh you weren't present this
19           morning when David an'I were talking with
20           (.) Milton. . h :
21  Ray:     No but I heard a little bit of
22           [what transpired, why don't ] you tell me
23  Vic:     [You heard something about.]
24  Ray:     what- heh!
```

25   **Vic:**   Okay, the problem is this, that
26   eh- eh John Ellis wants a computer. . . .

6.5   Research Group (2nd Call)

1   **Vic:**   Okay what we've (.) gotta do is get uh
2   *Ellis, you, me,* Ray Birch all together
3   in a room?
4   **Jack:**   Uh-huh.
5   **Vic:**   Discussing- before we make any application
6   to anybody?
7   (0.4)
8   **Jack:**   ⟦Yes.⟧
9   **Vic:**   ⟦.h:⟧ Uh- these kinds of things. *You* can
10   apply (0.2) for the kinda money that will- is
11   needed to cover you?

6.6   Research Group

1   **Vic:**   Uh *my* feeling is it should have uh- you, me,
2   Jack, Ray, uh and *John.* ⌈Okay?⌉
3   **Peter:**   ⌊Uh ⌋
4   **Vic:**   And that's enough. Is there anybody else
5   that *you* think should be there?
6   (1.1)
7   **Peter:** Uh Nathan, if he's in town?
8   (0.2)
9   Well, maybe he sh*ould'n* be there, I dunno.
10   (0.2)
11   I- I'd- I dunno.
12   (0.4)
13   Heh-heh⌈hehm⌉
14 **Vic:**   ⌊He's⌋ not gonna be teaching the
15   course?
16 **Peter:** Yeah. (0.1) That's true. I mean- I'd- I- I- I
17   prob'ly re- pr*o*bably you're right. Probably
18   the *fewer* people that are involved in this
18   the better,
19   (0.7)
20   ⌈(yeh)⌉
21 **Vic:**   ⌊And ⌋ the only reason, realistically . . .

Many elements of these calls deserve analysis here, but I want to
focus first on the information exchange and the structure of talk that
supports and facilitates it. Our central actor, Vic, actually made nine

phone calls that morning, to report *facets* of his initial conversation with the Director of the Research Center (example 6.2). He tells different bits to different people, streamlining the content to fit their interests and the way they are involved in the project. His talk is thus recipient designed at several levels of interaction: turn-taking, turn-making, and a quite broad organizational level of information update. Note, for example, that Vic makes quite extended "report turns" (for instance, in 6.3 and 6.4) through which he announces his updated information on research funding. In 6.4, he uses another contrastive device – a good news/bad news format – to highlight his own immediate agenda of setting up a number of related meetings and, again, to achieve immediate alignment.[2] He frames his report as: a good opportunity and a problem (lines 1–2); and at line 12 Ray waits for the other conversational shoe to drop: Yes? Again Vic provides the contrast with "Okay tha's the good news?" (line 14) and, with Ray tracking him (line 15), he begins the second phase of his report: "Now the bad news is . . ."

But the "bad news" isn't a genuinely parallel piece of new information; instead it consists of familiar internal problems related to how these negotiated resources are to be allocated. The conversational practice, however, provides a recognizable and readily oriented-to structure on which to frame a more subtle contrast, one of opportunity to tap scarce resources versus internal politics that may hinder that chance. The pairing of opportunity/problem, transformed as good/bad news, achieves instant alignment and the "problem" is then re-introduced (lines 25–6) as a particular co-worker and his need for a computer. In subsequent phone calls, Vic works to bring the internal team together. Timing is critical, as is internal agreement, before any further application for funding is made to the Research Center (6.5, lines 5–6).

It is in this way that the *sequencing* of talk paces the sequences of work tasks and organizational agendas. Similarly, the grouping of issues and actors can be seen as a decidedly local matter, indeed he says: "Probably the *fewer* people that are involved in this the better" (6.6, lines 17–19). Collectivity and sequence thus intertwine to produce the structuring of organizations. Moreover, if we recall March and Olsen's discussion of the temporal flow of autonomous actions up and down the organizational hierarchy,[3] we can begin to observe – quite directly – how the tension between loose and tight coupling actually operates. In incremental layers or even finer laminations, organizational actors simultaneously respond to the moment and attend to the larger picture.

The Discourse of Resource Allocation

In the organizational literature on resource allocation, the larger environment of action is seen as competition for scarce resources both within and, especially, beyond the domain of a single organization. This results in coalitions of organizational actors collaborating and competing within and across organizations. The struggle for control of resources, it is argued, results in an external control of organizations through those resources.[4] The availability (or scarcity or unevenness) of external resources is thus assumed to shape the actions of actors. Using the above strip of interactions between Vic and his immediate organizational environment, I want now to examine "just how" and through what *interactional resources* members articulate and actualize abstract external constraints and opportunities.

To do so, I need to draw on other conversational materials of Vic's many telephone calls, which simply cannot practically be displayed here. In his first telephone call (6.2 above), Vic calls Alan who, as the Director of the Research Center, is the gatekeeper of local funds for instructional and student research projects. Vic's purpose, clear from the extract, is to remind Alan of earlier accounting strategies whereby several line items in budget subcategories were bracketed in an earlier grant with an eye to the very moment he is now realizing. Specifically, Vic's subunit of the university, an academic science department with several interdisciplinary research projects under development, delayed applying for certain computer facilities, and made this delay a positive factor in "reducing" their grant total at the time. Vic is now engaged in "calling" that earlier favor, liened from one accounting year to another (6.2, lines 7–8), a critical organizational strategy for finessing otherwise "rational" but locally impracticable fiscal barriers.

Alan's control of local resources, however, is embedded in and part of the allocation of research and instructional funds in a public university system. That system, in turn, is embedded in a political system both local within the state yet actively connected to the federal level. Federal research grants, without here becoming unnecessarily embroiled in a complex topic, are funded in an elaborate dance with state resources and realms of responsibility; similarly, federal funding for higher education is delicately balanced with state obligations in the same domain. It would be difficult, if not impossible, to determine who is controlling whom in this arrangement. Indeed, in *most* embedded economic systems, the context of social and political opportunities and constraints *constantly* mediates any possible autonomy of a "market."[5]

If we follow Vic through his busy morning, we find that little of this is lost on him or on the other actors in his particular, for-the-moment "clatter" of collaborators. Embedded in his own reference to "accounting procedures" (6.2, line 14) and the "computing environment" (lines 16–17) are a number of local issues that delicately and consequentially elaborate the sort of global ties that interlace education and research with the national economy and even the endangered state of the physical environment.

To support this apparently sweeping claim, let me offer a number of further observations on the indexical particulars of Vic's several conversations, together with some general ethnographic information.[6] The academic department Vic represents has responsibility for extensive undergraduate and graduate teaching. Because it is a science, the instruction of more advanced courses requires fairly extensive computing facilities to teach students the modelling of environmental factors such as ocean temperatures, the flow of gases, climactic conditions, and so forth. For this, the department can apply for specific instructional grants mandated by the state for the maintenance and improvement of teaching at the university level.

"Instructional" grants are, however, "understood" by all concerned to serve multiple goals, among them a proportion of the research computing needs of faculty and graduate student research projects. The "accounting" must, at the same time, provide transparent "accountability" of how these funds are being dispersed, from the perspective of state legislators and their electoral constituencies. At the same time, the faculty of this department is also federally funded to do research on the environment and global warming, using materials from Landsat satellites. The "computing environment" Vic refers to (6.2, lines 16–17) is thus a complex one, involving high-resolution graphics capacities far beyond the needs of students. The local logic of the researcher/teachers' needs is hardly "determined" by external control, in this kind of analysis, but is instead deftly conjured out of opportunity and constraint. When, for example, Vic tells Jack that they need to examine just how this funding opportunity might work in their environment, he proposes an immediate meeting: "we've gotta meet together . . . an we'll have a meeting as quickly as possible if necessary this after*noon* to discuss the issues that are involved . . ." (6.3 above, lines 7–11).

And, when he goes on to call Ray (6.4), he elaborates both the issues and the timing further, again locating the opportunity in terms of a problem as indicated earlier. The "problem," in the most local sense, is that one of the faculty teaching the courses deserving of

instructional funding *also* does Landsat research and wants a particular computer (6.4, lines 25–6). In view of these familiar competing
interests, Vic goes on, in his next few phone calls, to construct a
meeting with *just* the right mix of people "all together in a room"
(6.5, lines 2–3), before the subunit rushes to "make any application to
anybody" (lines 5–6), working to avoid the intrusion of anyone who
will not be "teaching the course" (a further filtering or selective
membership categorization device, see 6.6, lines 14–15).

If we then reconsider the notion of external resource allocation and
control, we see that it is creatively, if discreetly, mediated by local
actors in terms of complex collaborations. Interaction, information
and institution are thus joined, as a single subunit gleans needed
funding in a both practical and accountable manner. These are
Garfinkel's structures of practical action and they are simultaneously
utterly local and quite general and thus neither unidirectional nor
determinative. This is, quite precisely, the business of talk. As we will
see further in the next chapters, local solutions to still further local
problems in fact seek larger problems they can appear to solve. The
nested and embedded nature of organizations in action is indeed very
like those Chinese boxes suggested earlier, but the boxes are often
transparent and everyone (or almost everyone) knows how to solve
the puzzle.

Reports in Action

So the success of this nested action matrix depends on information
and interaction. A tremendous amount of information is transmitted
verbally in organizations in the form of oral accounts, reports, and
assessments of both. Reports, accounts, summaries, and key position
statements further constitute a major element in the process of linking
groups and resources, in the maintenance of interdepartmental relations, and, ultimately, in the coalescing of a number of divergent goals
and agendas into "what happens" in the organization as a whole.
Here it will be useful to look across a few of these organizations to
see the shape of reports and the ways they are introduced and assessed
by specific actors in particular settings of action.

Doing Reports

Reports, long before they are typed, bound, circulated and left to
collect organizational dust, are verbal affairs, produced interactively
within one's own group or department and occasionally across

departmental or organizational boundaries. They are verbal accounts, descriptions, plans, assessments, complaints, summaries, accusations, and so forth. Few reports are purely informational, simply descriptive of some prior organizational activity or providing information, whether budgetary, legal, or otherwise, for some current or projected activity. Most also take positions on current issues. They are designed, as we have seen, to keep organizational members "in the know," and to enhance interdepartmental and intraorganizational information flow. Verbal reports are slow, uneven, erratic, inefficient and yet quite essential to what makes an organization "tick" (and keep ticking).

In terms of conversational structure, reports and the position statements and assessments they often facilitate are "extended" turns at talk, which is to say the turns are longer than is expectable in terms of the turn-taking model for conversation.[7] A substantial subset of "routine" reports are also produced as a position statement of some kind, on some subject, in relation to some parallel or related activity. Frequently, a report or round of reports will frame a telephone call or open a meeting, but recurringly they also occur in response to some member's question or query. Most reports begin as information items and conclude as position statements.[8] Like stories in everyday conversation, they have an internal structure that organizes both their production and reception. That internal format simultaneously signals that a long turn is in progress and marks the stages. A typical strategy, for example, is a list. Lists have been discovered to be a prevalent feature of mundane conversation, most often being produced as three-part formats.[9] In lectures and political speeches, the same pattern provides a structure for argument and rhetoric.[10] In the reports and position statements examined in this study, lists similarly work to "hold off" potential turn-taking by others.

Reports often open a meeting or telephone call, structuring them consequentially:

6.7   University Prov/2

1	**Dean:**	Okay,
2		(2.7)
3		Wanted t'talk to you about uh
4		(0.9)
5		Uh *first* item is this *sim*ple
6		matter on the Christmas sorting of
7		*mail*
8		(1.7)
9		Uhm

```
10                      (2.5)
11              The mailroom presently has (0.2) a
12              person (0.8) who comes in
13                      (1.1)
14              during the uh (0.9) period between
15              Christmas and New Year,
16                      (1.2)
17              for the purpose of *hand*ling pay checks?
18  Prov:      (Hmm)
19  Dean:      And what I want to suggest is-...
```

6.8 Kennedy

```
1   JFK:    Okay, should we proceed here?
2   Bell:   Yes sir, that there is (1.2) related (.)
3           uh (1.1) three party (1.0) monthly reviews?
4                       (1.4)
5           Uh (0.9) we *sent* you a copy on Friday
6           I don't know whether you had a chance
7           to look at it or *not*,
8                       (1.3)
9           *This* one uh (0.7) has the key element
10          in it (1.0) that uh looking forward into
11          fiscal sixty-*three*?
12                      (1.1)
13          we get a split *ver*dict (0.5) from the
14          Treasury and from the *Coun*cil. (0.6)
15          And uh that they make- that they have
16          *dif*ferent as*sump*tions about the-
17                      (1.2)
18          uh what the e*con*omy's gonna *do*
19                      (2.6)
20          in the early part (0.4) of calendar
21          nineteen-sixty-two
22                      (31.2)
```

In formal meetings, agendas are often structured to work their way explicitly through an *ordered* set of reports. Yet the production of the reports and their accompanying discussion also structure the meeting:

6.9 Council

```
1   Chair:  So, (0.8) uh, (0.3) anyhow now we
2           Have *i*tem *six* status report
```

```
3              on fellowships, (0.6) special
4              and affirm- I guess you're on Jim?
5    Jim:      Okay?
6                           (2.9)
7              The Special Fellowship Committee re-
8              ceived fifty (0.3) applications,
9              (0.2) and uh sent out twenty-seven
10             offers with eight alternates on- (.)
11             si : xteen have accepted . . . ( (continues) )
```

The extended length of opening reports is thus notable, as is the fact that they are unmonitored, that is there are none of the "uhuhs" and other continuers common in conversational production of long turns or story-telling.[11] This is even the case, to some degree, in Vic's telephone call reports examined above. And in both 6.7 and 6.8 the length of the actual pauses is also notable. An "average maximum" pause in everyday conversation has been established through the work of Gail Jefferson, and holds across a wide variety of conversational settings.[12] In these report turns and in quite a few position turns analyzed here, pauses significantly above 1 second are observable and do not elicit turn-taking by others.

But reports also involve turn-*making*. For instance, when positioned at the beginnings of interactions – whether telephone calls or meetings – they frame what follows, as well as providing an interactional springboard off which the first speaker can indicate or assess a position:[13]

6.10 Fellowship Meeting

```
1   Dean:      Ehm-
2                           (2.6)
3              After?,
4                           (0.9)
5              uh
6                           (1.3)
7              The most recent (.) meetings (.)
8              that we had I (.) c- came back disaffected
9              fected w'th the solutions that we were
10             looking at b'cuz in every case
11             (0.8) it involved ENDless juggling?
12             (0.9) each year? getting information from
13             students throwing balls 'n eventually coming
14             back? an'arm-twisting both you an'Ron
```

```
15                Agnelli? (0.7) with respect to people who are
16                marginally qualified (with the thing).
17                An'- an'ALways (.) faced with this
18                (0.7) endless (0.2) problem . h :: an'-
19                (0.6) try- trying to look at other ways
20                we can achieve the- thuh thing we're
21                after which is (0.8) to either find
22                another so ⌈urce'o money?⌉
23    ( ):                   ⌊( (sniff) )       ⌋
24                          (1.1)
25    Dean:      for campus fellowships? (0.8) so that we
26                don't have to engage in this shenanigans
27                (0.3) which cleans up everything (0.4)
28                unambiguously AND (0.6) in effect
29                really gives the aims- the institution
30                an opportunity to act affirmatively?
31                Cuz in the sensu strictu one c'd almost
32                say (0.7) that we have not acted
33                affirmatively what we've done is swept
34                the problem under the rug by using
35                (0.3) financial aid based monies? (0.4)
36                to do (0.5) uh on the- on the side
37                (0.9) uh include this initiative (0.4)
38                ri :: ght?  We'⌈ve  really⌉ not come ⌈out of⌉ our
39    Jean:             ⌊(Hm hmm)⌋            ⌊Yea : h.⌋
40    Dean:      hide/it's/come out collectively outa the
41                hides of students?
```

Here, the Dean opens a meeting with a report/assessment of his impressions of and dissatisfactions with earlier meetings. His opening position is a further lamination of a persistent organizational quandary related to graduate fellowships. Off this platform, he then proceeds to build an elaborate assessment of the limitations of present strategies.[14] Note again the unmonitored and uninterrupted nature of this long turn. It is not until "Right?" (line 38) that the Dean elicits and gets murmured concurrence from Jean (line 39). He continues in the same vein for a further stretch, laying down the framework for the meeting and his departmental position vis-à-vis the fellowship topic. The Dean is providing both his own and the organization's possible position on this issue, but is also framing the talk that follows with a substantially detailed "reason" for the meeting itself, a frame which is generally accepted by his coparticipants.

This meeting will be discussed in detail in the next chapter. For now, it will be useful to recall the earlier discussion of resource allocation and information exchange. Interaction and information are built, as I have suggested, in fine laminations, and used to evaluate past interactions, redefine earlier information, and shape next actions. Opening statements, in the "pole" position of any strip of interaction, set the tone to follow. They also project arguments and can even be used to plan upcoming interactions. We have already see this in the discussion of questions chained as queries in the last chapter, and in Vic's morning of telephone calls analyzed above. In the next example, a conference call is used as a meeting-of-the-air, to preplan an upcoming TV talk show. Scheduled participants are taken through the show format by the producer, who first introduces them, and then provides a clear position statement:

6.11 TV Show
       Conference call: simplified transcript

1	A:	Hello?
2	S:	Yes?
3	A:	Yes, yes, yes. Uh, gentlemen, I won't say ladies
4		because there are none here present, and I'm not
5		sure gentlemen is a good title either
		((laughter))
6		To those here, assembled, I'd like you first to
7		meet- uh- Jay Melvin. Jay, are you present?
8	J:	I sure am.
9	A:	You are. Jay Melvin is down in Menlo Park, uh
10		Lindsay Smith is down in Los Angeles,
11	L:	Hi Jay.
12	J:	Hi, Lindsay.
13	A:	And Sam Albers is up in- uh, Marin County,
14		Larkspur Landing or someplace.
15	S:	Sausalito.
16	A:	Sausalito.
17	S:	Hi, Jay.
18	J:	He's probably in his hot-tub. ((more laughter))
19	A:	Ah, there you go. Doing weird things with his
20		uh- peacock feathers and all the rest of it.
21		Yes, I've never trusted those types from the
22		northern end of the Golden Gate.
23	→	Well, gentlemen, the purpose of this conference
24		call, basically, is to get you all
25		familiar with what you all sound like and to get
26		some structure and order into our program of
26		Saturday afternoon at 3 p.m. at KKYA Studios.

27		Which I had better repeat, in case anyone
28		forgets, is found at 500 Lindburgh Street.
29		Corner of Sixteenth and Southmoor in San
30		Francisco. I'd like you to be there between 2:15
31		and 2:30. You'll be able to park right in our
32		lot. That will be no problem at all. We will
33		get you sitted down in the studio some time
34		between 2:30 and 3, and we'll be able to chat a
35		little bit before that.
35		I'll go through some basic housekeeping rules,
36		which are easier to cover at that time.
37	→	What I'd like to do . . . is to kind of give you
38		each a sense of the order of the procedure of the
39		program, We're going to start with our honored
40		guest, Jay Melvin, who has kindly come all the
41		way from Chicago, for this spectacular experience
42		((laughter from everyone))
43		Shall I call it that?
44	J:	Yeh. Not to be forgotten.

Here A uses his position as *de facto* chair of this meeting to make the opening statement. The reason for the conference call is announced at line 23 (recycled in expanded form at lines 37–41), and the local arrangements for the Saturday show are sketched. By controlling introductions and turn-taking, the show host is also reflexively controlling the projected structure of the program, as well as his valuable ability to place these participants in a key media outlet. Note, for instance, how he frames the guest speaker as coming "all the way from Chicago" for this "spectacular experience," thus invoking both involvement and shared laughter. Many of the "resources" allocated in a postindustrial society take just this form, namely access to influential social locations and informational settings. The talk, here and throughout this study, thus anchors and articulates the opportunity structure through which social actors accomplish the complex mix of personal and group goals.

That mix is often achieved through exchange of information which simultaneously exposes the interests and agendas of coalitions of actors. The many hours of verbal interaction of the organizational day thus finds individuals chasing bits of information at every available minute. It is, moreover, information that they must understand, not simply in some personal or cognitive sense, but in order to do their job. So opening reports and position statements are one mechanism for getting sizeable slice of information into play, and they are attended to as such. Moreover, as we have seen in the discussion of questions and queries, most information is gleaned through intense interaction and that requires careful conversational timing and tracking. If we extend the Kennedy example cited above (6.8), we see that Kennedy pursues just such a tack. After the opening report/position statement (and some paper-shuffling as the meeting settles down), he notes a discrepancy in the budget figures presented, one which shows a considerable gap between the Office of the Treasury and the Council of Economic Advisers (CEA):

6.12   Kennedy (continued)

22		(31.2)
		((much squeaking of chairs and some
		paper shuffling))
23	JFK:	It's a big difference, the CEA projection
24		for the (0.5) second quarter of sixty-three?
25		five-hundred-and fifty-*nine* billion?
26	Bell:	Right,
27	JFK:	While the Treasury projections for the
28		*same* is five-hundred and eighty-*one*?
29	Bell:	Yessir
30		(0.6)
31	JFK:	'S a *ma*jor-
32		(0.5)
33	Heller:	Yeah it's a-
34	Bell:	*Ac*tually the uh (0.4) the *diff*erence
35		of view as to what's gonna *ha*ppen to the
36		economy (.) after the first of the
37		year [( )]
38	Heller:	[The *detail* of] that is ((mike
39		static)) indicated on page two in (.)
40		the eco*nom*ic outlook under "Housing",
41		"Plant and *Equip*ment", "Inventories",
42		(1.4)
43	JFK:	(Hmm.)
44		(0.3)

The document being discussed is a quarterly review of the national budget, projected into 1963,[15] which shows distinctly different expectations of the economy's performance as viewed by the Treasury, represented by David Bell, and the CEA, in the person of Walter Heller. Kennedy's probing draws both these key actors into the discussion (lines 33–41), as he shifts from a "big difference" to an incomplete formulation of a "major" one (line 31). The discrepancy is one which is assessed by Kennedy in a theme he returns to recurringly throughout this and other meetings. Many of the reports in these Kennedy administration meetings, initiated as informational items designed to brief the President and often transformed into positional statements, are similar to the rehearsal-style position reports of lawyers in plea-bargaining sessions described by Maynard.[16] Politicians are ever conscious of future elections and of how something is going to play, whether on the Hill or in favorite corners of middle America.

Responding to another of Kennedy's probes about these soon-to-be-released budget documents, another adviser from the Treasury describes ways of legitimating the figures for the consumption of Congress and the public:

6.13   Kennedy

1	**Fowler:**	*We* haven't considered this
2		at any length, Mister President
3		over at the Treasury. I *have*
4		discussed it informally with Secretary
5		*Dillon* an-
6		(1.1)
7		And I have the feeling that *some*
8		consideration *ought* to be given to-
9		*if* (.) you *are* going to move
10		*for*ward on that, of having (0.3)
11		*some* kind of (0.7) outside (0.3)
12		uh (0.2) *economist*- (0.9)
13		*organiza* : tional analysis before you
14		(0.5) *jump*
15	**Bell:**	You mean as- as *win*dow-dressing? or (.)
16		for a *real* purpose,
17	**Fowler:**	Well . . . a little bit of *both*.

The impact of deficit financing on the economy, even in the predawn of an era of the federal deficits we have come to know so well in the intervening 30 years, is a deeply accountable and reflexive affair. Hence Fowler's support of "*some* kind of outside" assessment (lines 11–13) of the President's budget addresses a broad range of organizational and political issues. Position statements are heard and accomplished as collaborative strips of interaction, as Bell's political interjection (as a query) on window-dressing demonstrates (lines 15–16). Fowler is not merely reporting that an outside economic assessment is warranted, but that it is organizationally relevant: "Well . . . a little but of *both*" (line 17).

But opportunities to accept position statements and thereby the grounds of an exchange can also be declined, just as questions can receive responses that rekey, deflect, or reject their projected line of inquiry. As a final example in this chapter, the following fragment is taken from the opening skirmishes of the TV station meeting in which the station manager, Val, is attempting to draw out the producer, Ken, on his production plans and budget:

6.14 TV Station
      Simplified transcript

20	**Val:**	Now? Did you *think* any*more* (0.8)
21		uh Kenneth (0.4) on the
22		possibility of re*duc*ing the (.)
23		production hours,
24		(1.3)
25	**Ken:**	Tch. I thought that I should
26		come to this meeting and *hear*
27		all the good (.) ideas that are going to be
28		dis*cuss*ed and that then I'll go away and
29		*think* about all *sorts* of things
30		(0.3)
31		Uhm ((khn-khn)) Do I understand that we're
32		meeting here basically to find out
33		if we've got a viable project? (.) that
34		we can sell?,
35		(0.8)
36	**Val:**	Uh we're meeting [here b a s i c a l l y]
37	**Ken:**	[Is that the purpose of] this
38		meeting?
39	**Val:**	be*cause* you had *ques*tions
40		that I wanted to be sure you were
41		satis [fied]
42	**Ken:**	[No I] have *no* questions at
43		all. (0.2) U∷hm- d- all- all my questions
44		are answered (.) right here?

Note the pause after Val's query (line 24), signalling potential disagreement. Note, too, that Ken echoes only one element of Val's inquiry about his "thinking," side-stepping the question and moving sideways to his own definition of the meeting's purpose. "Did you *think* . . ." she says; "I thought . . . and then I'll go away and *think* . . ." he responds, his own stressed words matching the tone but hardly the trajectory of her opening move. He then shifts to *his* definition of the meeting, namely the viability of selling the TV show to local advertising sponsors.

The agendas of these meeting members vary widely, unlike the relatively homogeneous setting of the publicly funded university or handpicked team of economic advisers of the President. These meeting members are potential, if not actual, adversaries, struggling not over material resources so much as scarce airtime and limited local advertisers. Talk is the *primary* locus for these struggles and differences. Neither Val, who has convened the meeting, nor Ken, who may have most to gain from the ensuing negotiations, have an open platform on which to build their arguments. Each must invoke routine conversational procedures to accomplish their opening position statements and their characterization of the "reason" for the meeting. Val's initial query sets the tone. In asking Ken to reconsider "the possibility of re*du*cing the (.) production hours," she is, in one turn, laying blame for the high budget total at Ken's feet. It is, in effect, a position statement, couched as a query.

Moreover, there are others at the meeting, from different departments of the station, and these two adversaries are speaking as much for that "ratified" bystanding audience, in Goffman's sense, as for each other. Indeed, for the duration of the 55-minute meeting, Kenneth never directly answers the question of whether he would consider a reduction in the production hours, in effect a reduction of his fee-based income. Instead, from the onset, he converts a potentially routine reply into an elaborate indirect response (lines 25–9). In many words, he says little but communicates a good deal, using the contrastive structure of talk to do so, through pauses, inflections, shifts of topic, and so forth. But it takes two to talk, a kind of tango, and Val also uses pauses and selective formulations to retrieve her position. In response to Ken's query about what the meeting is "basically" about, she recycles the term and insists instead that the meeting is convened especially to answer Ken's questions (see also example 4.1, p. 88, where Val stresses how everyone has been brought in for Ken). Ken shifts the notion of "answer" to the budget, which he claims "answers" his questions, and a heated discussion follows.

In this combative environment, questions become statements and statements are produced as queries; conversational interaction becomes a kind of Alice in Wonderland affair with each turn masking complex and often opposite meanings. Val discovers from within the interaction that Ken has little intention of reducing the production hours, just as he has certainly not come to the meeting innocently to listen to "all the good (.) ideas that are going to be dis*cuss*ed." What he doubts, and demonstrates as doubting at the structural and interactional level of talk, is their competence to sell the package, and to do so according to his agenda (revealed later in this meeting). On the same lines, Val knows that Kenneth has not so much "questions" upon which he needs to be "satisfied" but instead has a considerable number of critical queries to which she, at this point, is organizationally unprepared to concede. Further, while Ken claims that "all my questions are answered (.) right here?", he then produces a number of very specific questions related to that very budget document (not given here). The business of talk can, in fact, be a very topsy-turvy affair, one which is nevertheless unproblematically recognized and accomplished by members in the business of the day.

Information and Institution

If we consider again the notion of collectivity, central to the work of Garkinkel as well as of Parsons and Durkheim, we can see that *collecting* – of people and activities, and even institutions – is an essentially local matter. Vic's telephone calls plan for a particular collection of people to meet to allocate scarce university resources, salesmen gather to compare stories on the affiliations and activities of others, and some participants invoke the structure of interaction to opt *out* of collectivities and collaborations, as at the TV station meeting just discussed. The coalitions of organizations are thus managed in the flux of talk. But they are also stable and familiar groupings that persist across time – through more talk.

Organizational collectivities are typifications, of people and actions but *simultaneously* of institutions. Vic produces *recognizable* and elementally *recursive* activities that instantiate educational goals and research agendas. Presidents realize the extraordinary complexity of a nation's needs, desires and politics by gleaning information, assessing strategies, weighing choices, and moving ahead in incremental steps, thereby creating the quite concrete conditions for next moves and next presidents. Actions now must *relevantly* fit into a larger context, but the actions, like politics, are always local. Individuals draw on their knowledge of the social world, its recognizable yet external quality, to make sense out of new conditions and contingencies, and to project their consequences, often, as we know, with unanticipated results.

The many coalitions of any organization or group of organizations thus depend not so much on physical resources as on information. The information *may* be related to material resources but it is usually far more diffuse and multivalent. Much "news" in organizations is *soft* – incomplete, fuzzy and flexible – and it is the *blur* that needs constantly to be clarified, refocussed, and occasionally completely realigned through talk. Meetings and telephone calls and the many corridor chats that make up the workday are central to this process and constitute it. Being in the right place at the right time is a matter of sequential placement – of talk and issues – and effective executives, politicians and even academics know that. Yet being where the news breaks depends, in turn, on a continuous updating of people and events just to be able to identify *which* information matters. Thus a purely structural explanation of networks or a consensual concept of collectivity hardly captures the phenomenon. What matters is the temporal and spatial flow of information and individuals, now mediated by complex yet interactionally based telecommunications devices.[17] The constant clarification and revision needed of "social facts" demand that we catch that facticity "in flight."[18]

7

Organizational Agendas

Much has been written over the years about the ways in which people in organizations manage interdepartmental relations, maintain boundaries, form coalitions, compete for resources, negotiate their environment, and generally muddle their way through the maze of organizational life. The "organizing" quality that Weick highlights is fluid, flexible, and ever-changing. Yet organizations are also very orderly places, stable and persistent across time and space. This mix of stability and flux is the fascination. The challenge is to capture and chart the fluidity by appreciating and analyzing the stability. It is a challenge for organizational actors themselves as they weave their personal ambitions, immediate goals, career paths, and even passing quirks into the interactional flow with others just as caught up in the immediacy of everyday existence. And all the while they are producing that reasonable and reasoned account of action that makes sense *now* and links past actions to only partially grasped futures.

For both member and analyst, organizations are assumed to be rational places. But rationality is managed quite differently *in situ* than in the heads of social or political theorists or in the models of revealed preference and rational choice favored by economists. The slippage leads many to assume "irrationality" on the part of individual actors, while locating the rational order as external to them. Indeed, even some of the most recent studies of *irrationality* simply take the nature of rationality as given, unquestioned and oddly under-analyzed.[1] Rationality is then presumed to "guide" individuals whose actions can be evaluated in terms of it.[2]

Another basic assumption of all bureaucracies, indeed built into the definition of the term, is that "rules" guide the actions of people who follow them. Find the rules and you have located the basic organization. The rules are, moreover, assumed to be external to individuals, internalized by them, and reproduced through them. Much of current organizational theory and research rests on this assumption, as we have seen. I have gone to some detail, of course, to try to dismiss this rule-governed assumption. People have indeed learned rules, including the decidedly subtle rules of conversational turn-taking. But the specific ways in which they draw on them to create particular moments, achieve discrete goals, coordinate concrete activities, and thereby sediment those local events into the ongoing history of the organization reveals that spontaneous quality that so bedevils aggregate-level analysis.

Rules, it turns out, are irreducibly local affairs.[3] This is not to say they have no general properties, indeed that is the whole point of rules, but their enacted quality is what gives fluidity to organizational behavior. The issue is not one of "appropriate" rule following,[4] because the adequacy of rules is always limited by the contingencies of the moment. People, too, are limited in their cognitive capacities, as March and Simon[5] and later analysts have insisted, but organizational members are not the bemuddled or merely strategic or self-optimizing entities suggested by many writers. Nor, I think, is it useful to characterize their local theorizing as "magical thinking."[6] They are instead those rather political animals that a substantial body of other writing attests – forming coalitions, establishing alliances, and jointly negotiating the always muddy, sometimes turbulent, and occasionally calm waters of the organization and its environment.[7]

The twist, as Tip O'Neill rightly insisted, is that all politics is local. And so it is with the practical enactment of organizational goals: they, too, are highly local affairs. The trick is to untangle the local logic of rules and the ways in which the *appropriateness* of particular rules and their immediate *relevance* at particular moments *consequentially* shapes the future and splices past policies on to present practices.[8]

The contingent manner in which the agendas of different organizational units and subunits are interwoven, elaborated and, at least superficially, merged through everyday organizational talk is the subject of this chapter. By tracking each other's verbal agendas, members manage organizational and departmental contingencies with adroitly fitted turns that accomplish position and counterposition, achieving apparent convergence by a meeting's end or in the closing sequences of a phone call, while continuing to mark and maintain their specific interactional and organizational strategies. Telephone calls are also, as we have seen, used to weave the substantial webs of connections between actors and agendas. Overall, the precise ways in which particular agendas are brought into and out of the flow of talk displays the sort of strategic interaction that so intrigued Goffman. More importantly, the accountability of action means that as actors fit what they are doing *now* to the larger flow of the organization, "vocabularies of rationality tend to cloak" the necessarily tense and shifting process of negotiation and decision-making.[9]

To produce that rational gloss, organizational agendas may be overtly announced, marked and projected, and thereby available in the opening skirmishes of interaction. More typically, though, they are embedded affairs, smuggled artfully into the sequential flow of interaction, used as affiliative framing devices or revealed stepwise through position statements, questions, queries, even through silences and minimal acknowledgments of announcements and pronouncements of others. Often they persist and are preserved over long stretches of meeting exchanges and across numerous telephone calls, remaining relatively intact at the conclusion of a stretch of interaction, although frequently rephrased to achieve alignment or *conversational collusion*.[10]

The many meetings and telephone calls of the business day are themselves layered or laminated successively, gradually building both argument and projected decision. Organizational agendas thus allow members to achieve degrees of immediate collaboration while deferring the examination of conflicting goals and differences of opinion to other times, other places, perhaps other meetings, phone calls or hurriedly snatched corridor chats. Deferring disagreement or debate is not a casual or random matter; it is central to the smooth and practical everyday enactment of the organization and to the recurrent patterns of interaction and activity that constitute and perpetuate that work organization. Discussion, debate and the process of position-taking and decision-making are *necessarily* fragmentary and incremental by virtue of these recursive practices. This again reflects the fragmentary work styles observed by Mintzberg,[11] but reveals them to be effective strategies for getting through the workday.

Organizational Agendas Defined

As we have seen throughout this study, people come together around some shared sense of current need or because of some pressing issue that is being discovered in the course of a series of work tasks or interdepartmental collaborations.[12] Verbal agendas are, in turn, the departmental and organizational plans, policies and strategies that locate *this* talk and *this* activity in that stream of organizational life noted above. They may ultimately be written, scheduled, planned and revised, but their initial appearance is primarily verbal and interactional. Out of the verbal exchanges come the memos and reports that are but loosely coupled to the incremental and often rather open-ended process of decision-making.[13] But these articulate agendas are, in essence, the day-to-day manifestation of collaborative coalitions within organizations and they track the equally essential drift with realtime precision. Agendas may also be interesting indices of interpersonal relations, career maneuvers and personal ambition, but such issues remain necessarily outside the present discussion.[14]

To define an organizational agenda is to define not so much a specific conversational procedure in talk as to describe a talk-based activity through which organizational members pursue local issues, maintain and advance departmental positions, and occasionally even follow a slated agenda. Their management is akin to topic management in that they are achieved through shifts of emphasis and rekeyings that are placed with precision in the ongoing flow of talk. Often, participants move "stepwise" toward or away from a particular topic,[15] while simultaneously "holding" their own agenda intact across these interactional shifts and across interactions.

Organizational encounters themselves are "built" in fine gradations, and organizational actors construct their serial quality out of their opening position statements and topic transitions, as we have seen in earlier chapters. Thus meetings and similar face-to-face gatherings around the work stations, photocopying machines, coffee dispensers, locker rooms, and cafeterias of the workday provide the key multiparty arena in which the "circles of affiliation"[16] that characterize organizations are developed. Quite a few so-called "hidden agendas" are available and oriented to in these casual but useful encounters. So, for instance, postmeeting discussions often reflect new working understandings and revised strategies, just as premeeting exchanges may project possible game-plans and coordinated moves, and generally frame the interactional forum.

In fine ripples, the effects of many interactions occurring simultaneously and across time in any organization shape the flow and direction of action, creating structure that is, in turn, affected by later cross-currents, sometimes from distant disturbances. The force of one exchange, moreover, recursively lays down the conditions of the next.

Most organizations further display a rather delicate balance between internal cooperation and competition.[17] These tendencies have long been noted by organizational specialists,[18] but in talk we can see the give and take *in action*. As members broker the *detailed* elements of budgets, policies, planning, revised deadlines, renegotiated contracts, immediate work goals, and so forth, the general long-range goals of the organization are finessed – quite literally.

Verbal Agenda Setting

The interaction we will examine here is the university meeting about fellowships that has featured in a number of earlier discussion. It will be remembered that the three university departments represented are the Graduate School, the Office of Financial Aid and the Provost's Office. The general topic of the meeting is the allocation of university funds for certain types of graduate fellowships. This is a recurrent *intra*organizational issue, since it regularly involves these three departments in allocating scarce resources available for funding graduate education in the state. It is also, again recurrently, an *inter*organizational problem because *this* institution's ability and flexibility in funding graduate students pivotally affects its potential to recruit suitable candidates, in particular those who meet specific affirmative action guidelines – these potential students being a scarce if different sort of resource.

Additionally, the state had at the time a new governor, whose "State of the State" address proposed large increases in certain areas of higher education, including affirmative action funding.[19] This particular campus had also received unexpected mid-year funding augmentation, and was further anticipating reallocation funds from other campuses. These, then, are some of the "external" organizational constraints which surface conversationally in this particular three-department meeting. The reason for the meeting is, however, much more focussed, and that focus is used collaboratively to structure the verbal fencing of the meeting *and* the meeting's outcome.

Agendas in Action

The Dean, as we saw in the last chapter, opens substantive meeting discussion with an extended position, providing a frame to the meeting and expressing a recurring stance of the Graduate School, namely that bureaucratic procedures have long hampered efforts to provide genuinely affirmative graduate funding to target groups. His organizational agenda is, in part, announced here. He wants, he says, to avoid complex "shenanigans" with a system "which cleans up everything unambiguously" (lines 25–30 in example 6.10 above, pp. 143–4). And he pushes this claim home emphatically, developing a lengthy argument in terms of broad university policies and goals, thus locating his own local organizational interests, such as control over local funding procedures, squarely in the context of the overall organization's best interest. He is operating here as a "solution monger,"[20] using his knowledge of his co-participants' shared stock of local organizational knowledge to couch his immediate need and proposal in terms of the larger picture, thus building his own organizational agenda into legitimate and acknowledged organizational goals such as effective affirmative action graduate funding.

Where any organization can be understood to operate in "a social context in which [its] interests are seldom clearly known,"[21] the ways in which conflicting internal and local interests shape the "larger" goals and presumed preferences merit our close attention. In many such practical settings, advocacy of various departments and subunits can shape both decision-making and resource allocation.[22] In this particular meeting, the Dean is interested in reestablishing the internal criteria by which certain graduate funds are allocated. The total amount available and even the real source of the funds are unclear to anyone at the meeting, but this does not deter the Dean. Yet he must build his discussion in an accountable manner. One strategy is to tie his own local plan to long-term affirmative action guidelines and related university goals:

7.1   Fellowship Meeting

44		. . . in the sensu strictu one can
45		*al*most say (0.7) that we have
46		*not* acted affirmatively what we've do : ne is
47		swept the problem under the *ru : : g* by *us*ing
48		(0.3) financial aid based *mon*ies (0.4)
49		to *do : : :* (0.5) u : : h on the- on the side
50		(0.9) uh including this initiative (0.4)
51		ri : : ght? We'[ve really] not come [out of] our
52	**Jean:**	⌊(Hm hmm)⌋ ⌊Yea : h.⌋
53	**Dean:**	hide/it's/come out colle*c*tively outa the
54		hides of students?

55		We find *no :: w* that in fact (0.6) there's le-
56		*less* legitimacy to it becuz in fact a
57	→	dispro*por*tional sha :: re of mino *:: r*ity
58		students *do ::* not meet ou : r *o :: wn* financial
59		ais- aids based *nee :: d*? crite : ria.
60		(0.8)
61	**Matt:**	At least this- this *cu :: r*rent (0.2) poo ::: l,
62		if we-
63	**Dean:**	The cu : rrent cro : p do ⌈esn'⌉
64	**Matt:**	⌊Ye :⌋ ah.
65	**Dean:**	O : kay. Now ⌈there're *SE : V*'ral WA :: YS in whi⌉ch=
66	**Matt:**	⌊There ma : y be a limita :: tion-⌋
67	**Dean:**	we can ha ::: ndle this- (0.7) . h :::: I a : sked
68		Jim to meet with Ron Ange : lli, (0.3) a : : n'*that*
69		was fairly unproductive, but Jim came up
70		with a *bloody* good ide :: a? (0.3)
71		which I've seized upon and somewhat modified?

Recourse to the general good – *per bonum publicum* – is a favored ploy of politicians and bureaucrats alike, one mirrored in the notion of aligning a local agenda with the good of the firm or corporation. Layered conversational agendas provide a legitimate mechanism for explaining the utility of a given organizational proposal, while pursuing quite specific departmental goals. Thus, at the level of talk, a particular organizational agenda is interwoven with the immediate topic at hand, at the local level, and linked to major institutional considerations, at a more global level. Just as jurors, lawyers and public defenders in legal settings are concerned that decisions or potential decisions appear unambiguous and rational, so with members of bureaucracies everywhere. Thus the Dean presents this initial position and proposal in a way that is appropriate both to the immediate meeting setting and to the larger institutional framework.[23]

Summing up the current woes of minority graduate funding, he notes that, despite their efforts, what he dubs a "disproportionate share of minority students" (arrow) do not fit into the university's own criteria. The reasons for this mismatch between regulations and potential recipients need not concern us here, although it is important to note that these meeting participants share sophisticated knowledge of the demographic and bureaucratic import of the Dean's claim. The issue revolves, in large part, around an elaborate multitiered system of assessing student "need" that results in the institution's: "financial . . . aids based *nee :: d* crite : ria." The Dean stresses "*need*" rather than "criteria," his own recruitment concern being much more with getting the best candidates rather than those with the lowest incomes.

He then moves his proposal several stages further:

7.2   Fellowship Meeting (continued)

72		. . . and what Jim said was
73		(1.4)
74		in essence
75		(1.1)
76	→	Can't we ex*tend* the pool?
77		(1.0)
78		to include also the Graduate Oppor*tu :* nity
79		fellowships
80	**Matt:**	(hmm)
81		(3.9)
82	**Dean:**	(tch) And in a very real (0.3) sense he's
83		ri : : ght. If we c'n- can crea *: : te* (0.4) what
84		am*ounts* to uh- Graduate Opportunity
85		Fellowship slash campus fellowships?
86		(0.6)
87		and we can *move* the money round and give
88		people campus fellowships one year,
89		GOF another year? (0.8) Right? (0.4) S'long
90		as we meet the sense- *strict* sense of the
91		re*quire*ments for GOF? which is *no* more than
92		two years, (0.1) and the *cam*pus're ( )
93		number t'three: (0.9) in other words what Jim
94	→	basically said was . h LET'S O : : PEN up the
95		categories. (1.2) Now there're other
96		things that- (0.6) '*mme : :* diately (.) occurred
97		to me
98		(1.2)
99		The criteria which we *operate* (0.5) were
100		established by us?
101		(1.3)
102	→	Let's goddamn well change (the crite : ria).
103	**Matt:**	For GOF?
104		(0.8)
105	**Dean:**	For *campus* . . .

Having announced that he has "several ways" in which the problem he has set up might be resolved, he now begins to list them. At the same time, using the sequential and iterative structure of talk, he reveals *stages* of his agenda. His first stage is to "ex*tend* the pool" (line 76, first arrow), namely expand the applicants eligible for various fellowships by blurring the distinctions between certain types. This allows him to move to a second proposal, to "*O : :* PEN up the categories" (lines 94–5). Where Matt is concentrating the issue to an immediate and temporary timeframe, that is, the current pool (line 61 in example 7.1 above), the Dean builds out to a more general plan, which also involves, as his turn unfolds, a substantial redefinition of fellowship categories. Conversational laminations are thus employed to quite solid organizational ends, and the Dean thumps his message home:

7.3   Fellowship Meeting (continued)

```
105  Dean:    WE CREATED THE
                ( (thump-thump) )
106              DAMN campus fellowships?,
107                      (1.2)
108              What Henry Childers wrote into the
109        →     damn thing, can be UNWRITTEN by
110              this Provost (right?) IF (.)
111              in order-
```

This sequence explicates some interesting issues related to rules and their accomplished nature, both interactional and across time. Rules, he is saying, can be *rewritten* ("*UN*WRITTEN," line 109) by the organization that created them, *and* specifically by the organizational members whose *present* organizational goals deem such rule change necessary and meaningful. All social rules are "transformational" in the sense that they are subject to human agency and thereby to production, reproduction *and* change across time and space.[24] Competent membership in an organization involves what Zimmerman has called the "competent use of a given rule or set of rules" which is "founded upon members' practiced grasp of what particular actions" will achieve a normal and reasonable state of affairs.[25]

For good organizational reasons, the Dean now explicitly suggests, the campus fellowship regulations need to be brought in line with the times, or at least, with the times *as he is defining them*. Current contingencies, moreover, can be conjured locally so as to provide solutions to problems set at the broader organizational level. In a vivid local enactment of "garbage can" reasoning, the Dean proposes a favorite solution of his, namely that of "opening up the categories" (line 94 of 7.2) and "changing the criteria" (lines 99–102) as a way of "really" allowing the organization to "act affirmatively." By position-ing the organizational goal of affirmative action *ahead* of his own agenda, the latter can be heard as a solution to the former.

And here we enter a new phase of the Dean's elaborate position. In a manner akin to Maynard's analysis of lawyers engaged in plea bar-gaining,[26] the Dean and Matt start to negotiate over so-called "pots" or "pools" of university funds, a debate which persists throughout the meeting and provides a key arena for the construction of separate organizational agendas:

7.4 Fellowship Meeting (continued)

```
112                      (0.8)
113   Matt:    How eh- how- how uh- those are funded
114            out of uh-
115                      (1.0)
116   Dean:   They come outa your pot, sport.
117            We're talking 'bout the campus fellow-
118            ships?
119                      (1.0)
120   Matt:    Well- well you mentioned Graduate Oppor-
121            tunity
122                      (0.2)
123   Dean:   That's a separate po⌈t?        ⌉
124   Jean:                    ⌊That's⌋ separ⌈ate  ⌉
125   Matt:                               ⌊Right.⌋
126                      (0.4)
127   Dean:   What I'm basically saying is ⌈if we⌉
128   Matt:                              ⌊Sure.⌋
129   Dean:   treat the Campus and G.O.F. (0.4) as a
130            consolidated pot (0.3) . hh and simply
131            MOVE the students around internally
132            within those two pots, . h to satisfy
133            the financial criteria . h so that
134            we're ALways moving students in to
135            the Campus Fellowship (.) pot who meet
136            the financial (0.5) assistance need?
137                      (0.2)
138            and moving them OUTA that (.) when they
139            meet the other....
```

How, Matt wants to know, are the campus fellowships funded (line 113), a query to which, as noted in chapter 5, he is likely to know the answer. But since the issue is one of pots and pools as yet unclassified by the Dean, there are good and organizationally relevant reasons for pinning this down. Indeed, the Dean's next turn highlights just how close the issue is to the domain of the Financial Aid Office (line 116). The Dean has, however, been blurring distinctions between the two fellowship categories, and Matt protests (line 120–1). Matt is now getting his own departmental agenda under way by tracking fellowship categories and "pots" or "pools" of funds with considerable care. Again, it is worth noting that who is drawing what amount out of which pool is important to these interactants and, in the case of campus fellowships, it is the Financial Aid Office's own pool of monies designated for students in financial need that is being discussed. Later it will be seen that the issue becomes confounded with further pots and pools of money and Matt's organizational agenda carefully tracks these issues, while holding a clear line on the role of financial need assessment in the process.

It suits the Dean's agenda to merge two categories of fellowships, but Matt's concern is related to the limited resources which, in part, fund the campus fellowships out of a so-called pool controlled by the Provost's Office and primarily channelled to the Financial Aid Office for regular student aid. Any threat to the pool is a threat to department control and sphere of influence. This is boundary maintenance at the verbal level and it is a pervasive feature of organizational agendas.

As the Dean proceeds to develop his theme, the Financial Aid director is maintaining a different line, treading the verbal waters with some care. Presented below are each of Matt's turns from this segment of the meeting. Since an integral feature of organizational agendas at meetings is that they are sequentially achieved within and through the structure of talk, it becomes useful to isolate each speaker's turns to understand the connective thread. It is the sustained quality of organizational agendas which highlights their subtle, multilevel accomplishment:

Matt: At least this- this *cu :: r*rent (0.2) poo : : : l,
if we-   (7.1, lines 61–2)

Matt: Ye : ah.   (7.1, line 64)

Matt: There ma : y be a limita : : tion-   (7.1, line 66)

Matt: (hmm)   (7.2, line 80)

Matt: For GOF?   (7.2, line 103)

Matt: How eh- how- how uh- those are funded
              out of uh-   (7.4, lines 113–14)

Matt: Well- well you mentioned Graduate Oppor-
              t*u*nity   (7.4, lines 120–1)

Matt: Right   (7.4, line 125)

Matt: Sure.   (7.4, line 128)

Matt is, in effect, not saying much at this early point in the meeting; indeed this is a conversational and interactional pattern he sustains consistently throughout and there are good organizational reasons for this verbal strategy.

I have been suggesting all along that the business of talk and the business that gets done through talk is accomplished incrementally and sequentially across turns at talk. An important aspect of this is that, while talk is collaboratively produced turn by turn, members, whether in courtroom, doctor's office, plea-bargaining session or bureaucratic meeting, also have organizationally relevant reasons for pursuing specific tacks in talk. In a meeting such as this fellowship discussion, certain members may employ the structure of the meeting to advance and elaborate their complex organizational agenda, while others may use the same structural procedures as a resource for holding an existing position in the face of the other's marked moves. This is Matt's primary meeting stategy, and I will return to this point below.

Agendas as Achieved Phenomena

People build layers of discussion, debate and eventual decision on a given topic or activity, diffusing possible disagreement while molding decision through multiple occasions of interaction.[27] Their conversational collusion is a matter of weaving, turn by turn, one agenda into another. In this way, talk at work weaves the kinds of affiliations and coalitions that are central to tranforming abstract organizational entities into going concerns. Circles of affiliation are spun out of layers of agendas and shared yet blurred goals, rather than strictly out of organizational hierarchies. In a tight, temporal sequence, the Dean's turns build toward an organizationally relevant argument for giving the Graduate School increased access to and control over the allocation of minority graduate student funding. Both action and argument are built through an incremental series of proposals, each adding greater degrees of administrative flexibility to his plan. But his affiliative strategy must, first and foremost, be built conversationally, thus reflexively tying talk and task.

The Dean had opened the meeting with analysis of problems related to fellowship funding and internal accounting procedures, and built his proposal, with Matt's cooperative monitoring turns, to note all the repetitive and unnecessary work involved. He goes on to lay out the descriptive foundation on which he will soon construct his larger plan for still more flexible arrangements. By now he has warmed to his theme and the notion of opening up the categories, a conversational account of a bureaucratic problem involving individual students and groups of students, has been transformed into an objectified or reified "consolidated pot." Students become objects, or more precisely, objectified groups to move about according to *new* bureaucratic rules. But certain institutional constraints must still be removed, an iteration of just what it is the Provost has, in effect, to rewrite:

7.5   Fellowship Meeting (continued later)

141	Now in *OR*der to *effec*tuate
142	that . h we've got to *eli*minate-
143	in *or*der to effec*tuate that-
144	(1.3)
145	we have to m- mo- remove is the stricture
146	(0.8) on (0.4) the *Cam*pus Fellowships
147	that they can *o : : n*ly be used (0.7) for
148	*in*coming gra : : duate students

And, after more discussion, the Dean presses home his point:

7.6   Fellowship Meeting (continued)

167	in other words . h : : I'm saying
168	(0.5) what we do is remove the barriers
169	which create a *SYS*tem (0.4) which has
170	its own internal inflexibilities

At this point, the Dean's organizational agenda is also becoming more transparent. The system he is proposing is flawed, and seems, in this new account, to be almost as problematic as the existing system. Indeed, he is far from enthusiastic with the general nature of the solution. He does not, in fact, "*care* for *any* of those sol*u*tions at all":

7.7 Fellowship Meeting (continued)

249 **Dean:**   (Of course) What we're cre*a*ting is a (.)
250   *u*nified sy : : stem=
251 **Jean:**   =(Hmhmm)=
252 **Dean:**   =that has its o : : wn (.) *new* set of
253   imp*e* : : ratives. (0.6) Now t'be *quite* frank I
254   don't c*a*re for *any* of those sol*u*tions at
255   all
256 **Jean:**   Hmhmm
257   (0.8)
258 **Dean:**   Because (.) it me*a*ns (.) that we are (.)
259   eng*a* : : : ged (0.5) each *yea* : : *r* in a
260   *DIS*proportion*a*te (0.4) administrative
261   burden

A long discussion ensues about the flaws of his own proposed system. The Dean, it seems, is after bigger things, but *blurring* the fellowship categories has been an important stage. He then, fairly
precipitously, introduces a new phase of his own agenda. He brings
up the topic of the newly announced state budget, which appears to
have specific allocation for affirmative action in higher education. This,
after all, is the Dean's theme, and he moves stepwise from *possible* state
funding to expand on his local agenda. By moving "out" toward the
topic of the Governor's budget, he takes one step cl*o*sr to his own:

7.8 Fellowship Meeting (continued)

267 **Dean:**   Now look (0.2) in *thi* : : : *s* year's
268   budget (.) Duk*e*m*e*ijian has *seven*
269   (0.2) million dollars.
270   (2.4)
271   This seven (.) m*i*llion dollars gonna
272   go (0.2) into aff*i* : : rmative action,
273   (0.4) which has been (0.4) *used* . . .

After some side discussion on the recent budget announcement, the
Dean presses his point:

7.9 Fellowship Meeting (continued)

282 **Dean:**   Wha- EXPLI : : Citly what I wanna
283   find out (0.9) is

```
284                    (2.7)
285          What the university's gonna *do* with
286          that money that was relea : sed?
```

This recording was made some two weeks after the state's Governor's budget had been announced. No one could at that time do more than speculate as to how and where extra monies would be allocated for higher education, or in what ways affirmative action could and would be funded. But speculation and guessing about an uncertain environment is a *central* feature of organizational life, and it turns up as much in the Oval Office at the White House as a backroom in a travel agency or a during a university administrators' meeting such as the one we are observing. Speculation is, moreover, *interactional* rather than the cognitive phenomenon theorized and experimentally tested by many specialists in organizational behavior. Organizational actors speculate *together* and that collaborative or collusive quality actively shapes the way they act toward and react to information and events.

As the meeting proceeds, it emerges that the Dean also has identified two other potential pots of money which may ultimately give him and his department the kind of flexibility and levels of funding he needs. Matt, however, is concerned with protecting scarce resources and, as will be seen shortly, Jean, as representative of the Provost's Office, is politely skeptical of these sources. The Dean, nevertheless, persists:

7.10 Fellowship Meeting (continued)

```
377  Dean:   So ya can't have your cake and ea*t it too.*
378          I'm saying . h : : :  let *ME* get what I want
379          and *YOU* (.) *GET* what *you* want?
380                     (0.4)
381  Matt:   *Out* of a new pool you're saying?
382                     (0.3)
383  Dean:   Out'v ⌈uh (              )⌉
384  Matt:         ⌊NO : T *RAI : : D*⌋ing exi *:* ⌈st : : ing do *: :* ⌉ llar-
385  Dean:                                      ⌊ No : : , no=no⌋
386  Matt:   ⌈limited do *: :* llar⌉
387  Dean:   ⌊No no, o u t of⌋ a new pool=
388  Matt:   =That's ⌈grea : : t⌉
389  Dean:           ⌊I'm ta- ⌋
390          talking abou : : t ⌈*two : :* new⌉ pools
391  Matt:                      ⌊Brand ne- ⌋
392  Dean:   ONE THAT ROBERT *AL*ready has in his ha : : nds
```

```
393              (0.3) which he's agree :: d to give me a
394              hu : ndred K per a :: nnum
395                          (1.6)
396              of UNRESTRI :: CTED ed fee mo : ney.
397                          (1.2)
398    Jean:     He sai :: d it was unrestri-
399              that ⌈you could u : se it as⌉
400    Dean:         ⌊Y : : : e : : : : s ⌋
401    Jean:     you wa :: nt⌈ed ⌉
402    Dean:              ⌊Y ⌋ : e⌈: s
403    Matt:                    ⌊I don't know any money that's-
404              (0.5) any e : d fee money ⌈that's u : nrestricted⌉
405    Dean:                              ⌊We : : ll, he said-  ⌋
406              he said there wa :: s? He said thet so : me of this
407              money coming to-
```

He reveals that, contrary to Matt's concern, there are actually two
new potential funding sources, one of which he has learned about
from Jean's immediate superior, Robert. Here, finally, we come to the
core of the Dean's organizational agenda, namely to the commitment
of so-called unrestricted funds that do not carry the normal financial
need criteria. Such funding would transform his own earlier plan by
creating complex consolidated pots of money and pools of recipients
and still leave his department with the needed flexibility to fund
minority graduate students consistently and without undue administrative burden. This claim draws considerable discussion and objections from Matt and Jean, but the Dean is insistent:

7.11 Fellowship Meeting (continued)

```
420  Dean:    And Robert said some of that mo :: ney?,
421           (0.8) with the (0.8) constraint on it?
422           that it's financial aid based (0.3) money
```

And he provides an organizational warrant, arguing that so-called "ed
fee" money is used for a number of interorganizational fundings within
the university system:

7.12 Fellowship Meeting (continued)

```
426           He said there's mo : : : re than fi : nancial
427           ai : d being (0.5) uh- funded out of ed fee
428           monies?
```

With the revelation that Robert is prepared to allocate permanent funding which is unrestricted, the Dean goes on to suggest that the complex ties between the Graduate School and the Financial Aid Office be severed. He verbally draws together all the imagined pools and pots of money he has identified – from the state's budget, from a campus reallocation, from the Provost's Office – and recycles his proposal to create new categories, now defined in terms of academic merit (lines 450–1):

7.13   Fellowship Meeting (continued)

436	**Dean:**	and what I'm
437		*say*ing is (.) be*tween* what's gonna
438		be released from Dukemaijian's pot and
439		coming down to *thi : : s* ca : : mpus . h : :
440		(0.9) and if Robert's prepared to a : : ct
441		im*med*iately (0.9) now with what he's
442		got, (0.3) let's for Go : dsa : kes cut the
443		gau : : dian *kno : t* (.) on this (0.6)
444		*crazy* bizness that we're go- going
445		through, . h : and re*lease* money to *u : s*
446		(0.7) which *in e*ffect is free : : : (0.2)
447		o : f (0.3) what I ca : : ll the fi*nan*cial
448		(.) *aid* (.) albatross.
449		(2.1)
450	→	And let's create some ge*nu*ine merit
451		based money (0.7) that I don't hafta go : : (.)
452		*cap*-in-hand . h : and eng*age* in
453		this she*na : : n*igans *year* after year
454		after year (after year). Now *you*'ll
455		get what I re*lease*?

By combining the promised state-level allocations with the second pool of funds Robert has promised, the Dean proposes to free his own organization of an uncomfortable tie, while at the same time freeing up funds which will then recycle to the Financial Aid Office.[28] The Financial Aid Office, he argues persuasively, will automatically get the funds released by freeing the campus fellowships:

7.14   Fellowship Meeting (continued)

457	**Dean:**	You'll get every *penny*?
458		of it because it's *need*-based, what I'm

```
459            presently taking fro : : m you (0.5)
460            is need-based money
461                      (1.2)
462            So as fa : : : r's you're conce : rned it's
463            a wa : : : sh, . h : now . h getting
464            addi : tional money is your oth- is your
465            o:wn pro : blem (0.2) ri : : ght?
466                      (1.6)
467            Getting addi : tional money is something
468            that you're enti : tled t-
```

As far as he's concerned, Matt is fully entitled to pursue his own organizational interests in relation to the new state monies (lines 462–8), and in response to a query from Matt he continues to forcefully present his case:

7.15 Fellowship Meeting (continued)

```
469  Matt:    From this- from this new pool
470  Dean:    From the new poo : : ls is- is something
471            that you (0.2) are entitled t'try:
472            and do, o : ka : : y. But a : ll I'm
473            saying is . h : le : t's clear the wa : y
474            so that I : get what I nee : : d in the
475            fi : : rst instance becuz that-
476            look, let's put it this way
478                      (1.1)
479            Any money that I get
480                      (1.2)
481            releases
482                      (1.3)
483            Automatically what I'm presently
484            taking away from you (0.3) back to you so
485            you gai : n somethi : : ng
```

Essentially, he seems to be suggesting, the Director of Financial Aid is in a no-lose situation. As an exercise in interactional slow motion, let's look at a small section of this stretch of talk, stage by stage, so that the internal dynamics of talk-in-interaction can be more fully appreciated for both their interactional and their institutional qualities. The temporal flow of talk, as we have seen throughout this study, is critical to the structuring process. Structure-in-action has a temporality that is *internal* to the interaction, while simultaneously bracketing and thus constituting a critical part of the "larger" organization rhythm.

Early in 7.15 above, the Dean sums up his position to this point in the discussion, a routine and essential feature of conversations of all kinds.[29] Let us therefore examine the *segmental* constitution of this section of the Dean's proposal (here with simplified transcription):

clarification/ correction	From the new pools
Self-retrieval	is- is something that *you* are entitled to try and do
Agreement solicitation	Okay?
Reformulation 1	But all I'm saying is *let's* clear the way so that I *get* what I need in the *first* in*stance* because *that*
Reformulation 2	Look, let's put it this way
Pause	(1.1)
Proposal, stage 1	Any money that *I* get
Pause	(1.2)
Proposal, stage 2	releases
Pause	(1.3)
Proposal, stage 3a	automatically
stage 3b	what I am presently taking away from you
Pause	(0.3)
stage 3c	back to you
stage 3d	so you *gain* something

Persuasion is a sequentially organized phenomenon. Here, however, my focus is on the *structure* of the sequence rather than on the semantic load it carries. First, the Dean responds to a clarification request, in the appropriate next slot for such a response and in a relevant turn shape, that is by "echoing" the contours of Matt's turn. He also uses this first turn component to initiate his summary statement, by shifting stepwise from Matt's "this new pool" to "the new pools." He then retrieves his own overlapped and interrupted earlier turn, this time recycling it with greater emphasis (*you*). He then tags an "okay?" on this claim of Matt's entitlement, soliciting agreement. The Dean then projects a reformulation yet again, breaks off, and recommences. Reformulation 2 is, however, distinctly different from its predecessor. That is, he is not just putting it another way in the sense of *any* other way, but is significantly shifting the interactional footing, using a segmented series of steps. At the same time, he uses this measured announcement to move quite deftly from a self-serving stance of getting what he needs first to a version that converts benefits to him into considerable and trouble-free ("automatically") advantages to Matt's department. Slowing down his delivery to a deliberate rate, he spells out the deal in verbal increments. We are observing the structuring process of resource allocation in the real world, rather than as outcome.

This turn is also structured by the Dean as a nested set of contrastive claims. The first (bracket a) is simple: I gain/you gain. The second (bracket b) is more detailed: any(thing) I get/you gain something. The third (bracket c) is directly and adjacently contrastive: away from you/back to you. Further examination of this tiny strip of interaction reveals how the Dean's stress on contrastive pronouns further underlines his attempt at persuasion.

Matt, however, is not immediately persuaded. He has his own solution:

7.16 Fellowship Meeting (continued)

476		look, let's put it this way
478		(1.1)
479		*Any* money that *I* get
480		(1.2)
481		releases
482		(1.3)
483		*Au*tomatically what I'm *pres*ently 'm
484		taking away from you (0.3) back to you so
485		you *gai : n* somethi : : ng
486		(0.4)
487	**Matt:**	We- we have-
488		(1.3)
489	→	Uh we're in a ne : : w- new uh *era*- new
490		*pla : : n* (0.2) *b*ut kno : wing that that
491		was gonna be ha : : ppening we also (0.7)

```
492              uh (0.2) will carry forward
493              funds
494                       (1.1)
495              uh we provided a two-hundred-thousand
496              do : : llar
497                       (1.0)
498              commitment (0.4) also (0.5) or
499              there abouts
500                       (2.3)
501              In other words there's a : l⌈ready been-⌉ we
502    Dean:                               ⌊h : : : : m : :⌋
503    Matt:    already tr⌈ie : d to direct (       )-⌉
504    Dean:              ⌊Jea : n's proVI : DED COM⌋MITM'NTS,
505              you're providing commitments everybody's trying
506              to help us ou : : t? That's wonderful.
507              (0.7) Jean is using money which
508              is unrestri : : cted? money
509                       (1.2)
510              which comes ⌈out of the Pro : vost's hi : : de⌉
511    Jean:                 ⌊For this- this year's- your      ⌋
512              ne : : w Ca : mpus Fe : l⌈lows=⌉
513    Dean:                              ⌊Yeah.⌋ =this
514              ⌈year⌉
515    Jean:    ⌊that⌋ (.) Matt can't co : : ver?
516    Dean:    Yeah.
517    Jean:    As need-based has to come out of
518              unrestricted money
519                       (1.3)
520              that's what I liened?
521                       (0.5)
522    Dean:    (Ye : s, oka : y) So ⌈in e f f e c t-
523    Jean:                         ⌊An 'that's what I was to : : ld
524              to lien
525    Dean:    Yes I know (0.1) Robert basically ⌈s-
526    Jean:                                       ⌊Yea : h,
527    Dean:    said that was the only way we can ha : : ndle it
528    Jean:    Yea : h,
529    Dean: →  At this ti : me
530                       (1.3)
531              U : : hm
532                       (1.1)
533              And so, w- realistically what I want
534              to achieve out of this (0.5) is a
535       →      reduction (0.8) in the unnecessary
536       →      (0.9) bureaucratic (0.6) shenanigans
```

```
537              that we have to enga : ge in, year ahfter
538              year after year ⎡(after year)
539   Matt:                      ⎣It would be a tremendous
540              help to us too because it is- it
541              is a tremendous accounting and
542              (0.9) uh technical-
543                    (0.5)
544   Dean:    Of course
545   Matt:    Uh nuisance.
546   Dean:    Okay, so what I'm- . h : : gonna to suggest
547              to Robert is: Robert this is the time
548              (huhn) to cut the gaudian- and let's do it
549              in such way that it's quick,
550              (0.2) and clean? . h : before somebody
551              else (0.4) gets all (.) excited
552              (0.2) by this (.) pot of money which
553              is somehow or 'nother coming outa
554              no : whe : re.
```

Matt offers instead a solution from *his* garbage can, announcing: "we're in a new era," and he proceeds to elaborate on *his* way of controlling for these allocation-funnelling problems through his *own* department. His offer, under *his own* new plan, is to carry forward funds in his budget to cover the immediate problem (lines 492–9). It *matters* to the Director of Financial Aid which pools the Graduate Dean may be proposing to raid, for how much and to what purpose. But these department representatives are also frequent collaborators and co-participants in a wide range of institutional activities and goals, and the Dean goes to some length to acknowledge how generous everyone has been. Jean, for her part, is careful to contain the Dean's enthusiasm as well as his possible misinterpretation of her own department's intervention, pointing out that funds are for this year only, limited to new fellowship holders who do not come under Matt's "need-based" criteria. The Dean is quick to acknowledge his understanding of the situation and its limitations, and equally quick (lines 535–8) to take from this the opportunity to reiterate his hopes and plans for the future.

The collaborative and tightly fitted conversational organization of these intertwining yet hardly identical agendas is a display of organizational coalitions in the making. Matt takes the Dean's third-time-in-one-meeting description of the: "un*nec*essary (0.9) bureaucratic (0.6) *sh*enanigans that we have to enga : ge in, *year* ahfter year after year (after year)" to demonstrate his enthusiastic, but notably oblique concurrence (lines 539–45). Indeed, perhaps the most notable feature of this whole meeting is that neither Matt nor Jean ever actually agree with or directly comment on the Dean's rather radical proposal. They have asked questions, queried statements, provided brief information, acknowledged comprehension, even laughed and joked, but at no time during the meeting was overt agreement or even general assessment made of his most elaborately developed proposal. At the end of the meeting, the next moves in the discussion are set, but no decision has been made or agreement concluded. Theirs are parallel moves along the same trajectory, but in this meeting they are happy to track the action with a kind of caution.

Parallel Agendas

Before concluding this discussion on organizational agendas, it may be useful to consider briefly just how parallel interests can be achieved. I want therefore to look again at Matt's meeting strategy. As we have seen, the Dean's maneuver involves, effectively, severing important so-called "structural" ties between the two departments. His argument is built, in essence, on a proposed series of pools of money available to achieve this goal. He claims, throughout the meeting, three different funding sources: a pool of unrestricted education fee money, reallocation of funds from three other campuses in the university system, and the new Governor's proposed increases in funding for higher education and affirmative action.

Matt's tactic is one of marking time, as well as being a rather well-executed exercise in boundary maintenance. Both his turn-taking and turn-making throughout the meeting are limited primarily to questions, queries, brief acknowledgments, continuers, and so forth. As the Dean's multiple strategy relating to various proposed pots and pools of money emerges, his essential querying stance persists. Let us look at part of Matt's organizational agenda at this meeting. The brief turns presented below constitute all of Matt's turns that correspond to the general timeframes extracted for the Dean above:

1   What is the maximum amount you wanna gi- wha-
   whaddiz the *amou* :: nt ya wanna give *each* (.)
   of your fellowship recipients,
            (0.4)
   cuz I sense *tha* : t's (.) the dragging poi : nt

2   (Hm.)

3   So you're *no : : t* talking about forty eight hundred,
    You're talking about . . .

4   Who- who es*tab*lishes the two *yea :* r limit*a :* tion

5   *Out* of a new pool you're sa : ying?

6   NO : T *RAI : :* D*ing* exi : st : : ing do : : llar-

7   limited d*o : :* llar

8   That's grea : : t

9   Brand ne-

10 I don't know any money that's-(0.5) any e : d fee
    money thats unrestricted

11 Basically?

12 Hmhmm,

13 (Hmm.)

14 From this- from this new pool

15 We- we have-

16 Uh we're in a ne : : w- new uh *era*- new
    pla : : n (0.2) *b*ut kno : wing that that
    was gonna be ha : : ppening we also (0.7)
    uh (0.2) will *carry for*ward
    funds
                (1.1)
    uh we provided a two-hundred-thousand
    do : : llar
                (1.0)
    com*mit*ment (0.4) also (0.5) or
    there abouts

The above array of turns reveals that Matt is accomplishing his
participation at this interdepartmental meeting through the types of
conversational devices suggested in earlier chapters. That is to say
that he is constructing his turn-by-turn collaborative exchange through
queries about levels of student funding, control of criteria, credibility
of sources, pools of funding and position statements. Interwoven
through the Dean's strong and forcefully developed agenda is the

Director of Financial Aid's own organizational position, which is one of a watching brief. He has agreed to nothing. Despite closely fitted turns and topics, Matt never actually agrees or even assesses the Dean's creative idea for restructuring graduate fellowship funding. Even his position statements are, at best, subtle indirect responses, limited in their scope and noticeably and observably absent of approval or agreement. Isolation of Jean's turns, as representative of the Provost's Office would reveal a similar pattern, maintaining departmental boundaries of responsibility and control without committing either to the proposed project.

Collaborative Agendas

In this chapter, we have been looking at different organizational agendas as produced by different speakers. It is important to bear in mind that the reason for this meeting was not really to change radically the management of minority fellowship funding in this particular organization, but rather to explore ways of avoiding a *particular* and *local* accounting problem which had precipitated unusual intervention by the Office of the Provost. While it is true to say that these departmental interactants were seeking long-term solutions to these sorts of interdepartmental fiscal problems, the matter was seen as a practical one, with relatively immediate solutions. The Dean, on the other hand, had taken this organizational occasion of talk, that is, the meeting, to articulate a discussion of a larger departure from previous fellowship funding procedures. The ultimate success or failure of his proposed changes lay outside this particular meeting. He was, however, not simply *talking* about his plan, he was *talking it into being*. Although outside of the data presented here, later meetings tailored and trimmed the Dean's agenda to those of others (including the departments represented here) and the design and allocation of graduate funding did indeed shift, although "change" would be rather a large word for the results. Nonetheless, both organizational change and inertia are created, slowed, avoided and attentuated through the sorts of organizational moments presented here.

If the suggestion that organizational debate and decision-making are sequentially and incrementally achieved activities is correct, then we may at least suppose that the Dean's organizational agenda has moved one stage further along its trajectory by virtue of this meeting. By the same token, however, the organizationally relevant positions of both the Director of Financial Aid and the representative from the

Provost's Office have also held to their own organizational agendas, and thereby legitimated, in one small way, their department's role in the scheme of the organization and their own position within it.

And, most significantly, each has achieved these meeting-constrained goals collaboratively through talk, marking their shared orientation to multiple goals through routine conversational procedures such as questions, queries, replies, responses, long position turns, agreements, laughter, and so forth. Using the development of the meeting, the connective tissue of conversational agendas displays, for member and analyst alike, a given organizational stance. In the meeting we have examined, the Dean's overt and carefully developed plan to restructure minority graduate fellowship funding receives, at best, immediate minimal reception from two closely tied departments. At the same time, those two departments successfully hold their own line in relation to the topic, with the Provost's Office maintaining a sceptical stance and the Director of Financial Aid maintaining a cautious watching brief.

This is neither the first nor the last meeting on this topic; there will be others between these departments and between these particular interactants. Graduate fellowships, minority student recruitment and funding resources are recurrent features of public universities. The organizational agendas accomplished in one meeting are but a minor part of interdepartmental relations across time and space. They are necessary to achieve a given goal, but not sufficient to do so in a single meeting. The incremental accomplishment of organizational relations and of organizations is, of course, not only done in meeting settings but also in a wide range of interactional settings. Piece by piece, moment by moment, stage by stage and level by level, decisions are discussed, debated, diffused and ultimately resolved. In the next chapter, we will look at the significance of this essential incremental and local process for the enactment of everyday organizational rationality.

8

Local Logic and Organizational Rationality

As humans, we expect each other to be reasonable. Without such an assumption, everyday social life would be impossible.[1] Indeed, as we have seen throughout this study, we hold each other "unremittingly" responsible for attentive, meaningful, and collaborative activities. Through them, we solicit and reciprocate the fullest range of social solidarity. In so doing, we treat each other as knowledgeable agents, responsively and interactively constituting a shared social world. In ascribing rationality to each other, basic elements of trust are involved. We trust each other to act and react reasonably and morally. We tolerate departures, but within limits; we expect and demand consistency and reliability and even make allowances for consistently unreliable behavior. Above all, we expect and seek *accountable* action, joint actions that are reasonable in context.

In this chapter, the broad topic of rationality will be explored in a quite narrow and specific manner. At the same time, I shall rather explicitly pick up a number of issues discussed earlier in this study. In particular, I want to highlight the ways in which interactional materials such as those presented here can directly address the problematic of action and structure. I also want to suggest that our recurring preoccupation with human rationality needs to be examined as a sequential and *irreducibly* interactional phenomenon.

The essence of my position will be to argue that we observe our social world, select among options, interpret ambiguity, make decisions, and take action *together*. That togetherness matters profoundly to what "decision-making" is or ever can be. Advanced communications technology has, moreover, accentuated the interactional properties and the fine laminations of information, choice and contingency that build toward a "decision." I shall return to this point shortly. First, it will be instructive to look at the elements that constitute the *process* of rational action.

If we treat "action" as rooted in human "agency," that is to say in the ability to think and act freely, then the activities of human actors become a critical resource for observing "structure," what I have called structure-in-action. If, moreover, we wish to understand the mechanisms of rational action, we need to abandon false distinctions of "macro" and "micro," as suggested at the outset. Rationality isn't "big," nor is action "small." Scale, though useful methodologically, should not be confused with scope. Rationality is reflexive in the ethnomethodological sense in that it is instantiated in the actions of individuals who thereby provide a flexible grid through which those same actions are filtered, assessed and accounted for. The interpretations and accounts are, moreover, not simply *post hoc* rationalizations of action[2] but are continuously updated, revised, redefined and realigned, again *reflexively*. This ethnomethodological notion of reflexivity embeds institution in individual and vice versa. As a result, quite routine organizational action entails what might be called a *necessity of choice*, which is to say a bias toward action creating structure rather than the reverse. Throughout, we treat each other as *actors* in just this sense, as active participants and as competent collaborators.

Rationality in any abstract sense must thus be linked to everyday *rationalities*, here deliberately treated as plural.[3] Both the embeddedness of social actions *and* their collaborative and coproductive quality are critical. People, as I have stressed, create practical structures, which they then treat as external, factual and real.[4] The facticity of the social world, in turn, becomes the framework for the accounts provided. Thus the essential duality of structure-in-action lies in the tension that links immediate *reasoning* to relevant institutional *rationalities*.

We will be looking at organizational rationality close-up, as indeed we have been doing throughout these discussions. Initially, however, I want to attempt to disentangle a few important strands of the considerable current debate on rational behavior and rationality. My purpose is neither to review nor to critique the better discussions on these topics, but rather to relocate the debate within the domain of concrete human behavior.

The Discourse on Rationality

From Weber on, and in the utilitarian tradition that preceded him, the rise of rationality[5] has been seen as an essential feature of modernity.[6] In turn, modern organizations are the essence of rationality, both in terms of their basic rational-legal structure, and in the purposive pursuit of goals through reasonable and apparently consensual means. That Weber was, in large part, concerned with "ideal type" formulations while most modern researchers are studying real organizations never seems genuinely to deter anyone.[7] One way or another, observable behavior is made to fit the models, or is found decidedly wanting. *Idealization* is what the modern notion of rationality is based upon, and it is, almost by definition, unattainable.[8] But much of the current debate over rational choice and rationality tends to ignore this.[9] Instead, a single, external and abstract rationality is assumed to guide action from above. Or, similarly, human behavior itself is defined as rule-governed[10] and dictated by internalized social norms[11] and rationality is then assumed to reside in the rules or norms.

Differences between rationality in the abstract and the nature of rational action in practice have, of course, not been lost on social researchers and theorists. Some of the economic literature, for instance, catches a glimmer of the problem when it notes that there are shifting points of reference that may affect individual decision-making. But the glimpse is quickly lost in decontextualized assumptions of preference under conditions of uncertainty and change.[12] Much of the better work in this area is based on experiments that tend to ignore either the temporal urgency of social life or the inherent intensity of interactional settings of decision-making. Most such models of rationality are based on rather rarified assumptions and, by tapping interesting "threshold" conditions of decision-making and interpersonal influence, attempt to map the near "chaotic dynamics" of decisions.[13] A system of reciprocal interaction is sometimes acknowledged,[14] but preferences are assumed to be personal, and rationality, in this case, is located *inside* the heads of individuals.

Much decision theory and the research based on it also depends on basic assumptions of rather singular rationality and the manner in which degrees of uncertainty of both environment and outcome influence the process of decision-making. A whole "science" grew up around and about the topic of decision-making,[15] which is hardly surprising given the central role decisions (and nondecisions) play in all organizations. Yet most research on decision "making" actually studies the *outcomes* of decisions, these being the sorts of data that lend themselves to statistical modelling and manipulation. And social psychological studies of the "process" of decisions are largely limited to experimental settings[16] and frankly phony "decisions" with little or no long-term consequences for the subjects.

In general, then, there is a considerable paradox about all the recent interest in rational choice and the fuss over rational action. That paradox positions rational theory in the behavioral sciences as "the Newtonian theory of matter in motion stands in the physical sciences," namely "the law that behavior would obey if it were not for various disruptive influences, the behavioral analogues of friction, wind, measurement error and the like."[17]

In the study of organizations, this paradox persists. The organizational literature on decisions also places considerable emphasis on the amount of information both available and employed by actors in seeking a solution to a concrete issue. Again, much of this work depends on cognitive models of processes that are largely inferred in real situations and whose elements are either modelled statistically or simulated in experiments. Lost in these approaches are two critical factors that are readily observable in virtually all interactional data drawn from organizations: (1) the information generally available, in whatever form, however good or bad, must also be made *interactionally* available and thereby relevant: and (2) decisions are virtually never stand-alone affairs but rather are part of a sequence of "tinkering" with some organizational problem or policy. While these observations are likely to seem obvious, their consequences – if taken at all seriously – are considerable and could greatly illuminate the mechanistic "decision-tree" models of much current research. I am not suggesting here that the decision-making strategies suggested by much of the organizational literature are "wrong," so much as that their assumptions – for good methodological reasons – side-step the issues of context, sequence and contingency to such a degree as to be of limited value.

So while a number of these approaches certainly reveal cognitive elements to choice processes, they seem unable to illuminate and theorize the multiple layers of information, realtime constraints, and dynamic *interactional* contexts of most organizational action (or failure to act). In the real-life intensity of human affairs, most models of rationality, in a recent understatement of Herbert Simon, "deliver somewhat less than they appear to promise."[18] They do so, I believe, just because of the persistent absence of temporal, spatial, sequential and interactional aspects that *dominate* social life.

Again, social science convention haunts not only the academic literature but, through what Giddens calls the "double hermeneutic" or double involvement of sociological findings in the ongoing real world, it permeates the training and day-to-day assumptions of managers and workers. Trained in the "rational actor" model, organizational members, and especially middle and upper-level management, account for their own and others behavior in terms of it. This is at one level merely an extension of our everyday and abiding insistence on reasonable and accountable behavior, that has been underlined by the work of the ethnomethodologists. Yet at another significant level assumptions of rationality and rationalization are inherent in modern organizations, and organizational actors draw on this resource to account for the actions (and inactions) of others.[19] This, too, entails reflexive layers of rationality and has considerable consequences in terms of both accommodation and misunderstandings in the day-to-day affairs of an office or team or division. The structures of everyday life underpin and at times undermine "formal" and "institutional" frameworks just because they are the bedrock of social existence.

A central problem is that decision-*making* is incremental and fragmentary. Actual decisions in organizations are virtually invisible, yet they are the "quanta" out of which pivotal choices are made, undesirable strategies avoided, and critical paths taken. The result is best described as that "drift of decision-making" suggested by March and his colleagues, rather than the crisp, goal-oriented, value-maximizing assumptions of many theories of rational action. Decisions, as identifiable items, become clear only *after* their constitution. Moreover, for all their attempts to provide ongoing rational accounts, actors constantly adjust their understandings. In his elegant study of the Cuban missile crisis, for example, Graham Allison points to the way analysts and strategists shift from one variant of a model to another "occasionally appropriating in an *ad hoc* fashion aspects of a situation that are logically incompatible with the basic model."[20] Using the "many ways to skin a rabbit" approach, organizational actors are, after all, there to get a job done, and they do. Most of the time. All these factors, and more, shape those activities we call "strategies" and "decisions."

Furthermore, because organizational actors themselves have that pervasive sense of idealized bureaucratic rationality just noted, it has considerable consequences for how they proceed and, most especially, for the accounts they provide. Jackall's vocabularies of rationality are an integral part of how organizational actors move through the business of the day.[21] The everyday discourse on rationality is thus a significant mix of accountability and practical ethics.[22] The concept, noted at the outset of this chapter, of independent, responsible and responsive individuals acting freely and reasonably is deeply held and central to social order.[23] It is the basis of the articulation of action and structure.

Everyday Rationalities

To explore the empirically pervasive qualities of everyday rationalities, consider one brief fragment of organizational talk. It is a moment of interaction taken from a meeting between three hospital administrators who have been discussing billing procedures in a large urban medical facility. Questions of the timing of admissions as a basis for billing maternity patients have been raised at an earlier meeting with consulting physicians, who have been dealing with billing queries from their patients and from insurers. In 8.1, Peggy is reporting on this earlier meeting and is simultaneously providing a kind of "running account" of the general problem for the purposes of *this* meeting, laminating present issues on to past problems:

8.1 Hospital-1

1	**Peggy**:	What- what is happening is that (0.5) a census
2		is being taken for ev- *by- on* every shift.
3		(0.8)
4		So it's not a specific *m*idnight census (.)
5		count
6		(0.6)
7		'Mean they *call* it the midnight census but it's
8		not actually (.) being counted (0.3) *at*
9		midnight. . h : So it's being counted at three-
10		thirty
11	**Lucy**:	⌈Hm hmm⌉
12	**Peggy**:	⌊On one⌋ shift, it's being counted at eleven
13		o'*clock* on another one, and in the *morn*ing
14		as well. (0.4) Sometimes- ideally (0.4) all
15		these re- reports should add up (.) to the
16		(.) total *cen*sus, but sometimes there's a r-
17		a *prob*lem with it. (0.4) Problem occurs when . . .

She goes on to describe how, in *practice*, ways of arriving at a daily inpatient census are expressly "calculating" in their constitution. The "midnight census" is neither done at midnight nor is it a precise reflection of the patient population at that time. Problems, as she says, often occur such that the "census" of patients in the hospital is technically inaccurate yet "complete" for all practical purposes. Problems arise, she continues, because an expected patient is longer in labor or in recovery (different billing categories in the hospital accounting scheme) and is thus not tallied when "heads" in beds are, or a patient may be suddenly admitted just after the count, or transferred to another ward between counts, or unexpectedly released.

Note, in 8.1, the precision of Peggy's initial characterization of this bureaucratic "routine," delineated through a delicate series of semantic modifications. A census, she explains, is done, not *for* each shift, or *by* each shift, but *on* every shift. The total "somehow" should add up to an idealized total done simultaneously at midnight. In practice, however, a rushed nursing staff does the counting *within* the logic of their own local priorities: sometimes at half past three, sometimes at 11 o'clock, and in the morning as well. This practice is, however, thoroughly rational in the sense that these local practices are *known* to be produced in this way. It *works*. And it also makes sense. Billing clerks', accounts managers' and even insurance adjusters' own local work practices and assessments of hospital costs are *constituted* through this achieved fit between local and larger rationalities. Nested one within another and taking their meaning indexically from each other, local logics interlock to provide larger accounts.

So everyday rationalities are *built in* as local logic and yet *made external* as organizational rationality.[24] The fit between the two is reflexive and dynamic; they are mutually elaborative. For organizational analysis, *how* the spatio-temporally intense logic of everyday rationalities are made to work with and articulate a larger, normative view of "how we *should* be doing things" becomes critical. By conceiving of rationality as singular and as a single standard that is held to be universal and trans-historical, analysts have found social objects like the "midnight census" to be deviant cases. But if we turn the problem upside-down, we can instead see that rationality pervades human activities. It may not be ordered to our liking, but that is another matter.

By inverting the analysis, rationality in action can illuminate insights into rationality writ large. To explore this claim, it will be useful to return to a more ethnomethodological approach to the general topic of rational action. By turning the problem of social order upside-down, ethnomethodologists do not just achieve a bottom-up or "micro" view of conventional social structure,[25] but an oddly radical insight into the local organizing properties of action *and* structure, seen as one quite seamless whole.

Garfinkel's own initial ideas on this are developed in the jury study discussed in chapter 2. They are an extension of his critique of Parsons's abstract analtyic theorizing.[26] It was Parsons's espoused intention to identify the "intimate interrelation of general statements about empirical fact with the logical elements and structure of theoretical systems."[27] In the process, and on behalf of sociology, Parsons also appropriated rationality for his scientific enterprise. Despite his goal of studying "human action in society" and observing the "subjective aspect" of social life,[28] he conjured "acts" out of action, and both disappeared, as is well known, into the thin air of grand theory. Garfinkel, for his part, set out to develop a genuine theory of action. To do this, he had to rescue rationality from the grand positive science proposed by Parsons.

First, building on Schutz's classic work, he notes an essential difference between everyday amd scientific rationalities. He observes, for instance, that scientific standards for rationality require four basic elements:(1) a commitment to a means–ends relation as defined by formal logic; (2) semantic clarity and distinctness in defining a situation in which action is to be taken; as well as (3) an interest in clarity and rules of procedures for their own sake and not just the task at hand; and finally (4) a willingness to act according to a body of scientific knowledge.[29] These Garfinkel, following Schutz, calls the "scientific rationalities." And he goes on to point out that they are held up as ideal standards of everyday behavior when the sociologist proceeds to investigate the "realistic, pathological, prejudiced, delusional, mythical, magical, ritual, and similar features of everyday conduct, thinking and beliefs."[30] The mismatch between scientific and everyday rationalities results in the routine discovery that people do not follow such pure, general procedures when they make decisions about where to go to dinner or how to make revolution.[31] This is the paradox noted earlier.

Having found the scientific guidelines and rational properties they set out to investigate empirically ellusive, sociologists are accused by Garfinkel of having "preferred instead to study the features and conditions of *non*rationality in human conduct. The result is that in most of the available theories of social structure and social action rational actions are assigned residual status."[32] The properties of practical rationality and the organization of rational action are thus ignored in the interests of investigation of presumed departures from the ideal. Despite discrepancies between the scientific ideal and lay persons' knowledge, however, society displays quite effective, persistent and stable patterns of action and structure. Even if people rarely, if ever, demand the standards of formal logic, semantic clarity, general procedural rules, and scientific rigor, social life is remarkably orderly.

By switching from analytic theorizing to grounded observation, Garfinkel's approach emphasizes the organization of ordinary, everyday actions and their local qualities of rationality. In his early discussion, he, too, noted that most rational models in the social sciences "are models of rational actions but not of actions performed by living human beings in situations defined by them," which is to say that the rationality is defined by the social scientists and not by the social actor *in situ*, or *in vivo* as he likes to term it.[33]

To explore how everyday rationalities work, Garfinkel draws on the general phenomenological notion of "bracketing." According to this approach, social agents immersed in an intense world of experience bracket out extraneous detail and selectively constitute a here-and-now mix of meaning and action. In Schutzian terms, situations of action are characterized by a "purpose at hand" which defines *just* what elements of organizational and biographical background features deserve attention and are thus *made* relevant.[34] Everyday situations of action turn actors into "practical theorists" who understand, to a profound degree, what Garfinkel came to call the "etcetera principle," namely that in the real world *no* set of rules, no matter how general, clearly defined, or logically formulated, can *ever* be "complete."

There is also that *temporal* dimension to daily life discussed earlier; moving constantly along a social timeline, meanings, relevancies, and their relation to one another change. A scientific logic of causal relevance is, in practice, replaced by a simultaneity of problems, solutions and decision-makers.[35] As a result, any strict means–ends relationship or attempt to fix the properties of rationality is doomed. Yet this is also an opportunity since, according to Garfinkel, the very fact that scientific rationality (such as a strict means–ends relation) cannot be applied successfully to everyday rationalities "has the important and paradoxical consequence of permitting us to study the properties of rational action more closely than ever before."[36] Indeed, by bracketing scientific idealizations of rational action, we can genuinely examine Weber's neglected distinction between formal and substantive rationality. Practical conditions demand flexibility. Practical rationality has, in fact, many degrees. On this view, far fewer everyday activities come to be labeled as "nonrational" or "irrational," since their local properties are understood. Attitudes, accounts, and activities of daily life contain within their own logic the rational properties of the larger organization or society.

Organizational Rationality in Action

This approach to the problem of rationality also opens up opportunities for organizational analysis. By examining rationality with a self-conscious myopia, we begin to see that the timing of many different individual actions and the changing context of those acts matter greatly to what organizations are and can be. In particular, we can observe that the "contexts" of action are always shifting across time and space and that it is organizational actors themselves who smoothe the wrinkles and fill the holes in the social fabric. Much of the organizational literature treats context as relatively unidimensional and stable; it is people who are seen as the source of confusion. Close up, however, we can see that the reverse is actually closer to the case. Instead of giving "context" a "blanket" or "bucket like" quality[37] and assuming that it "contains" action, we can note that concrete moments of action are primarily *interactionally* based, and that they branch out in multiple directions, connecting to an interlocking set of people, problems and solutions.[38] Rationality in this sense is not a unitary measure of behavior; it has many degrees, multiple dimensions.[39] Even as an ideal, it is a *moving target* with which organizational actors align from different positions on a fast-moving scene that is constantly being renewed. And in their efforts to *produce* the organization as a real and reasonable entity, they fit local elements *into* that largely idealized rationality discussed above. Even "efficiency" is produced as a finely graded set of actions rather than a deterministic economic solution.[40]

The "smoothing" of the social fabric is not, however, a cover-up. In their assessments and actions, organizational members continuously position their current activities and emerging agendas in terms of the larger stream, and they do so through that constant retrospective-prospective analysis discussed earlier. In the process, that recursiveness of action lays down the steps of the organizational dance that others must, with their own variations, follow. Notice, for instance, in the following brief example (from the end of the fellowship meeting), how the recursive features of organizational life reflexively shape present *and* next actions. Here, the Dean notes that his office has forgotten, yet again, to request certain information from potential fellowship recipients, information that was obtained late the year before and is late again this year. This announcement elicits an acknowledgment from the Financial Aid Director, Matt (lines 4–5), with a kind of organizational lament: "the fellowship people again":

8.2 Fellowship Meeting

```
 1  Dean:     We've screwed up again. We didn't ask fer
 2            that material- we ask'd f'r it last year (.)
 3            late in the pie⌈ce   r⌉ight?=
 4  Matt:                   ⌊Yeah.⌋    = The fellowship
 5            people again
 6  Jim:      'S there a March fifteenth dead ⌈line?⌉
 7  Matt:                                      ⌊Yes. ⌋
 8  Jim:      That' ⌈s sad, ⌉⌈we'll ⌉ have all- all these
 9  Jean:           ⌊. h : : :⌋⌊of all-⌋
10  Jim:      people's applica : tions (.)
11            ⌈by the time (you need 'em)                      ⌉
12  Dean:     ⌊MAY I MAKE (.) ⌈the       fo : llowing⌉ su(.)ggestion? ⌉
13  Matt: →                  ⌊WE CAN DA : : NCE⌋ around the March⌋
14            fiftee : nth . . .
```


The "again" motif (lines 1 and 5) provides the essential thematic quality of all organizations, namely that the "routines" that appear so repetitive are actually deeply recursive in the sense that they contain the seeds of next actions and, at the same time, require constant *in situ* fine-tuning. The ad *hoc*ing quality of the moment is also distinctly institutional: actions (and their reasons) *now* must fit into a stream of responsible and responsive reactions to past events for what Garfinkel calls "another next first time." They must, simultaneously, provide an immediate context that will also make sense *later*. When, in the above example, Jim notes that it is "sad" that there is a March 15th (national) deadline for graduate fellowships, he is verbally rehearsing the need for his *particular* institution to fit federal guidelines while *these* applicants' materials, though late, could be available by the time they are (really) needed by the local Financial Aid Office (line 11). The issue, it will be remembered from the last chapter, is that *some* of these fellowship applicants may fit affirmative action guidelines both within the university system and in terms of an emerging agenda at the state level. Any "fit" is thus a multidimensional yet irreducibly local matter.

In the conversational simultaneity that follows Jim's brief pause (line 10), the Dean starts up noisily with one solution while Matt, as the organizational actor directly responsive to external deadlines in his role as Director, jumps in (arrow, line 13) with a classic bureaucratic proposal, namely to "dance around" the deadline. Dancing around deadlines, rules, regulations, and presumed formal structures is what gives dynamism and, over time, vitality to organizations. Note that Matt's offer (line 13) comes in at just the point where Jim has explained that the applications will, for all practical purposes, be in "time." In local terms, that is all Matt needs to know.

But the proposed dance is not deviant. It is a quite practical affair. Nor is this rational adjustment similarly *ad hoc*: just as the graduate applications were "screwed up" two years running, each local solution indexically embeds and enacts "formal" practices in such a way as to ensure a smooth flow of *legitimate* funding and students. In this way, the very nature of a public institution's accountability creates the narratives through which immediate problems are solved smoothly and take on that retrospective and external reality discussed earlier. Any deadline, even a federally mandated one, contains within its *enactment* on any particular occasion the "etcetera principle," namely that it is incomplete and must be worked out on the spot. So the loose coupling often noted in this sort of educational setting marks not so much *departures* from rules and official procedures as extraordinarily creative and *consistent* ways of shoring up those locally unworkable rules.

When organizational actors "look up and around," it is just this "locally achieved goodness-of-fit" exercise that is, I think, involved. What they are doing under unavoidably local conditions must be (and be seen to be) of a piece with the organization or organizational field as a whole. The process is not really "mimetic" in any precise or analytically useful sense, although actions are indeed "rehearsed" for the sort of ratified audience Goffman identified and "matched" to other organizations or subunits. The "rehearsal" quality of much backstage organizational talk certainly suggests that parallel procedures and policies within and beyond organizational boundaries are produced as "another" of "those" actions in the sequential process of creating the organization and its environment, but they are also produced "anew" – every time.

Time, Space and Local Logic

March and Romelaer have noted that the history of organizations rides on "minor actions, minor decisions, and minor changes."[41] Using an interactional sort of analysis, we can see that this quality is even more finely graded. The incremental process of constituting organizational practices has a number of interesting consequences that are both interactional and institutional. As layers of small "decisions" build, and various alternatives are actively discarded or simply sidetracked, time passes. Attention also shifts.[42] What "looks good" or practical or desirable at T1 often looks different a few days or weeks later, in the light of intervening information and events, seen against that rapidly moving backdrop discussed above. While this observation may seem a bit banal, the unfolding logic of decisions-in-progress is dominated by a local focal point that is constantly shifting along a dynamic and often multidirectional time horizon. As social actors look over their shoulders at past actions and decisions, they also look sideways, fitting their current activities with parallel points and agents on their organizational landscape. Simultaneity is a critical contingency of action. Nor are these local relevancies of various aspects and stages of a decision-in-progress simply constrained by temporal contingencies; they are also *constitutive* of them, creating timelines, controlling, to a high degree, the practical enactment of organizational actions and even goals.

Space is also involved in a way rarely appreciated in organizational analysis. While information now leaps large distances through advanced technology, and documents speed to their destination digitally, key personnel are caught in quite physical constraints. Moreover, despite elaborate spatio-temporal maneuvers, not everyone can be in the right place at the right time. Just as often, they are working with distinctly incomplete information and, as we saw earlier, in chapter 4, with a need to chase documents and people from place to place. In virtually every potential decision setting, social actors are forced to work with *just* what they have, at just that moment, with just whoever is available. The persistent urge to deal with complex activities in face-to-face settings means that space matters centrally to decision-making and to organizations in action.[43]

The interpenetration of time, space and the inevitably interactional medium of decision-making operates in several ways: (1) meetings and other interactional connections, as noted in earlier chapters, must be precisely timed and coordinated, even those that are "slipped" in between scheduled encounters; (2) in modern organizations, the tense connections of information systems commit social actors to be in virtually constant potential contact with each other; (3) the serial ordering of various settings of decision-making has consequences for who participates in which parts of the process, as well as for who

must be kept up-to-date with the emerging result; and (4) the "accu-
mulated" decision needs to be timed to fit and facilitate a more distal
flow of events and crises occurring both within and beyond the organization. To a considerable degree, each of these dimensions of
temporality and spatiality is anchored in the interaction order of the
organization, paced by telephone calls and grounded in informal and
formal meetings. At each stage, fine sediments are laid down. At each
moment, we catch the organization in action, on the move, if only
stumbling or blundering along. Any "decision" must be woven through
this transparent yet dynamic time-space grid. The transparency of
action is, as we have seen, an accountable matter; it is open to appraisal,
revision, condemnation, repetition.

Local logic is thereby opportunist and fluid.[44] It is in just this way
that organizations can, must and *do* enact their environments, linking
local and highly contingent micromoments to the exigencies of town
hall, marketplace or global village. Underlying the local readings of
organizational members is an often profound sense of the "larger"
picture, but how it is framed depends on what Schutz calls the
"congruency of relevances." The logic of local action and decision is
centered on the relevance of that action, there and then, to an un-
remitting temporal and moral unfolding of events in which actors are
caught. "Real rationality" is thus, in Molotch's apt phrase, "tense." It
involves "the capacity to appear appropriate under diverse settings
and ever-changing circumstances" and, through this accountability,
"to display and recognise [an] attitude of practical ethics."[45]

Organizational actors are, constantly I suspect, of two minds: on
the one hand, they subscribe to a Weberian rational/technical
framework for their actions, yet *simultaneously* they know that those
actions only "work" if they are fine-tuned and adjusted in a highly
local manner. Formal and substantive rationality are complementary
yet separate, as Weber has indicated.[46] But the matter is even more
complex. It is not so much that local conditions are ambiguous, although, to be sure, they may be. The point is that reflexive tension
between ideal and practical action that Molotch highlights.[47] *Making*
the organization "work" means supporting (not subverting) rules,
policies and goals at the formal level through a *constant* process of
considerable informality. It is in this sense, as I indicated at the outset
of this study, that organizations operate in an informal mode *all the
time*. They do so because they *must*.

In sum, the ability of social actors to talk the organization into being,
make it happen, and carry it forward is embodied in the following
sorts of skills. People in work settings, from top to bottom, have:

1   a powerful sense of the temporal corrdination of their joint activities;
2   a still more pressing concern for the "what nextness" of work tasks;
3   a preoccupation with their own ability to identify and intelligibly
    act upon specific knowledge of the work environment;
4   an understanding that any official set of "rules" or "regulations"
    or "procedures" are simply partly formulated recipes or slogans
    that have to be worked out *on the spot*;
5   an ability to act in such a way that those same rules or procedures
    are *made to work* and the organization thus is made to *look good*,
    that is, rational, efficient, competitive, correct, and so forth;
6   a paramount skill in recognizing *which* rules are relevant on the
    particular occasion of their use.

The list could be longer. The skills interlock. Modern organizations, from the corner dry-cleaning establishment to the national government, depend *utterly* on local talent.

In an interesting way, the partial result of all this is negative: organizations are always out-of-date just because their constituent members are busy fitting informal solutions to official goals. The informality is lost in the moment and goes unrecorded in the many memos and files that provide the formal record. The shifting sands of organizational agendas traced in the last chapter and the lively coalitions and cooperations-of-convenience that typify organizational life are largely verbal. In the process, much innovation may also be lost, a point I shall return to speculatively in the next and final chapter of this study.

The dynamism of all organizations is a multidimensional affair; the everyday rationalities needed to make the organization happen are similarly multifaceted. Long ago, Dalton noted that: "the logically conceived plans at one executive level are variously altered by subordinate levels to fit their shifting social relations, as well as the emergencies of work. Inspired by the fear of unofficial reprisals, the alterations are usually concealed and therefore not incorporated into future planning . . ."[48] The drift of decision-making may thus be more adaptive than it appears. Future work-settings may have to take interactionally bounded rationality more fully into consideration.

Bounded Rationality Revisited

It will be useful, at this point, to reexamine briefly the idea of bounded rationality. It is an idea that has proved one of the most durable approaches to the practical problem of rationality. As originally formulated, it is a cognitive notion applied to an individual theory of action.[49] Rationality is assumed to be located in the heads of individual actors and is "bounded" by their capacity to process information and complexity. Individuals move iteratively through solutions until one works or fits, rather than searching exhaustively for the maximum benefit/minimum cost solution. By grounding the problem in behavior, Simon moved, in effect, from omniscient rationality to a practical set of steps through which actors make decisions. He has a good sense of the sequential properties of rationality and the ways in which people "approximate" classical rationality by moving iteratively through a search process. The serial quality places, in Simon's terms, *limits* to rationality which may well be rooted in good evolutionary reasons.[50] Yet this emphasis on individual characteristics in an essentially organizational process seems to blur the two.[51] Individuals in work settings rarely act alone. *Together* they make decisions or, more typically, enact *parts* of a decision-producing process. They do so as part of the organizational dance just observed.

The incremental pattern often further creates the sequential context for interactional shortcuts that effectively constitute a more coherent work environment. Offers such as the one to dance around a deadline are working examples of what Weick calls "small wins," namely the positive process by which people create "scaled-down problem environments" that facilitate collaboration and build commitment. These local action stations, in turn, allow organizational actors to focus on here-and-now recognizable goals with jointly specified features.[52] Coordinated, coproductive activities are thus bounded *interactionally* rather than simply cognitively and atomistically. As March's work has been especially effective in demonstrating over many years, solutions chase problems whose solution creates problems elsewhere in time and space. But there is a kind of syncopated rhythm to it all, one which catches and propels people and organizations forward, again and again.

As a final glimpse of this multilayered process, we can look again at an early example in this study. This is another meeting of administrators at a different hospital, extracted in chapter 3 (3.1 on pp. 59–61 above). Linda, a consultant working on a cost-cutting program in this large research hospital, has been reporting on a meeting with orthopedic specialists who have been persuaded to arrange for patients' routine preoperative X-rays to be done before arriving for surgery. At the beginning of the example, she is assessing their response and apparent willingness to give up long-standing procedures in the interests of reducing costs on their unit. The physicians in question are medical faculty at "UHH," the research hospital. *Their* local logic, as the orthopedic department, is different from the local logic of radiology:

8.3   Hospital-2 (Ortho)
      Simplified transcript

```
 1  Linda:   The- the point is that- that was the
 2           only area we talked about,
 3  Paul:    (Yeahm)
 4  Linda:   So far about whether or not (0.2)
 5           through what (.) we've
 6           accomplished which in this case?
 7           is- was getting the- (0.2) hearing what the
 8           physicians were willing? (.) and able- to
 9           give this up
10  Paul:    (Mm ⌈hum)⌉
11  Linda:       ⌊This-⌋ this type of practise up if in
12           fact they were offered some organizational
13           help in getting these ⌈tests⌉ do : ne.
14  Paul:                          ⌊Yeah⌋     And that
15           kinda astonishes me (it really does)
16                      (0.6)
17  Hal:     ⌈⌈What-
18  Linda:   ⌊⌊Well- ⌈shall we jus'⌉
19  Paul:           ⌊Well, I mean⌋ it's services that-
20                      (1.0)
21  Hal:     (right)
22  Paul:    I- we're talking r- U.H.H. (.) faculty
23  Hal:     Huh-huhn
24  Paul:          phys⌈i  c  i  ans⌉
25  Linda:        ⌊(Hm-hmm)⌋
26  Paul:                      who are willing to
27           give up U.H.H. services? Give away business?
28                      (0.9)
29  Hal:     (Yehm) Oh ⌈t h e y don'- but I-⌉
30  Paul:           ⌊Yeah, for the hospi⌋tal
31           you're right. The hospital is basically
32           neutral. ⌈Or re-    or benefits for Medicare⌉
33  Hal:            ⌊Yeah, but you don't underSTAND⌋
34           that THESE GUYS don't see any of that revenue
35                      (0.2)
36           that they understand
37                      (1.0)
38           see they- they only see the reve⌈nue⌉
39  Paul:                                 ⌊Heh⌋
```

```
40                    heh-heh-hun
41      Hal:                        No, no, no, you understand that
42                    it's- they don'- they only see it as
43                    revenue, if it comes back to 'em that way.
44                    But this relationship is with the U.H.H.
45      Paul:         (Right)
46      Hal:          Not with the orthopedic division
47                                  (0.7)
48                    so that percentage is so far away from
49                    their hands
50                                  (1.2)
51                    arright?
52                                  (0.3)
53      Paul:         (Hm-hmm)
54      Hal:          that they don't say – Oh we're not gonna do
55                    that, that's money in our pockets, I mean-
56                    you're assuming that ⌈they have uh⌉ private
57      Paul:                             ⌊Oh.  I s e e.⌋
58      Hal:          physician mentality that they see the money,
59                    they ⌈don't SEE⌉ the money!
60      Paul:              ⌊Well th-  ⌋             ((Khn-khn))
61                    Yeah, but you're talking to uh- uh- you-
62                    okay. The- the UHH physicians you're
63                    talking to? then,
64      Hal:          Yeah.
65                                  (0.2)
64      Paul:         Are- uh are not the ones who would get
65                    the pre-op- the pre-admission (0.2) money
66                    any ⌈w   a   y,    that's⌉ whatcher
67      Hal:              ⌊THAT'S RIGHT-      ⌋
68      Paul:         saying.
69      Hal:                    That's right.
70      Paul:         (right)
71      Hal:          Now, y'see- if we would say- if we'd go to
72                    Meyerson and say what do you think about the
73                    idea of us ⌈sending these⌉
74      Paul:                    ⌊Heh-heh-heh⌋
75      Hal:          they'd say what the hell are you talking
76                    about? That's our money!
77      Paul:         Yeah.
78      Hal:          We're not talking to them. We're not
79                    talking to Radiology, we're talking to
80                    Orthopedics, okay?
90                                  (0.7)
91      Paul:         ⌈⌈Hah- huh- huh⌉
92      Hal:          ⌊⌊And they don'⌋ And they don't think as a
```

```
93                    (0.8)
94        mega-organization that has lost money to
95        them as a group. They think of their
96        practice (0.4) in maintaining whatever
97        incentives . . .
```

They are, in the words of Paul from the Finance Office, willing to "give away business" (line 27), that is to say X-ray work. The "business" is the *hospital's*, not the subunit's, and "they don't *think* as a mega-organization" (lines 92–4) that is losing revenue by having X-ray work done elsewhere. These doctors think as an orthopedic practice. To them, in terms of *their* cost incentives, revenue is only real if it "comes back to 'em" (line 43) as such; revenue to other hospital units is "*so* far away from their hands" (lines 48–9) as to make little sense. If Hal, as Chief of Physicians, were to go to the head of radiology (lines 71–2) and propose sending patients to their local doctors for X-rays, he would say "what the hell are you talking about? That's our *money*!" (lines 75–6). Each group is cooperating with the cost-cutting scheme, however, for their own local purposes. Circles of affiliation thus cut into issues of organizational rationality as solutions chase problems to solve more distant dilemmas. The many meetings and telephone calls of the day provide the medium through which working *together* creates both local logic and collective conscience.

In this meeting, Linda, Hal and Paul are themselves reflexively building their own collaboration and, at the same time, maintaining their own organizational agendas. The conditions and consequences of their next actions are murky at best, but in *pooling* information, updates and interpretations they move forward, often along slightly different lines but with renewed insight. The small wins at one level are layered upon others. Some, of course, are built on organizational quicksand, but generally these fine sediments lay down the foundations of later collaborations. Rationality as a single standard intersects with many everyday rationalities and is supported by them.

Even an advanced modern hospital, as we have seen in the earlier example, cannot come up with an accurate count of the number of patients under its roof. Yet, with genuine local ingenuity, nursing staff and billing clerks produce figures which, woven through the rational accounts that organizations routinely provide to each other, meet the needs of the medical insurance environment. These figures are neither "socially constructed" in some vague way, nor are they "symbolic"; they are practical structures of action out of which *next* actions – actions by the hospital, actions arising in its organizational environment, and actions prompted by the now global crisis in medical costs – will be built. Layer by translucent layer, social actors create the fine web of interlocking structures to which they and others must respond.

The interpenetration of agency and structure is thus necessarily dialectic, simultaneously contingent and contradictory. What is done *now* must make sense immediately, retrospectively, and, to a consequential degree, in the future. This again is the essence of the ethnomethodological position, namely that as social actors discover *from within* the local logic of their actions, they *reflexively* – which is to say, consciously, interactively, and indexically – locate those activities within a stream of events that, taken together, constitute the rational production of the organization. In so doing, the local logic of action creates and recreates the smooth and reasonable surface of organizational rationality.

9

The Business of Talk

"Life doesn't hold still," as Eudora Welty, the American essayist, likes to say. It is that dynamism that is the wellspring of social life. It has also been the topic of this book. The tension between discrete and immediate local activities of individuals in organizations and that synergistic mix of collective effects we call "*the* organization" is not simply a matter of the *reproduction* of social arrangements and structures. The enacted organization is *produced* through the actions and inactions of its constituent members.

In this concluding discussion we are now in a position to draw together both the theoretical and practical consequences of studying organizations in action. Organizations are apparently objective systems colliding with the practical contingencies and rationalities of everyday life. The dynamism and flexibility of action and response that is a routine feature of conversational interaction grounds idealized bureaucratic structures in concrete moments of human experience. If we look back to the much earlier discussion of current research on organizations, it is easy now to see how devoid of this dynamism are most of those approaches. The urge to abstract away from the "blooming, buzzing" busy moments of organizational life has proved almost irresistible.[1] By standing back far enough, it is hoped, individual activities will blur into institutional patterns.

Yet organizations are composite groups of *individuals*, collaborative to varying extents, interdependent to various degrees, operating in variable ways toward a variety of goals, both shared and, not unusually, divergent. Groups within organizations are therefore further subdivisions of these intersecting and colliding systems. The ways in which the agendas of different organizational units and subunits are interwoven, elaborated and merged in interactional settings is critical. The groups are dynamic, tense, and at times volatile. The "dance" enacted by people in organizations cannot thus simply be analyzed as a "small group" phenomenon, rather obviously because the "group" itself is an enacted entity, shifting across time and space.

People are the organization. Their actions make the trends.[2] But many social science theories of organizations develop "slogans"[3] about what people do and these become the taken-for-granted assumptions of theory and research. The slogans rapidly come to stand for what people do, yet they are constituted through the social scientist's own, inevitable and unavoidable, participation in the unfolding everyday world of experience.[4] So everyday resource is confounded with research topic. In the process, the slogans take on a self-important life of their own. Glossing a complex multidimensional phenomenon of, for instance, "loose coupling" or "institutional isomorphism" *loses* the actual phenomenon. Across the bubbling surface of organizational life, the very process by which structure is created, over and over, is lost. So, to achieve a genuine theory of action, we need to retrieve the details of actual events. Too much reduction or abstraction loses the phenomenon of order, the very organization we want to theorize.

Organizations: In Theory

This is *the* pervasive problem of social theory today: most human action is made to disappear into the solid walls of structure that are presumed to surround it. And, in many social science traditions, there is the further analytic problem that "action" and "agency" are often taken to be located at the institutional level, in collective interests and in the polity.[5] Institutions are assumed to be "actors" who "think" and "act" and so forth. Agency then resides in those institutions, rationality is, as noted in the last chapter, collective and social order is a constraining container in which individuals reproduce patterned relations. Alternatively, the emphasis may be on lone, individual actors who make atomized "choices" based on personal "preferences" under optimal or suboptimal conditions, thus reproducing institutions through their aggregate actions. Either way, institutions triumph over individuals.

Any reformulation of organization theory aimed at incorporating the dynamics of action within structure thus needs to respecify the basic components. If organizations are us and we are them, then this duality should be central to theories about both. The theoretical impasse in organizational theory and research suggested at the outset of this study can be overcome, I believe, through genuine engagement of how action creates structures which then shape action. The seeds of this solution are germinating in the careful studies of the neo-institutionalists, in the dense connections of network analysts, and in the sophisticated models of the population ecologists. Similar ideas emerge strongly in the work of Clegg, Van Maanen, Morgan, and like minds, as well as in the continued probing of March and his colleagues, and in work that combines social psychological findings with a structuralist approach.[6] But these nascent ideas could easily whither away. It is, I think, facile to say that one person's structure is another's process. Social reality is seamless. *Society* does not happen at different levels, research does. If so, attempts to characterize organizational structure need to theorize how variability in the conduct of individuals changes it. The action component, in other words, cannot be one in which individuals merely reproduce an existing order which then acts alone (somehow) on their behalf.

The importance of action and agency are assuredly being reconsidered and reformulated in organization theory. Some of the earliest work in this area was Silverman's theory of organization, which incorporated an action frame of reference into the then-current vogue of functionalist theory.[7] Over the past 20 years, a variety of avenues have been explored, some tracing "structures in motion,"[8] some advocating multiple paradigms as a way of isolating interpretive/objective features of organizations,[9] and others borrowing from Foucault as the poststructuralist and later postmodernist critiques caught up with organizational analysis.[10] The works of Giddens and Bourdieu have also been variously adapted to the perceived needs of organization theory, and there has been much recent borrowing from ethnomethodology and phenomenology.

Nonetheless, the borrowing is piecemeal, and a central problem of organization theory remains one of *respecifying* action as an *active* component of structure and not simply as an outcome. As this study has proposed, one way of analyzing organizational behavior and ultimately whole networks of organizations is at the level of everyday actions and the talk that shapes them. This suggestion does not entail a fascination with language, nor does it recommend the idea that individual action "builds" toward some larger entity that "is" the organization in some cumulative sense. The recurring theme of this discussion has instead been to propose that organizational talk both shapes and is shaped by the structure of the organization itself. Refracted through the talk and created within its unfolding dynamism is the organization in action.

This analysis is intertwined with an ethnomethodological insistence on reflexivity. The retrospective illusion of social structure, reflexively understood and realized in immediate action, is not some monolithic backdrop against which tiny human actions are played out, but a highly dynamic, at times even dramatic, social tapestry whose details are picked out and elaborated by succeeding generations of human actors. As people talk organizations into being, they simultaneously pick out the particular strands of abstract order that can relevantly instantiate the moment. In so doing, they significantly support, shape and occasionally subvert the organization, which will then move forward into next moments through other actions with other actors.

The duality of structure and action that results from this reflexive and local process transforms individual into community. Simultaneously the myths, languages, cultures, and conditions of past social structural arrangements come alive again in the choices of the moment. If organizations *are* the people who comprise them, then it is rather clear that structure is dynamic and shaped from within, rather than static or moving independently of action. Action, in turn, is only meaningful through language. Not the abstract system of *langue* of the structuralists, but the lively and interactive *parole* of everyday speech. Looking at language-in-action, we get a quite direct, close-up view of human agency. Since organizations form the matrix of modern societies, it seems reasonable to say that there is some urgency attached to expanding our understanding of this dual operation of action and structure.

The findings of this study can only begin to explore one avenue of such a research agenda. Conversational procedures invoked by members, characterized as members' practices, operate as both *interactionally* and *organizationally* relevant activities. While the current analysis is limited to talk in meetings and other common work settings, these interactional encounters have been treated as organizationally occasioned events through which members generate both immediate interaction and larger organizational agendas. These are reflexively shaped by the same contingencies and conditions. Talk is not *just* talk, but rather the mode and medium through which the structure of the organization is constituted and reconstituted. It is one dimension along which organizational behavior can be observed directly and analyzed with a high degree of accuracy.

One way of thinking of an organization, as Mintzberg[11] and Stinchcombe[12] have suggested, is as a system of information flow. If so, talk is assuredly the primary medium of transmission. Conversation analysis provides an unambiguous method for careful observation of such issues, since the intersubjective accomplishment of meaning in interaction is readily available at the level of talk. Information, of course, does not simply "flow," nor has communication in organizations anything like the rather simplistic cybernetic quality often proposed. More important than any analysis of stages or steps in the communication process is the fact that it flows *through* people *via* everyday talk in just the sorts of settings presented here. To understand the "system," then, we must track the talk. It is the practical locus of organizational action. The business of talk is thus a multi-layered affair, located and accomplished simultaneously at the structural, interactional and organizational levels of verbal exchange.

Respecifying Action

To propose to study organizations in action, as I have done here, has a certain arrogance, since we are unable to observe all types of organizations or, rather obviously, all actions within any given firm. Yet my intention, as has been indicated all along, is at once more modest and more grandiose. On the one hand, by observing the unfolding of talk-based *organizing*, we can, as it were, take the pulse of an organization, at that moment in time, with just those particular organizational actors coming together in quite specific and local ways. Modestly, what is being proposed is that the observed rhythm, however cross-sectional and momentary it may appear in conventional research terms, is a strong indicator of "business as usual." By understanding the basic beat of business as usual, through the *details* of action, we discover what organizations "really" are, and thus, in one quite uncomplicated move, can tap directly into the most abstract and theoretical level of organizational analysis.

This transformation is, moreover, not the sleight of hand or theoretical bedazzlement it might appear. The issue is not structure *versus* process, but rather that seamless web of structure-in-action. This recurrent claim, in its turn, merely proposes that organizational "structure," so called, comes alive and is directly observable in the actions of organizational members. To repeat, this is not to say that actors simply reproduce pre-existing and "larger" structures, but that *as agents* they are forever (and necessarily) breathing new life and direction into existing arrangements. In their ability to do so and to account for their activities as such, they create formal structures of practical action.[13] Reflexively and retrospectively, they then treat those structures as consequential, constraining and real. The single web of reality is woven, moment to moment, out of the practical structures of everyday life.

The problem of recent social science has been to treat abstract patterns of social relations as structure and everyday processes as *something else*. Instead, they are one. Or rather, more challengingly, they are mutually elaborative within a highly dynamic space–time matrix. Their elaborative coproduction is, moreover, subject to *constant* interpretation and continuous updating.

This is the essential message of ethnomethodology.

In its own way, it is a strong and ultimately radical position, one whose elements have been smuggled into mainstream sociology but many of whose incisive insights have been lost in the process.[14] This is a pity since it is the genuinely alternative approach of ethnomethodology that can uncover organizatio*n* in organizatio*ns*. Moreover, normalizing ethnomethodological concepts by incorporating them into mainstream theory merely neutralizes them.[15] My own approach has been to retrieve the reflexivity inherent to ethnomethodology as a way of capturing structure-in-action. In organizational terms, the local logic and immediate efficiency of events and actions are then taken to be inextricably *part* of the goals, practices and procedures they embed and embody. People don't follow rules, they *do* them. Rules, in this sense, do not "govern" behavior but are an active constituent of what people *do*; they are a resource not a template.[16] In the process, the contingencies of the moment shape not only immediate action but the organization itself over time. When an organizational actor says "we have a quorum" or "we screwed up again" or "they don't think like a mega-organization," they are not marking simply *their* idiosyncratic or momentary understanding of some organizational practice, they *are* that practice.

This is the basic inversion of the problem of order discussed at the outset. The central question of social order is not how social actors respond to some set of rules but instead how they make the inherent incompleteness and elasticity of any rule set *work* on any given occasion of its use. It will be remembered that the temptation to assume rule-governed behavior leads many investigators to then suppose that departures from official policy or rules are deviant and that systematic transformations lead to informal rules.[17] Since organizations run in multiple, overlapping informal modes all the time, that is not very illuminating. It also blocks from view, and thus from analysis, what is observably typical in all organizational settings, namely the considerable skill which members bring to making relevant rules work on relevant occasions.

Indeed, rules are transformational by their nature; they are continuously the product of and subject to human agency.[18] They can, once written, as we saw in chapter 7, be *un*written by present actors for both immediate and future purposes. Even more typically, everyday informal practices are built into the practical enactment of bureaucratic procedures.[19] The most rigid of bureaucracies, the military for example, works because local command makes local action look like headquarters policy. When this local sense is disallowed, inaction, inefficiency and even collapse may occur. At the very least, the sort of "work to rule" procedures used, for instance, by trade unions results in trains at a standstill, telephones unanswered and whole industries frozen.[20] In contrast, the collaborative dance that enacts successful organizations embodies fluidity and flexibility. It involves, in the words of two organizational experts of recent years, "rich ways of communicating informally [and] . . . special ways of using *ad hoc* devices" to keep things and people moving, responding to complexity with fluidity.[21]

By producing a complex matrix of actions and interactions spun *simultaneously* and *collaboratively* across time and space, actors create and recreate their organizations and the links between them: local TV stations with national networks, research hospitals with other medical facilities, university administrations with state legislatures, or governments to other governments. *Cross*-multiplied over still broader stretches of time and space, these actions and reactions may indeed appear as "structure," as enduring, solid and real. That "reality" is, however, reflexively and contingently tied to the *continued* actions, commitments, and constituencies of other actors, both past and future. Criss-crossing the surface of any apparent organizational structure, and underpinning it at every point, are real social agents drawn together in real time. Some may be caught on an assembly line or at data-processing station, while others roam the corridors, sit in air-conditioned meeting rooms, or catch each other's eye in airport VIP lounges. Their talk may thereby be differentially occasioned and occasionally even forbidden, but it is the center of their coordination. Coordination of complex activities is what organizations are all about. Certainly, as I shall explore briefly below, in the complex interactive settings of *future* workplaces, finely tuned and coordinated talk-based activities will continuously breathe life into organizations.

Discovering Sequence in Experience

The key to this continuity of structure-in-action is *sequence*.[22] Action *coheres* as sequence. Through coherent sequences of coordination we discover the structuring quality of all social life. This structuring feeling comes from a multiplex mix of personal, physical and psychological features that give us an embodied sense of self, on the one hand, and from an interlocking set of social, spatial and societal sensibilities, on the other. As social actors fit *their* agendas and time-frames into those of others, they discover *together* what is possible – in fact. The practical structures of everyday life and their achieved sequence embody and enact the abstract structures of organizations and of societies.

By discovering the significance of sequence, we can as analysts, I believe, also greatly enhance the abstract theorizing so typical of the social sciences. The utility of conversation analysis to theories lies in its structural and interactional emphasis on sequentially achieved social action. By directly observing the sequential context *and* consequences of quick verbal exchanges, analysts can track quite distinct interactional processes that are simultaneously organizational. The structure of turn-taking and the finegrained fluidity it provides locate the sequential flow of interaction at the center of human affairs and, as we have seen, at the heart of organizations. The everyday exchanges, created and facilitated through talk, in turn, derive their existence and persistence over time from the recurrent and recursive activities of organizational members acting within and reacting to their internal and external environments. The point, for organizational analysis, is not so much that talk is produced on a turn-by-turn basis but, by extension, that the sequential pacing talk gives to tasks is deeply implicative of organizations themselves. The ways in which verbal rhythms *anchor* the unseen organization make that abstract entity available and directly observable.

Turn-taking mechanisms reveal the *articulation points* of action and thus its structuring properties. Take, for instance, the notion of "paired objects" and "adjacency organization." Turns at talk, paired and adjacently organized such that one gives meaning and direction to the next, provide a kind of revolving prism that highlights each discrete point of this apparently microscopic social order. Similarly, the *positioning* of organizational objects – tasks, goals, decisions, even catastrophes – is also critical. Where, when, how and with whom particular actions occur in a sequential flow of tasks and events is pivotal to what happens *next*. The *adjacency* of action analytically captures the importance of next-positioned tasks and outcomes. Since *all* organizational behavior involves *joint* action, it follows that adjacency organization and turn-taking are central to that "togetherness" of action introduced at the beginning of this study.

Joint action is, furthermore, pervasively problematic to notions of single rational actors and individual preferences. This is because it entails *reciprocity*; not the vague, normative structure-functional approach to reciprocity, but the tense and tightly organized reciprocity of perspectives theorized by phenomenologists and revealed by conversation analysts. Intersubjectivity is *built in* to conversational turn-taking.[23] As organizational actors move through the multiple agendas of meetings or tie together talk and task in a stream of telephone calls, their immediate actions cohere as sequences of action. In the process, actions and meanings are woven into structure.

To come together in a coordinated way, over and over, requires the temporal attention to a *course of action* that Weber also emphasized. Reciprocity cannot thereby be simply normative but is, much more importantly, interactional and sequential. Moreover, as actors also look "sideways" and adjust their actions to those of others across the organizational landscape, they are acutely, if incompletely, aware of their coordination. When someone says "how are they handling this in Tucson" or "we're not talking to Radiology, we're talking to Orthopedics," they are "flagging" that sensibility, marking their parallel activities in time and space. By positioning their local actions in the sequential flow of related departments or organizations – by dancing around (yet accommodating the practical demands of) a federal deadline, for instance – they similarly mark the essential recursive quality of all organizations.

The result is not the fragmentary breakdown of organizational life posited by the postmodernists, but the conscious montage of action and reaction that produces the organization *from within*. As knowledgeable actors segment their work tasks, decisions and even long-term strategies into units, they also collect them into significant participatory streams of action. And as they provide a continuous flow of accounts of those actions, they sediment local acts into dynamic structures of action. These, in turn, become the *next* conditions to which they and others must respond. Operating under intense and often simultaneous conditions, sequence matters greatly to social agents. Simultaneity, sociability and local rationality produce, in their turn, those "satisficing" qualities so insightfully theorized by Herbert Simon decades ago.

The practical consequences of recognizing turn-taking as a central property of organizations is that theorist and researcher can build *sequence* into their own analysis. As should be clear at this point in the discussion, I am not recommending the mechanistic use of lagged variables in multivariate analysis, or the manipulated datapoints of event history and sequential analysis. In these and related techniques, what Duncan calls "statisticism" easily comes to drive the analysis and what *can* be usefully "computed" becomes the social phenomenon of preference. Instead, I am proposing that real advances in both theories and research on organizations will be achieved by taking members' knowledge of position, pace, and overall sequence seriously. What we need is "a theory that considers the timing of different individual actions, and the changing context of each act," so that we can understand a "much more interactive, branching, and contextual set of connections among participants, problems, and solutions . . ."[24] If we recall briefly Vic's chained series of telephone calls (examples 6.2 to 6.6, pp. 134–6 above), his sense of sequence, collaboration and collectivity are clear. To *get the job done*, he needed a quite specific, nested and selective series of interactions, which also had to be enacted in a distinct sequence. In the process, and *together* with others, he outlined an opportunity, isolated a problem, built a team, excluded possible collaborators, set a schedule, and pursued an internal goal that meshed smoothly with external guidelines and resources. In one fine move, he blended local with global. Increasingly, the practical enactment of both organizations and their environments will entail this precise sort of realtime "online" interactional pacing and sequencing.

Organizations: In Practice

I suggested earlier that organizational rationality is really a moving target with which actors align their local actions and accounts. It may also be worth conceiving of an organization itself as an idealized objective which becomes flexible and dynamic through the actions of its constituent members, deriving its stability across time not from "structure" but from the recursivity of reflexive action.[25] In the practical arenas of everyday organizations, rapidly changing conditions require constant attention and quick reflexes.[26] Increasingly, managers, workers and even academics operate in a synchronous and often nonlinear information environment. The informality stressed in this study is thus accelerating, and Garfinkel's insistence on the "once through" and "no time out" organization of experience has taken on new dimensions. The implications for organizations in future are considerable. In this concluding section, it will be useful to look at some of the practical consequences of studying the interface of interaction and information and at the possibilities for more innovative workplaces.

The Office of the Future

The modern office is alive with communications technology these days, far more even than when the data for this study were collected. In addition to established channels such as telephone and telex, increasing numbers of organizations in both the private and public sectors, in the United States and around the world, are also linked by facsimile machines, electronic networks, video conferencing capabilities, and a wide range of advanced telecommunications techniques based on the average touchtone telephone. In government offices and financial centers, satellite television has also become a standard information source, while many multilocational firms also use open-line conference calling and "shout boxes" to maintain both interactional and unidirectional contact with their executives and middle management. McLuhan's prophecies of an information-saturated and message-syncopated global village have, in many ways, become reality.[27] To paraphrase Madison Avenue wisdom, the office of the future is here today.

With increased telecommunications technology in a largely service-oriented economy, both verbal and electronic turn-taking are likely to expand rather than replace necessary communication. At the same time, the human preference for face-to-face exchanges and personal phone calls is likely to persist. And as long as that is the case, the study of organizational interaction – in meetings, on telephones, along the corridors, and in the lunchroom – will illuminate organizations as realtime places. Since all kinds of executives, administrators and workers generally show, as Mintzberg's managers did, "a strong preference for the verbal media of communication"[28] and for a variety of informal information settings, it seems reasonable to suggest that such sociability will continue to be central rather than epiphenomenal to organizations. Just as an earlier generation of organizational analysts drew comfort from Blau's study of bureaucracy,[29] it may be time for careful reconsideration of what people actually *do* in organizations rather than contemplating the residual traces of these activities in the aggregate. The "dynamics of bureaucracy" turn out to be located not in structure but in action.

Information and Innovation

The materials presented here have highlighted a fundamental feature of the workplace of the future: the need for greater flexibility. As is well known, the industrial and even postindustrial economies of the twentieth century have depended on large, centralized decision-making bureaucracies and broad-based, relatively deskilled workforces. Past workplaces of industrial societies depended, in large part, on standardizing, simplifying, and not infrequently stifling individual flexibility in the interests of production efficiency and organizational effectiveness. Organizations of the future will essentially invert this trend.

Effective work settings and thus successful organizations will increasingly depend on *local, decentered, on-the-spot* decision-making. The rapidly changing economic and social conditions projected by virtually every contemporary study will reflexively be created out of just the sort of dynamism of social life alluded to at the outset of this chapter; it will be a dynamism of genuinely global dimensions. Managers and workers of the future will operate in information-rich environments and with the kind of interactionally bounded rationality discussed in the last chapter. They will, as a matter of daily "routine," be confronted with consequential, realtime choices. To explore these issues in any full sense would obviously be beyond the scope of these closing remarks, but, as I have tried to indicate, transformations and innovation in organizations occur at the intersection of information and interaction.

That intersection is, as we have seen, finely organized and massively dependent on what might usefully be called "just in time" understandings of organizational agendas. Those in turn are developed not as abstract pseudo-rational goals but in the intense settings of everyday interaction. Increasingly, people in organizations will have to move ahead with quick interpretations of rapidly changing events. Those understandings will be just enough, based on just enough information at just the moment they must respond to events and create new conditions. Organizations of the future will, to be sure, need impersonal, long-term strategies, complex and anonymous accounting systems, multiple mechanisms for resource allocation, and a variety of efficient ways of dealing with their environments. But those systems and plans will be enacted, with ever increasing intensity, by managers and workers (and their "smart" machines) operating in local environments linked *simultaneously* to global events, which will be anchored in and articulated through other local actors, however distant.

In the local/global workplace of the future, current emphasis on "just in time" production processes will be critically connected to "just here, just now" interpretations of incoming information and understandings of unfolding events. Workers at *every level* will be affected by a speeded up, interactive work environment that will be not simply technologically complex but interpersonally demanding. In the workplace of the future, there will be no hiding places, no time out.

Once-mighty corporations with centralized cores, in the US for instance, are already losing their force and direction as information technology, global production processes, and financial linkages bypass the centers. In the process, direct global links between key actors may well undermine the utility and even the meaning of "headquarters." The borders of national economies are dissolving and with them much of the logic of huge multinational conglomerates whose strength lay in playing one market off against another, whether in terms of resources, labor or consumers. Capital is footloose. Work processes are decentered. Information is instant, and the global workplace is buzzing.

It has been said that "the threads of the global web are computers, facsimile machines, satellites, high-resolution monitors and modems – all of them linking designers, engineers, contractors, licensees, and dealers worldwide."[30] To this must be added the interactional web of telephone calls from ever more mobile phones, meetings of co-present and distant participants, and the near ceaseless chatter in the corridors of the global business community. The fine, often invisible, *technical* links between people and networks across time and space need – *at every point* – even finer interactional and interpretive processes that constantly update the meanings of "what's happening" and the "facts of the matter." The facticity and flexibility of an intensive-extensive global web of business, government and the people who comprise the organizations and institutions of world societies are woven through turn-by-turn interaction. That facticity is structure-in-action.

An emphasis on flexibility need not assume that organizations will turn into "adhocracies,"[31] though obviously some will become overly flexible and many may fail. A clear finding of all ethnomethodological studies of organization, including this one, is that "ad hoc" flexibility occurs within the framework of sense-making and order-making activities. This local flavor need not and, as we have seen in the last chapter, does not mean that either understandings or actions are freefloating or necessarily loosely coupled. Quick exchange of information, however uneven and incomplete, means in the future that "coupling" will be more tense yet elastic. Information will still depend on intensive interpersonal interpretations, but the multiplicity of messages and connections will also mean extensive exchanges with distant collaborators. Some organizational units may be loosely coupled, others tight, but my suspicion is that this misses the point. Organizations in future will be *tensely* coupled because the linkages between them will be far more multidirectional.

The key is that information itself is neither neutral nor unidirectional. It flows not only *into* the organization from the environment, but *within* and *between* subunits. Its transmission may occur in many modes, but its interpretation and incorporation into action is verbal and local. The link between information and action is decidedly "soft,"[32] yet it is critical to the accountability of action that plays such a central role in organizational rationality. Fluid interactional settings that create, encourage and enhance information absorption and adoption will play an even greater part in future workplaces, whether on high-tech factory floors or in the crisp executive corridors of the next decades. Worker skill and management flair alike will depend on quick and varied information about products, services, markets, costs and competitors than ever before. This need for information, once controlled by top management and manipulated by middle managers, will span whole organizations, demanding flattened hierarchies, broadened job categories, and greatly restructured training programs for on-the-job updating of both knowledge and responsibility.[33] Each will, nonetheless, need intense and quite basic turn-by-turn environments of intersubjective understandings and interactional flexibility. Workplaces that facilitate (rather than contain or constrain) high levels of interaction in many modes will thereby be able to build on shared understandings and innovate through quick finegrained decisions.[34]

Where workers of the past could be treated as deskilled cogs in a largely autonomous machine run by distant management, successful firms of the future will have to seek out and retain literate and *communicative* employees whose job satisfaction and contribution will depend on a sophisticated understanding of and involvement in their work. Just as the organizational conversations and meetings presented throughout this study suggest, the interaction order of organizations will be more (not less) important in future, as tele-conferencing, interactive tele-media, pocket telephones, document transmission, and ever more portable computers link people to people on a 24-hour basis. Effective use of these and other information technologies will require increased capacities for collaboration as well as interactively managed abilities for judging the environment, planning ahead, seizing opportunities, and analyzing outcomes. Those outcomes will be the result of a fast-moving and largely unscripted sequence of actions. The unfolding dynamic elements of organization and environment will require a quick competence to identify and assess their local relevance and necessarily immediate logic. Organizational "learning" and "thinking" will thus involve managers, workers and technologies in a far more intrusive mix than earlier years, when they lived in largely separate worlds.

What is at issue, I believe, is a distinct redefinition of the basic division of labor that has shaped the industrial age and persisted well into the postindustrial period. As we move into the age of the smart machine, in Zuboff's apt phrase,[35] we also need smarter workers and more interactive work settings. In this new mix of action and structure, machine and moment, "hot" information can fuel flexible thinking and shape effective planning *only* if the flood of data can be usefully and relevantly made to work. Traditional distance and difference between management and workers will not facilitate this. The workplace of the future must be highly interactive, not just with technology, but with people. The pacing and sequencing of work tasks will continue to be talk-based, but in ways in which technologies complexly mediate both talk and task.[36]

The ability to innovate and thereby change will, at an ever brisker pace, depend on good communication and quick integration of information. Given the momentary attention spans of modern management and workers, successful organizations will be those that recognize and facilitate high levels of interaction and ready opportunities for quick contact. Local, on-the-spot decision-making and planning will require physical environments that facilitate the informality that is central to flexibility.[37] It may well be that the "small is beautiful" theme needs to be reintroduced; flat hierarchies and small work groups enhance communication and build community. The kind of "bubbling" effect necessary for innovative management and general problem-solving needs the synergy of the moment. By allowing the structuring feeling of collaboration to simmer, the inherent creativity of human beings can flourish. It may thus be that *dis*economies of scale will be critical to organizations of the future, as social agents work their way through realtime decisions. What may seem later as *post hoc* rationalization is actually *in situ* reasoning, and this immediate quality will become increasingly important under global conditions of action.

Organizational actors, as we have seen, routinely invest considerable time and energy clarifying the working understandings out of which they craft agendas and actions. This often involves the symbolic and mimetic practices noted by institutional analysts, but the process is not "ritual." By drawing symbolic attention to their activities and aligning themselves with other organizations, local agendas are cloaked in the trappings of official goals and guidelines. As markets and institutions go global, politics will remain local. The steps of the local organizational dance are, however, familiar, part of the folklore of all organizations, everywhere. In this sense, the findings of this study, with their reliance on the finegrained yet universal properties of conversational turn-taking, also apply to "any" organization. In the details of action, we find the complex, purposive, flexible yet durable social properties that define any organization.

Talk and Organization

The central themes of this study can now be drawn together. Talk is not "micro" nor are organizations "macro." The micro–macro distinction is neither empirically observable nor theoretically sensible, though it is certainly useful methodologically. Reality is a seamless web of actions, reactions and inactions. Using the reflexive prism of ethnomethodology, we can now see that all actions are embedded in a continuous stream of social relationships, which, in turn, are framed by a historical context. But it is human agents who must select out relevant aspects of immediate structure and distant history. In so doing, they spin and weave the fine membrane of the web, smoothly, sequentially and seamlessly.

Separating action and structure may thus be more an analytic academic exercise than an empirically grounded strategy. Action and structure are not simply mutually enriching and complementary, as Merton once suggested; they are one. Action creates *and* builds on patterned practices. In so doing, discrete human activities and the intersubjective achievement of meanings they trace take on retrospective rationality and stability. The essential accountability of action locates individual interpretations in the wider social arena, thus creating community out of moment. The issue here is not one of incorporating the "individual moment" into some collectivist whole.[38] Institutions are talked into being[39] in particular moments and at relevant historical conjunctions; the *relevance* is a local matter, the consequences may be global.

This study has been developed very much within the joint orientations of ethnomethodology and conversation analysis, but it also marks a departure from them. I have been especially concerned with the *reflexive* relation of talk and organization, and this breaks with current practice in conversation analysis. In treating reflexivity seriously, the strict adjacent positioning of turns at talk and what Schegloff calls "procedural consequentiality"[40] must be understood in their appropriate theoretical and methodological context. Interest in adjacency organization has, as we have seen, led most conversation analysts to focus on questions and answers as a primary locus of social organization. As the field grew, "institutional" settings were included as more and more researchers had access to talk-based work activities. These too have, however, tended to be examined as ways of understanding variants of turn-taking and the central role of questions and answers.[41]

In the current analysis of organizational talk, I have been more interested in the ways in which the reflexive properties of talk *necessarily* instantiate and creatively extend organizations. These qualities of all interaction are, in turn, extended in time and space "back" before a particular verbal exchange and "forward" into the life cycles of those organizations (and others in their sphere). Interaction is thus an autonomous domain of action in that it unfolds independently, but it is *simultaneously* embedded in a sociocultural world. Goffman's tangible and consequential interaction order embodies faceless organizational principles and transforms abstract goals into lively, *lived* practices.

Talk is *intensive* in its local and delicately balanced turn-driven organization. It is *extensive*[42] in that the lifeblood of organizations flows through it. In this way, everyday talk and the business that gets done through it is doubly contextual. Talk creates its own local logic, turn by turn. At the same time, everyday interaction creates the contexts and interprets the contingencies out of which next actions spring. The *organizing* qualities of organizations are located in the organization of talk. This is the business of talk.

Appendix:
Methodological Notes

I started this study with an interest in organization. I use the singular quite explicitly because what interests me is how life is organized, in particular the relation between language and social organization. I decided to study talk in organizational settings and to attempt to analyze where and how the organization of experience proposed by Hanold Garfinkel actually organizes these pervasive places.

My first attempts to gain access into organizations failed miserably, despite good introductions and well-placed contacts. The initial plan, overly ambitious in every way, was to study one organization at many levels. Instead, I found myself going up and down in elevators. The executive suites were not always, I found, at the top of impressive buildings, nor were the executives themselves much taken with my idea of studying multiple levels of their organization. They could not imagine, it seemed, that anything would be worth studying in their production department, or accounts, or even in sales. On the other hand, while they agreed that talk was the very essence of business, they were uncomfortable about the thought of any tape-recording done of *their own* talk, which they clearly assumed was terribly important and worthy of study.

Almost too late I realized that, like Alice travelling through the Looking Glass, I had quite forgotten to walk backwards into situations and to ask for the opposite of what I really wanted. This was a lesson I had learned at the very beginning of my film career; 10 years of academic abstraction had knocked the commonsense of it out of me. Both the trust and ease of access essential to either good fieldwork or successful location filming depend on asking for simple things first, leaving complex and more demanding requests to later.

I began again, using small, local organizations where I had a close personal contact: a travel agency, a sales office, a local TV station. Instead of asking to tape, I asked what sorts of things they already routinely taped. Instead of asking to study the whole organization, I asked simply to study a department, or to follow one person. This resulted in some fascinating tapes of settings such as the investment banking house, where sales meetings, conference calls, and certain internal telephone calls are regularly taped, and in meetings and informal conversations in the travel agency with an owner-manager who had no reservations about the research or preoccupations with the importance of what she and her staff were doing. The television station was a similar situation, though ultimately rather little data got recorded there for reasons altogether unrelated to the research request. My biggest break came on my own doorstep, where the lively and attentive Graduate Dean of my university came to my aid, and his staff (who knew me well as a part-time employee) generously put up with my tape-recorders. In 18 erratic months of initial research, only one participant asked for a tape-recorder to be turned off. I also offered everyone the opportunity to screen tapes and erase anything or everything. No one did. In the end, the lesson was clear: be flexible and modest in early arrangements, work locally, use friends and close contacts as much as possible, build trust by seeming to want very little and "grow" into the research site.

Overall, the data for this study were collected over four years, 1983–7; the Kennedy materials were recorded in 1962 and 1963. The organizations studied include the Oval Office of the White House during the Kennedy administration, a university administrative department, two research offices, a travel agency (with branches in northern and southern California and Tucson, Arizona), a banking and brokerage institution in southern California, two hospitals, a sales office and a small TV station. The interactional settings include meetings, telephone calls, corridor conversations, doorway exchanges, chats around work stations and photocopy machines, and even a few elevator exchanges. I was present at most meetings, sometimes as participant but mainly as researcher. Telephone calls and casual conversations were more often recorded by participants who were collaborating in the research and through the use of small Walkman-style recorders. All participants were aware of taping periods and often consulted.

The only exception to these general conditions were the recordings made in the Oval Office, for obvious reasons. These are available to any researcher through the archives of the Kennedy Presidential Library in Boston.

A concern of all social science researchers and especially those who do qualitative work and thus have direct contact with real people, places, times, and organizations is that of maintaining the anonymity of subjects and their settings. My own strategy in this regard was straightforward. I renamed and relocated all personal names, places, departments, organizations, and affiliations as I did the first rough transcriptions of the data. In the process, I created, and later extended, a log of these transpositions so that, rather like novelists or the writers of long-running television productions, I could remember where and how the changes had been done as I transcribed additional recordings or made use of my rather limited fieldnotes. In the case of two organizations, I developed charts to keep track of the names/characters. This was necessary because, as noted above, I worked continuously with the audio recordings where, rather obviously, people were using their own names and those of others in their "original" form. Over time, I came to think of all of the interactants in terms of their research names. The only exception to this procedure was with the Kennedy materials, where I made no attempt to disguise the speakers as the materials had been explicitly cleared for public use by the National Archive staff at the Kennedy Presidential Library.

Finally, the transcription notation system used by conversation analysts has been developed, over many years, by Gail Jefferson. Those presented here are a small subset of the large and growing system of symbols used to document the materials of conversation analysts, standardized to facilitate scholarly exchange of materials, and used by researchers in conjunction with audio or video recordings. Using standard keyboard symbols, the conventions are intended to capture for the eye the way the talk is heard by the ear. Transcripts are always analyzed together with relevant audio or video materials and are not intended as substitutes for the data they record. For more extensive discussion, see Atkinson and Heritage (1984), Button and Lee (1987), and Boden and Zimmerman (1991).

A: Ye⌈s, two.   ⌉   Brackets indicate the point at which
B: ⌊Oh goo:⌋d.   simultaneous speech starts and ends.

A: ⌈⌈How-   Utterances starting simultaneously are
B: ⌊⌊When did you hear?   indicated by double left brackets.

A: Hello= **B**: =Hi.	When there is no audible gap between one utterance and the next, equal signs are used.
(0.8)	Numbers in brackets indicate elapsed time in tenths of seconds.
(.)	A dot in parentheses indicates a slight gap, typically less than one-tenth of a second.
A: *Right*.	Italics indicate emphasis in delivery.
B: HOW MUCH?	Capital letters indicate that a word or phrase is louder than the surrounding talk.
A: So : : :	Colons indicate that the immediately prior syllable is prolonged or "stretched"; the number of colons denotes, approximately, the duration.
A: We added to-	A hyphen represents a "cut-off" of an immediately prior word or syllable.
.,?	Punctuation marks are used to capture characteristics of speech delivery rather than grammatical notation.

A: Sure.
  B: Issues,
  C: Ca : mpus?
	– downward contour
	– sustained contour
	– rising contour

.hh : :	A dot prefixed "h" indicates an inbreath; without a dot, exhalation.
Heh-heh-huh-huh	Laughter particles
I'll ju(h)*st* ski : : p that pa (. hhh)rt!	An 'h' in parentheses denotes breathiness or a plosive delivery.
('r something)	Items enclosed in single parentheses or empty parentheses indicate transcriber's doubt of a hearing.

((cough))
((ring))
((loud bang))
((softly))

Double parentheses are used to enclose a description of some phenomenon that characterizes the talk or the scene.

→ *H*ang on

Arrows are used in front of key lines of transcription to highlight analytic phenomena.

Notes

Introduction

1 An important move toward a more holistic view of social order is contained in Randall Collins's important papers (1981a; 1981b) that trace what he terms the "micro-foundations" of order; see also Nancy DiTomasi's discussion on the core danger of reducing "(inter)action and structure" to each other (1982: 15) and Ritzer 1990.
2 Weick 1979.
3 See Gouldner 1970: 51–4.
4 See also Zimmerman and Boden 1991.
5 See, for example, March 1988.
6 Lieberson 1984.
7 On this point, see also Berger et al. 1989.
8 To be fair, Merleau-Ponty (1945) is concerned with much broader and more durable conventions of thought than that of "social structure." He is addressing the ways is which we perceive objects in the world as independent of ourselves, and, thus separated, assume that they actually pre-exist us (hence "retrospective illusion"); see a more extended discussion in chapter 1 below; see also Schutz 1962; Pollner 1987.
9 For an extended discussion of space, time, and modernity, see our discussion in Friedland and Boden 1994.
10 Ethnomethodology, both directly and indirectly, has greatly influenced structuration theory; see Boden 1990a; cf. Cohen 1989.
11 For an extensive discussion of the multiple ways modern actors still contrive to get together to talk, see our "compulsion of proximity" discussion, Boden and Molotch 1994.

12 This theme has been best elaborated by Thomas Wilson (1982) and picked up by Giddens (1984); for an empirical application see also Molotch and Boden 1985.

Chapter 1 Talk and Organization

1 My sense of this concerted sort of action and the ways in which human action involves people gathering to do things *together* has grown greatly from reading, and talking with, Howard Becker (e.g. 1986). The claim that "togetherness" is bound up with and bound by *talk* is my own approach (e.g. Boden 1990b; see also chapter 6 below), although it also has roots in the phenomenological notion of "consociation" or mutual lived-in experience of the world (e.g. Gurwitsch 1979).

2 See e.g. Garfinkel 1967; Zimmerman and Pollner 1970; this point is elaborated below.

3 Schutz 1962.

4 Zimmerman and Pollner 1970: 82–4; see also Garfinkel 1967: 35.

5 Wilson 1989.

6 On the agency/structure question, see Giddens 1976; 1979; 1984; Abrams 1982; Bourdieu 1977; Sahlins 1985; for authors approaching the role of agency in this spirit, see Alexander 1988a; 1988b; Collins 1988b; DiMaggio 1988; Sztompka 1991; see also Alexander et al. 1987.

7 By organizations "in action" I mean something far more concrete and specific than earlier formulations of this idea (e.g. Thompson 1967); see ch. 2 below.

8 This has been argued in a variety of ways by a considerable range of writers, e.g. M.W. Meyer 1979; Pfeffer 1982; Clegg 1989; DiMaggio 1988; Daft 1990; Stinchcombe 1990; and so on.

9 E.g. Homans 1966; Baron and Bielby 1980; and Friedland and Alford 1991; see also Collins 1988a: 393–9.

10 See especially Heritage 1984a: 311.

11 For an extensive discussion of the duality of structure, see Giddens 1984: 297–304; see also Cohen 1989: 42ff.

12 Giddens 1979: 5. The relationship between the institutional order and social practices was earlier developed by Berger and Luckmann (1966), though much of the phenomenological underpinnings of that path-breaking work have been oddly misunderstood by many subsequent fans; for an illuminating discussion of this misreading, see Eberle 1992.

13 Maynard and Wilson 1980. The idea that the reflexive interplay of talk and social structure unfolds in the turn-by-turn production of interaction is developed in some detail in our earlier study of the Watergate hearings, see Molotch and Boden 1985.

14 Cf. Cohen 1989: 44–5.

15 Garfinkel 1967; and see especially Sacks 1963; 1972a; 1984; and Garfinkel

and Sacks 1970; my own views on these matters are developed in some detail in chapter 3, and thereafter throughout this study.

16 This classic view is offered by, among many others, Neil Smelser in a recent essay (1988), whereas a quite alternate view is held by all ethnomethodologists, e.g. Zimmerman and Boden 1991.

17 Coser 1975.

18 Typified by, but not limited to, the views often expressed by Peter Blau, e.g. 1970.

19 See also Zimmerman and Boden 1991: 6ff.

20 Tilly 1984.

21 This point is made by Freeman 1978: 341, but occurs in various forms in many discussions of the issue, e.g. Collins 1988a: 386.

22 E.g. Goffman 1983a: 2.

23 E.g. Coser 1975; but Randall Collins has developed a more eclectic position in recent writings which posits an interplay of first micro and later macro phenomena, e.g. Collins 1981a; 1988a.

24 Part of Gouldner's polemic in his well-known book (1970) is an insistence that all forms of microsociology are ahistorical and therefore flawed. The notion that people make history in and through circumstances they creatively reconstruct seems oddly misapprehended by many sociologists. I am indebted to Howard Aldrich for reminding me of this, yet again.

25 Heritage 1984a: 110.

26 The retrospective illusion, as noted earlier, is central to Merleau-Ponty's work (e.g. 1945: 274–80) and rather more obliquely in the writings of Garfinkel as the notion of "facticity"; it has also been developed especially well recently by Pollner (1987: 108).

27 Heritage 1983.

28 Heritage 1984a: 290; see also chapter 3 below.

29 See especially Molotch 1990; Zimmerman and Boden 1991: 17–19.

30 This notion of "reflexive tying" of action and organization has been a theme of Hugh Mehan's work, e.g. Mehan 1979; Mehan et al. 1986.

31 A wide range of writings deal with this theme, see e.g. Weber 1968; Parsons 1937; Blau 1963; Thompson 1967.

32 E.g. Simon 1957; March and Simon 1958; March 1962; March and Olson 1976; Weick 1976; Pfeffer and Salancik 1978; Stinchcombe 1990.

33 Parsons 1951.

34 See Pfeffer and Salancik 1978.

35 E.g. Mintzberg 1973; Kanter 1977; Pondy 1978; Gronn 1983.

36 Mintzberg 1973: 58.

37 Gronn 1983; see also Gronn 1985.

38 Again, a variety of researchers have studied these various areas, such as Kanter 1977; Sproull 1981; Clegg 1976; Pettigrew 1979; Daft 1983; Boje 1991.

39 E.g. Giglioli 1972; Trudgill 1974; Grimshaw 1981; 1990.

40 Especially Goffman 1981; 1983b.

41 Goffman 1983a.
42 See on this point Clayman 1989; Heritage and Greatbatch 1991. Schegloff has become particularly exercised about the, as he claims, inherent dangers of considering the reflexive relationship of talk and structure (e.g. Schegloff 1987a; 1991) despite the fact that analysis of the sort he advocates sometimes winds up isolating structures of talk that seem to operate behind the backs of actors.
43 See Giddens 1987: 153.
44 See, for example, Boden and Zimmerman 1991; Drew and Heritage 1992.
45 See Heritage's discussion of "continuous updating" in interaction (1984a: 259).
46 This part of the model developed by Harvey Sacks and his colleagues is discussed more fully in chapter 3 below; see Sacks et al. 1974.
47 See e.g. Goffman 1976: 310; also his many discussions of talk drawn together in *Forms of Talk*, 1981.
48 March and Simon 1958.
49 For a rather splendid, though, he claims, incomplete list, see March 1978.
50 Cf. Elster 1989.
51 March and Olsen 1976: 10.
52 Ibid.: 11.
53 Ibid.: 11–12.
54 Ibid.: 11.
55 March and Simon 1958.
56 Zuboff 1988.

Chapter 2   Organizations in Action

1 Georg Simmel's central point in *The Philosophy of Money* (1978).
2 Eric Wolf's (1982) discussion being the most elegant account.
3 See e.g. Scott 1987a; there is in organizational analysis a fascination with typologies, although often they are typologies of *theories* of organizations, rather than organizations themselves, cf. Morgan 1986.
4 E.g. Hall et al. 1967.
5 Stinchcombe 1965: 142; see also Aldrich and Marsden 1988 for a useful definitional discussion, e.g. pp. 362–3.
6 For excellent yet abstract definitions see Etzioni 1964: 3; Aldrich 1979: 242; Scott 1987a; Hall 1987: 37–41; and Pfeffer 1982.
7 Gareth Morgan (1986) has written particularly effectively on the use of metaphor to capture the essences of various forms of organizations; see also Morgan 1980.
8 Simon 1962.
9 Here I appreciate Howard Aldrich's comments on an earlier draft of this discussion, but am stubbornly ignoring his good advice.

10 E.g. Hannan and Freeman 1977; Aldrich 1979.

11 E.g. Pfeffer and Salancik 1978.

12 E.g. Tichy et al. 1979; Galaskiewicz 1985.

13 E.g. Clegg and Dunkerley 1980; Clegg 1981; Pfeffer 1981; Fligstein 1990.

14 This is, in relation to the theme of this study, an especially relevant area and a growing one, e.g. Sproull and Larkey 1982; Dingwall and Strong 1985; Donnelon et al. 1986; and Finholt and Sproull 1990. In this regard, Stinchcombe's recent analysis (1990) is likely to become a classic and should, at the very least, spawn new studies in organizational research (see also chapter 6 below).

15 E.g. Carroll 1987; Fligstein 1990.

16 E.g. Deal and Kennedy 1982; Sproull 1981; Barley 1983; Van Maanen 1979; Fine 1984.

17 See Pfeffer 1982: 254–6; see also Benson 1983; Daft 1990; Hassard 1991.

18 See also Hilbert 1987; Sica 1988: 24–33.

19 Weber 1968; see also Cicourel 1964: 189–91; Giddens 1987; 1990.

20 Weber 1968; Granovetter 1985.

21 Weber was, in many ways, primarily concerned with state bureaucracies and the emergence of the nation-state and national governments, rather than the sort of organizational society we now contemplate; for recent studies of the bureaucratic form, see e.g. Williamson 1975; DiMaggio and Powell 1983; Fligstein 1990.

22 See e.g. Colignon 1989.

23 Rationality is taken up in detail in chapter 8 below.

24 Weber 1968: 312.

25 It is worth noting that the subtitle of *Economy and Society* is: *An Outline of Interpretive Sociology*. Even this impressive compendium of Weber's writings collected by Guenther Roth and Claus Wittich in 1968 routinely defers to the Parsonian translations or treatments of such critical terms as *Verstehen, Deuten, Sinn, Handeln, Verhalten*, and especially *Sinnzusammenhang* (understanding, interpretation, meaning, behavior, action, and complex of meaning).

26 For a far more elegant discussion of this point, see Hilbert 1987.

27 Parsons 1951; for more recent related discussions, see in particular Zucker 1977; cf. Alexander 1988a; 1990.

28 For a variety of excellent overviews from different perspectives, see Aldrich 1979; Pfeffer 1982; Scott 1987a; Hall 1987; Perrow 1986; cf. Hassard and Pym 1990.

29 These developments are sketched for the US and Britain by Scott 1987a; Argyris 1965; and for continental Europe by Bonazzi 1989; Chanlat 1990; and, more selectively, Bouchikhi 1990.

30 Perrow 1986: 63.

31 March and Simon 1958; Blau and Scott 1962; Cyert and March 1963.

32 E.g. Clegg 1976; 1989; 1990; Clegg and Dunkerley 1980.

33 Especially Silverman 1970; Silverman and Jones 1976.

34 Chanlat 1990 has provided an excellent overview of organizational research in France and Canada.
35 My rough translation of Chanlat's point; more fully in the original, Chanlat argues: "Étudier les dynamiques humaines telles qu'elles surgissent et les interpréter à la lumière de ce que les principaux acteurs font et disent, tels sont les objectifs poursuivie par la majorité des chercheurs de langue française" (Chanlat 1991: 20). See also Ballé 1990.
36 Gouldner 1954.
37 E.g. Fligstein 1990.
38 See e.g. Etzioni 1964: 59.
39 This notion of "explaining away" human action is borrowed from Wilson 1989, as noted earlier.
40 See especially Barnard 1938; Dalton 1959; Blau 1963.
41 This theme is central to Dalton's work, and appears in various guises across the length of the text, e.g. 1959: 8–17, 194–215, 218–40.
42 Blau 1963: v.
43 See also Blau and Scott 1962.
44 See also Blau 1970.
45 For example, in Pfeffer and Salancik 1978; Clegg 1981; Pfeffer 1982; and DiMaggio and Powell 1983; but recently Fligstein (1990) and, more surprising, Stinchcombe (1990) have been developing more articulated theories of the role of action and contingency in organizations.
46 See e.g. Burrell and Morgan 1979: 120; and the discussion in Scott 1987a especially.
47 As discussed by Gouldner 1959; Thompson 1967.
48 Scott 1987a.
49 Thompson 1967.
50 See Scott 1987a: 121–32.
51 See Aldrich 1992.
52 This will be offered in part as a corrective, though hardly a complete one, of a number of brave but flawed attempts to characterize this work, e.g. Burrell and Morgan 1979; Pfeffer 1982.
53 See Giddens 1987 for a related discussion, although not from an ethnomethodological perspective.
54 Pollner 1987: xvii.
55 This idea of structure-in-action is developed in some detail in Zimmerman and Boden 1991; see also Molotch 1990.
56 Thompson 1967. The reverse has not too often been the case although recent work, especially Granovetter 1985, has begun to stress the ways in which organizations *shape* their environments, including the economy.
57 For example, Lawrence and Lorsch 1967: 9–14.
58 Ibid.; M.W. Meyer et al. 1978; Aldrich 1979; Meyer and Scott 1983 (these authors are working from an institutional approach, but are similarly interested in the interchange between organizations and their environments); Hannan and Freeman 1989.

59 Indeed, some of these major proponents of the technique seem unconcerned by an ecological effect of a different kind that occurs when results at the population ecology level of aggregation contradict their own findings at what they call the "subpopulation" level, see e.g. Freeman et al. 1983; Hannan and Freeman 1989.

60 Scott and Black 1986.

61 This important point is developed quite differently by March and Olsen 1976; Stinchcombe 1990: 2–7.

62 E.g. Pfeffer and Salancik 1978; see also Aldrich and Pfeffer 1976.

63 E.g. Granovetter 1985.

64 E.g. Meyer and Scott 1983.

65 Selznick 1948.

66 Pfeffer 1982: 239.

67 See DiMaggio and Powell 1983.

68 For example, Kamens 1977; Powell and Friedkin 1986.

69 Meyer and Rowan 1977: 340.

70 Ibid.: 346.

71 See Weick 1976: 2; "coupling" holds a great deal of fascination for some institutionalists, with loose coupling providing a useful analytic escape hatch from the untidy performance of many real organizations.

72 This notion of "typifications" is central to the work of Alfred Schutz. Many organizational readers of these materials seem to depend on rather singular readings of Berger and Luckmann 1966, a not uncommon problem with that most successful little book; see the discussion in Eberle 1992.

73 Meyer and Rowan 1977: 349; for an even more sweeping statement, see J.W. Meyer et al. 1987.

74 Zucker 1977: 729.

75 See especially Schutz 1962; see also Smith 1978.

76 Zucker 1977: 731.

77 E.g. DiMaggio 1988: 5.

78 See e.g. Zimmerman 1971; see also Clegg and Dunkerley 1980: 292–3.

79 See Wittgenstein 1958: 56–66; cf. Giddens 1984: 19–21.

80 Indeed, the frequent appeal to routine or ritual practices on the part of social theorists (e.g. Collins 1981a; 1981b; 1988a; Giddens 1984; Cohen 1989) or organizational specialists (e.g. Stinchcombe 1990) is really an appeal to "rescue" the formal rules or norms assumed to guide behavior, while social actors actually *sustain* that "routineness" as a central matter in their life and work, and that is Wittgenstein's point.

81 Within the institutional literature, even the meaning of "isomorphism" seems to vary across the literature; I am indebted to Walter Nord for this insight.

82 See e.g. Zucker 1977; DiMaggio and Powell 1983.

83 Or rather, to be fair, it is both, hence the reflexivity of both accounts and action, see also Perrow 1986: 174–6.

84 Scott 1987b.

85 E.g. Giddens 1976; 1984; Heritage 1987: 25–65; Heritage and Greatbatch 1991; see also Cohen 1989: 38–40.
86 Cicourel 1964: 178.
87 DiMaggio 1988: 2.
88 See Scott 1987b.
89 See especially the discussion, in Meyer and Rowan 1977: 356–7, which is much cited in organizational literature as a way of justifying the need to study structure instead of action.
90 The success of these attempts is relative, see e.g. DiMaggio 1988 and, in the same book, Zucker 1988a; old habits die hard, even when "agency" has become somewhat trendy, at least in theoretical circles.
91 Simon 1962.
92 For example, Simon's *Models of Man* (1957) and his work with March (March and Simon 1958).
93 Simon 1972: 161.
94 The idea of decision-making entailing an essential "drift" is developed in March and Romelaer 1976 and is explored further in chapter 8 below.
95 See e.g. March 1988.
96 March and Olsen 1976: 16.
97 See Cohen et al. 1972; see also March 1988.
98 Weick 1979: 1.
99 Ibid.: 1–2.
100 Ibid.: 43.
101 See DiMaggio 1988: 13.
102 E.g. March and Olsen 1976.
103 Ibid.; see also Zimmerman 1969.
104 Garfinkel 1967; Weick 1979: 44–8.
105 Here is not an appropriate place to attempt even the most minimal review of this excellent study, see Stinchcombe 1990; the works of Chandler and Williamson which Stinchcombe analyzes with considerable originality are, respectively, *Strategy and Structure* (1962) and *Markets and Hierarchies* (1975).
106 Stinchcombe 1990: 2–3.
107 Ibid.: 342.
108 Hobbes 1968: 728.
109 For example, Parsons 1951: 36–7; cf. Heritage 1984a: 20–2; Giddens 1987: 59–61.
110 Durkheim 1982.
111 This view of order is discussed as "Parsons' plenum" in Garfinkel 1988.
112 Contrary to much writing on ethnomethodology, Garfinkel did not reject the work of his mentor; for Garfinkel, to this day, "Parsons' work . . . remains awesome for the penetrating depth and unfailing precision of its practical sociological reason on the constituent tasks of the problem of social order and its solutions" (1967: ix; see also his discussion of "Parsons' plenum" in Garfinkel 1988).
113 Garfinkel 1967: 1ff.

114 For those who find Garfinkel's apparently convoluted prose rather labor intensive, there are now a number of lucid and highly readable current accounts of ethnomethodology and its companion traveller, conversation analysis. See, for instance, Heritage 1984a; Zimmerman 1988; Hilbert 1990, 1992; Zimmerman and Boden 1991; Maynard and Clayman 1991; as well as my own attempts, Boden 1990a; 1990b.

115 Pollner 1991.

116 Garfinkel 1988: 105.

117 See also Roth 1968: xxxi.

118 Garfinkel 1988: 76–115.

119 See Garfinkel 1967: 1; see also Hilbert 1990, 1992.

120 Garfinkel himself has tended to take the view that the word "ethnomethodology" has itself become altogether emblematic, e.g. Garfinkel 1974.

121 Pollner 1987: 13.

122 This is a common enough confusion, e.g. Turner 1988: 49.

123 Garfinkel 1967: 79.

124 Bittner 1965.

125 See also e.g. Lynch 1985; Garfinkel 1986.

126 Bittner 1965: 241.

127 E.g. Selznick 1948.

128 Bittner 1965: 244.

129 Including Cicourel 1964; 1968; 1974; Garfinkel 1967; Sudnow 1967; Zimmerman 1969; Zimmerman and Pollner 1970; Silverman 1970; Wieder 1988; Atkinson 1978.

130 For a recent and innovative examination of the inherent interactional quality of even survey research findings, see Suchman and Jordan 1990.

131 Kaufman 1944.

132 Garfinkel 1967: 106–7.

133 Ibid.: 114.

134 Ibid.: 74; see also Heritage 1984a: 137–41.

135 See the discussion in Sudnow 1967: 61–9.

136 Garfinkel 1967; Sacks 1966; see Atkinson 1978: 110–47; Heritage 1984a: 168–76.

137 See especially Cicourel 1964.

138 Zimmerman 1969: 237.

139 Feldman 1989: 79–96.

140 For example, Harper 1988.

141 For example, Cicourel 1968; Wieder 1988; Pollner 1987.

142 This misreading is common in the organizational literature, see e.g. Pfeffer 1982: 209; or the more general misreading in Zucker 1977.

143 E.g. Lynch 1982; Garfinkel et al. 1981.

144 See e.g. Mehan et al. 1986.

145 Mehan 1979.

146 Pollner 1987.

147 Bittner 1967a; 1967b.

148   Wieder 1988.
149   See e.g. Anderson et al. 1989.
150   Mintzberg 1973: 35; see also Kurke and Aldrich 1983.
151   In Mintzberg's coding scheme, time and activities were coded sepa-
      rately (indeed presented considerable coding difficulties), so that the
      distribution of clock time might overlap an activity or *vice versa*. For
      example, "tours" of the work site and "desk work," as activities, *included*
      time spent talking. Mintzberg's activity codes were: desk work, tours,
      unscheduled meetings, scheduled meetings, and telephone calls; almost
      40 percent of activities were meetings, accounting for *70 percent* of time
      allotted, for instance (see below, chapter 4).
152   Gronn 1983.

Chapter 3   Talk as Social Action

1   Mead 1934.
2   For an illuminating discussion of child/adult interaction using a con-
     versation analytic approach, see Maynard 1985.
3   Saussure 1974: 14.
4   E.g. Chomsky 1957.
5   See e.g. Boomer and Dittman 1965.
6   One of the earliest writers on this topic was, of course, Charles Saunders
     Peirce; in contemporary writing, see especially Cicourel 1974; in the
     organizational literature, see also Silverman and Jones 1976; Pondy et al.
     1977; Sigman 1980; Barley 1983; Smirich 1983; Gray et al. 1985.
7   Baccus 1986: 7; see also a more general discussion in Mehan and Wood
     1975.
8   The discussion of "signed" objects appears mostly in unpublished recent
     work of Harold Garfinkel, which itself seems often in a direct line of
     intellectual consideration of signs and especially *signing*, from Peirce via
     Merleau-Ponty. Its *sociological* relevance, however, moves beyond
     philosophy and linguistics into a practical everyday realm that merits
     much more attention than it receives from most social scientists.
9   Clegg 1989: 151.
10   See also Mehan 1987: 298–300.
11   Sacks 1972a: 32.
12   The repetition of "organization/s" is consciously articulated to express
     the reflexivity involved, with apologies for the stylistic consequences.
13   Garfinkel 1967: 184.
14   Ibid.: 185.
15   This transcript contains a limited number of transcription conventions,
     which indicate, for example, simultaneous speech with "[---]"; pauses
     timed in tenths of seconds as: (0.9); a "cut-off" word denoted with a
     dash ("-"); and volume of delivery in capital letters; the transcription
     methods of conversation analysis are described in detail in the appendix.

16 Observations based on video analysis in a recent "Workplace Project" conducted at the Xerox Palo Alto Research Center clearly demonstrate this inhabiting quality of action as, for example, coworkers in an airline operations room coordinating high-technology communications systems with aircraft in flight, airport gate arrivals and departures, and a host of other activities all mediated through talk-based coordinations of both local and distant events (e.g. Brun-Cottan 1990).

17 Garfinkel 1967: 185.

18 This is not, of course, the real name of the hospital or of the faculty group.

19 This is a position Paul maintains throughout the meeting, withholding full alignment with Hal's proposal through a series of topical side-steps that maintain a "finance" perspective; for further discussion on organizational agendas, see chapter 7 below.

20 Here echoing Weick's discussion of the ways in which actors make sense of common goals and meanings *through* their actions together, rather than in advance (1976; 1979).

21 Sacks 1984: 22.

22 Ibid.: 23.

23 Ibid.: 26–7.

24 Sacks 1984: 26.

25 Sacks 1966.

26 For extended discussion of questions and answers and their adjacent positioning, see Schegloff 1968; Schegloff and Sacks 1973; and especially Heritage 1984a.

27 E.g. Sacks 1984.

28 E.g. Sacks 1972b; 1987.

29 Sacks 1987: 56.

30 Sacks et al. 1974.

31 This apparently general claim has proven most durable; across all Indo-European languages, for example, conversational turn-taking reflects the basic elements of the Sacks et al. model (e.g. Boden 1983), and there is good evidence that it holds for "any language" (e.g. Moerman 1977; Ren 1989).

32 Sacks et al. 1974; see also Jefferson 1974; Wilson and Zimmerman 1986.

33 See e.g. Schegloff 1987b.

34 See e.g. Heritage 1984a; 1985; Atkinson and Heritage 1984; Wilson et al. 1984; Button and Lee 1987; Wilson and Zimmerman 1986; Zimmerman 1988; Goodwin and Heritage 1990; see also Boden 1990a. A number of these and related writings have also explicitly addressed the linkages between conversation analysis and ethnomethodology: see e.g. Heritage 1987; Zimmerman 1988; Boden 1990a; Hilbert 1990; Maynard and Clayman 1991. For an early discussion of turn-taking in organizational settings, see also Rawlings 1982.

35 See Heritage 1984a on the "primacy of mundane conversation."

36 Sacks 1989: 211.

37 Schegloff and Sacks 1973.
38 See especially Pomerantz 1984.
39 See Schegloff 1980.
40 Sacks et al. 1974: 726–7.
41 Goodwin 1979.
42 Schegloff et al. 1977.
43 The term "talk-in-interaction" was coined by Schegloff and used over a number of writings, see e.g. 1987a. The term "interaction analysis" has been developed especially by Jordan to apply to a wider analytic frame than is typical in conversation analysis, see e.g. Jordan and Henderson 1992.
44 For more extended discussions of these interaction/institution linkages, see Heritage and Greatbatch 1991; Drew and Heritage 1992; Boden 1994.
45 For a more specific discussion of the "comparative" approach in conversation analysis, see Drew and Heritage 1992.
46 This is detailed in a collaborative article by Garfinkel and Sacks (1970).
47 For a more extended discussion of this point, see Boden 1990a.
48 Jefferson 1979.
49 Jefferson and Lee 1981; Jefferson 1984b; Maynard and Zimmerman 1984; Button and Casey 1985.
50 Drew 1987; on jokes generally see Sacks 1974.
51 Schegloff 1987b; Maynard 1991.
52 Maynard 1985.
53 Drew and Holt 1988.
54 See especially Schegloff et al. 1977.
55 McHoul 1978; Mehan 1979.
56 Atkinson and Drew 1979.
57 Maynard 1984.
58 Molotch and Boden 1985; Halkowski 1989.
59 Garcia 1991.
60 E.g. West 1984; 1992; Heath 1986; Ten Have 1991.
61 E.g. Zimmerman 1984; Whalen and Zimmerman 1990.
62 E.g. Mellinger 1990.
63 E.g. Harper et al. 1991.
64 Heath and Luff 1991.
65 See Greatbatch 1986, 1988; Heritage and Greatbatch 1986, 1991; Clayman 1989.
66 E.g. Suchman 1993.
67 Boden and Zimmerman 1991; Drew and Heritage 1992.
68 This apparently handy, technical convenience has, as noted earlier, theoretical relevance since it allows the researcher to observe – quite directly – what Garfinkel calls "facts in flight" or what I have elsewhere termed the-world-as-it-happens (Boden 1990a).
69 The boundaries of organizations are, of course, much debated in the literature; for members, the issue is far less opaque and they routinely accomplish variations on the boundaries as part of their quite consciously

enacted environment. This everyday variation may, in and of itself, be the primary source of the organizational researcher's frustration.

70 See also Zimmerman and Boden 1991.
71 Powell 1988: 119.
72 Giddens 1987: 155.

Chapter 4   The Interaction Order of Organizations

1 Goffman 1972; this is a problem Harold Garfinkel likes to call "bumping into bodies," namely that the embodied or incarnate social world is a recalcitrant problem for social scientists. I am grateful to him for several highly amusing conversations of our own through which he has taught me a great deal about this problem and its consequences for social science theorizing.

2 Goffman first developed the notion of the interaction order in a slim volume entitled *Encounters* in 1961 and returned powerfully to the theme in his presidential address to the American Sociological Association, which he was too ill to deliver and which was published posthumously (1983a). I am grateful to Spencer Cahill for guiding me to these parallels in Goffman's work.

3 As Becker likes to put it, e.g. 1986 and elsewhere.

4 See also an extended discussion of the interaction order *sui generis* in Rawls 1987.

5 Goffman 1983a: 2.

6 See Gronn 1983.

7 See Mintzberg 1973; 1979; Kanter 1977; see also Schwartzman 1988: 158–9; Anderson et al. 1989.

8 Mintzberg 1973.

9 This also applies, indeed strikingly so, for firms in the aggregate, see Friedland and Palmer 1994; see also Boden and Molotch 1994.

10 Absence, which might conventionally be assumed to be nonproblematic in a Weberian bureaucracy of rules, roles, and files, actually involves complex mechanisms of trust, which are in turn built and bound up in situations of co-presence, see Giddens 1990; Boden 1991.

11 This is discussed more extensively in Boden and Molotch 1994.

12 See Schwartzman 1988: 110.

13 See Dalton 1959: 227; if meetings are described as skirmishes, organizations are often described as battlefields, e.g. Freeman 1978. Such metaphors often strike me as decidedly male, as do notions of "cutthroat competition," "concrete jungles," and "back-stabbing" behavior. More often, organizations seem, as suggested in my opening remarks, like the encounters of Alice in Wonderland, ambiguous and arbitrary, filled with secret language and local logic. Sometimes they operate like

"organized anarchies," as March is fond of noting. They are often capricious to be in, yet only occasionally and briefly violent.

14 Dalton 1959: 227–8.
15 See p. 66 above; Sacks et al. 1974.
16 See also March and Olsen 1976; Schwartzman 1988.
17 See also Mehan et al. 1986: 115–31.
18 Schwartzman 1988; Mintzberg 1973.
19 Here I would exclude the pervasive two-party call from a "meeting" definition, although their role in *producing* and retrospectively assessing meetings cannot be underestimated.
20 March and Romelaer 1976: 251–76.
21 For example, President John F. Kennedy has said: "The *essence of ultimate decision* remains impenetrable to the observer – often, indeed, to the decider himself . . . There will always be the dark and tangled stretches in the decision-making process – mysterious even to those who may be most intimately involved." Cited in Allison 1971, emphasis in original.
22 March and Olsen 1976: 11.
23 For a more extended discussion of "formal" vs "informal" turn-taking, see Atkinson 1982.
24 See quite extended discussion of these issues in Atkinson and Drew 1979; Atkinson 1982. Greatbatch 1988 has a related analysis.
25 It is odd that many researchers who study "organizational communication" are rather minimally interested in the *process* of transmission, focussing instead on "channels" or frequency of contacts in a network, or, less wisely still, on the multiplicity of information in a system. Most people get most information verbally and orally. It is a slow, time-intensive process but a "social fact" of organizational life. See also chapter 6 below.
26 I am indebted to Doug Maynard for pressing this point.
27 It would be interesting in a larger organizational study to include a textual analysis of written materials related to meetings, memos to other parties summarizing decisions, reports to superordinates, instructions for action, requests for funding, and so forth. Cicourel has frequently emphasized the importance of relating talk and text (e.g. 1985). Mulkay (1984) has conducted a most effective analysis of descriptive and sequentially organized remarks in written speeches, using conversation analytic techniques. The role of bureaucratic documents in general is also beginning to receive critical organizational analysis, e.g. Feldman 1989.
28 On an anecdotal level, a Rome film colleague returned some years ago from a co-production in Tokyo with a large Japanese documentary film company. A substantial section of the film was held up because the local graphics company (subcontracted to do certain design work) persisted in sending the president of their company to each production meeting because of the importance of the meeting (and because of my colleague's high rank in his own company), instead of the requested graphic

designer who was not deemed sufficiently important to attend these
early meetings.

29 Sacks 1966.

30 Schwartzman 1988.

31 See Turner 1974; Atkinson et al. 1973; and also below.

32 See especially Atkinson and Drew 1979; Atkinson 1982; see also
Halkowski 1990a.

33 The other two "paired" representatives being from the Graduate School
and the Provost's Office.

34 Failure to attend a meeting is also notable *after* the event, as in the
following discussion between Italian film producers (recorded for a different study, Boden 1983):

Mario: L'altra cosa e : : : hm : : che ho raccontato a Fran*ce*sca é
sta : to il mio inco *:* ntro : : – cioé la riunio : : ne nella quale
non *hai* participato perché pare che hai *c*ompletamente
di : : menticato!
(0.2)
Mario: [[(   )]
Angelo: [[Ho telefona : : to] eri [uscito   da] dieci=
Mario: [Huh (h) huh]
Angelo: =minuti

Mario: The other thi : ng e : : : hm : : that I told Francesca about
was my enco*u : :* nter- that is the mee : : ting in which you
didn't participate because you seem to have *c*ompletely
for*go*tten!
(0.2)
Mario: [[(   )]
Aneglo: [[I telepho : : ned] you had [left   just] ten
Mario: [Huh (h) huh]
Angelo: minutes before

Mario teases Angelo for having, he claims, "completely forgotten" a
meeting. Angelo responds with a straight and serious claim that he tried
to catch Mario but he had already left (the office). He does not join in
Mario's laughter. This is a typical interactional handling of a tease, as
Drew demonstrated (1989).

35 March and Olsen 1976: 12.

36 Jackall 1988.

37 The problem of attention or interest is not a primarily *cognitive* matter in
the way the work of Simon and others tends to overstress. What is dis-
tracting about organizations is the near-constant interactional diversity
and the multiple channels through which social actors are required to
communicate. It is *interactionally bounded* shifts of attention, interest,

time and energy that account for much of the apparent flux in organizational life, see chapters 6 and 8 below.
38   Cf. Atkinson et al. 1978.
39   Cf. Schegloff 1968.
40   Atkinson and Drew 1979: 91.
41   A number of these openings also involve bids to cut off side chatter, but each also explicitly invites focussed attention on the opening topic of the meeting; see also Atkinson et al. 1973.
42   Terms such as "reports" and "position statements" are similar to Maynard's "position-reports" (1984: 81–4). However, as meetings and telephone calls are much more *general* settings of talk than the specific negotiation setting of plea bargaining studied by Maynard, there are important differences that will be explored in more detail in chapter 6. *Reports*, in organizational settings, are *informational* and not typically produced as opening statements in an unfolding negotiation. Position statements, on the other hand, are potentially *decisional* and are located and constituted as opening gambits or strategically inserted elements in a discussion that is moving toward a decision or, more likely, defining the organizational arrangements for a decision. What Maynard calls position-reports are more narrow devices that, in effect, use a proposal of some position to initiate or advance a specific plea-bargaining stage.
43   Schwartzman 1988: 137–8.
44   This is, at times, a powerful resource: see our discussion of John Dean's testimony of Nixon's knowledge of the Watergate break-in, Molotch and Boden 1985.
45   See also Atkinson and Drew 1979; Maynard 1984.
46   On stories in everyday conversation, see e.g. Sacks 1974; Jefferson 1978.
47   For an extended discussion on the placement and achievement of "continuers," see Schegloff 1982.
48   For an early analysis of how a meeting gets started (or restarted after a break), see Atkinson et al. 1973; 1978.
49   Atkinson and Drew 1979: 85.
50   Ibid.: 91.
51   See Sacks et al 1974 and Atkinson 1982 for discussion of variants of the turn-taking model and, in particular, the ways in which some formal speech settings require that turns be "pre" allocated.
52   Congressional hearings and court settings are also decidedly "pre-allocated" in their turn allocation procedures, but even there social actors struggle, often successfully, to get their own points across, see Molotch and Boden 1985; also Halkowski 1989.
53   See Schegloff 1980.
54   Ibid.: 120–8. See expanded sequence in example 1.1 on p. 19; see also example 5.2 below.
55   See also Greatbatch 1988.
56   This somewhat cumbersome term draws on the linguistic or pragmatic notion of conversational "implicature," see Schegloff and Sacks 1973.

57 For an interesting discussion of "role" achieved through conversational turn-taking, see Halkowski 1990b.
58 Schegloff and Sacks 1973; see also Zimmerman 1984; Button 1991.
59 Goodwin 1987.
60 See Button 1987: 102–9; also 1991; Drew and Holt 1988 also has an interesting discussion on the ways clichés can interactionally "bound" and close down topics.
61 See Goodwin 1981: 209.
62 For an extended discussion of this issue, see Boden and Molotch 1994.

Chapter 5 Conversational Procedures and Organizational Practices

1   Schutz 1962.
2   Meyer and Rowan 1977.
3   Cf. Weber 1968 on the issue of how social actors orient to action over the course of its enactment.
4   This notion was introduced in some considerable detail by Schegloff and Sacks 1973, and expanded in terms of its role for the turn-taking model in Sacks et al. 1974; Goffman, in his elegant essay "Replies and responses," critiqued this insistence on adjacency organization, see Goffman 1976; 1981.
5   Sacks 1987: 55.
6   See Jefferson 1972; 1973; Jefferson and Schegloff 1975.
7   See also Atkinson and Drew 1979: 173–81.
8   Cf. Atkinson et al. 1978.
9   See also Whalen and Zimmerman 1990.
10 This confirms, using talk-based data, the impressions and ethnographic observations of authors such as Dalton (1959) and Mintzberg (1973) discussed earlier; see also Schwartzman 1988.
11 Interestingly, in the increasing number of organizations using internal electronic mail systems, similar exchanges have been noted between members who meet many of times per day:

CT: WT

```
1   Dan:  →  Hey! I jus' sent you a message 'bout
2              thet- that new software?
3   Randy:    Oh yeah?
4   Dan:      Here. ((hands stack of papers))
5   Randy:    'M tha : nks. (0.2) What software?
6   Dan:      Oh, you know? the AMT program?
7   Randy:    Oh yeah. I- I'll read it inna minnit.
8   Dan:      It's no big- y'know, no big deal. I jus'
```

9   thought you'd be innerested,
10 **Randy**:   *Sure.*

12 There is a related example in chapter 6 below, pp. 132–3.
13 See, among others, Maynard and Zimmerman 1984; Button and Casey 1985; Button 1987.
14 See also, Whalen and Zimmerman 1987; Heritage and Drew 1992.
15 Examination of the full transcript (Boden 1984), rather than the simplified version provided in 5.25, will reveal that Matt comes into this turn at full speed: "Whaddiz=thuh=ma : : : ximum=amount" and selectively stresses key words throughout the composite utterance: ma : : : ximum, amou : : nt, ea : : ch, and tha : t's, with each word stretched out for effect as well. This leads, after a 0.4 second pause, to the rationale behind the query: "cuz I se : nse tha : t's (.) the dragging= ((delayed)) point" (cf. French and Local 1983).
16 See, especially, an early discussion of "chained" questions in courtroom settings, Atkinson and Drew 1979; see also Goffman 1976: 259.
17 See Zimmerman 1969.
18 Goffman 1976.
19 See Goffman 1974; see also Maynard 1984: 61–9.
20 See also Molotch and Boden 1985; Jefferson 1984a.
21 Goffman 1976: 310.
22 See Heritage 1984a, especially chapter 8.

Chapter 6   Information, Interaction, and Institution

1 See also Zimmerman 1984 and Whalen and Zimmerman 1987 on the "interrogative series," which seems to operate in a similar manner.
2 For a much more extended analysis of conversational alignment in the delivery of news, see Maynard 1991; 1992.
3 March and Olsen 1976.
4 Pfeffer and Salancik 1978.
5 This is Granovetter's central point in his elegant analysis of the embedd- ness of economic structures (1985).
6 Again, it is important to note that "ethnographic" here means informa- tion gleaned from other stretches of *talk*, of these and other interactants in this university setting, rather than from conventional ethnography.
7 The bias toward *short* turns in casual conversation was initially pro- posed in the classic Sacks et al. work of 1974 and has been amply sup- ported by 20 years of subsequent research; see the discussion in chapter 3.
8 Maynard's (1984) study of lawyers in plea-bargaining sessions details this conversational strategy in considerable detail. More recently the

work of a number of conversation analysts studying TV news interviews has examined a related yet inverse phenomenon where new interviewers tag their purportedly neutral questions on the end of leading statements, e.g. Greatbatch 1988; Clayman 1987; Heritage and Greatbatch 1991.

9 This has been documented by Jefferson 1990 but is also discussed in Sacks's lectures (1992).

10 See Atkinson 1984; also Clayman 1987; Heritage and Greatbatch 1991.

11 See especially Schegloff 1982.

12 See Jefferson 1989; it is worth noting, however, that where telephone calls are concerned they vary somewhat from face-to-face conversations in this.

13 This kind of conversational structure is reported extensively by Maynard 1984.

14 Sacks has an early discussion on the distinction between indicating and assessing a position, in his lecture of Spring 1971, see Sacks 1992.

15 This Kennedy meeting took place on June 30, 1962.

16 Maynard 1984.

17 For a more extended discussion on the role of interaction, space, time, and communications technology, see Boden and Molotch 1994.

18 Garfinkel 1967: 67.

Chapter 7 Organizational Agendas

1 E.g. Elster 1983; Sica 1988.

2 See e.g. Blau 1963; Pfeffer 1982.

3 This point is raised, in a tentative way, by Sproull (1981), who points out that rules that seem rational in the abstract lack the specificity to guide effective decisions. My position is a firmly ethnomethodological one: rules can *never* have the specificity to guide complex occasions of their actual use. Their enactment thus can *never* simply "reproduce" some institutional order, but must produce it anew, for each succeeding "next first time"; the same problem applies to those who would argue that "rules" guide rationality.

4 Cf. March 1981.

5 March and Simon 1958.

6 Elster 1989.

7 Cf. Pfeffer and Salancik 1978.

8 E.g. Allison 1971.

9 Jackall 1988: 76; see also Molotch 1990.

10 See e.g. the series of telephone calls examined in the last chapter, examples 6.2 to 6.6.

11 Mintzberg 1973

12 Cf. Schwartzman 1988.

13 For a very interesting analysis of this issue, see Feldman 1989.
14 Similarly, notions of "goals" are variously defined and negotiated by members as they pursue their own interactional and organizational agendas. Those solutions in search of problems are readily observable in the fine yet structured interaction of organizational settings.
15 As described, for example, in Sacks 1984.
16 Jackall 1988: 39.
17 See, for example, Morgan 1986: 155–8.
18 E.g. March 1962; Pfeffer and Salancik 1978; Pfeffer 1982; Mintzberg 1983.
19 This political speech has been reported in the *Los Angeles Times* as the participants of the meeting subsequently discuss.
20 March 1988.
21 Pfeffer and Salancik 1977: 643.
22 Ibid.: 642–6.
23 See Garfinkel 1967; Atkinson and Drew 1979; Maynard 1984.
24 Giddens 1979: 104.
25 Zimmerman 1971.
26 Maynard 1984.
27 Cf. Grimshaw 1990.
28 This interdependency in resource allocation has critical consequences for subunits, providing a limit on subunit power in the process of organizational decision-making; Pfeffer and Salancik 1974: 149–50.
29 Heritage and Watson 1979; see also Atkinson and Drew 1979; Maynard 1984.

Chapter 8 Local Logic and Organizational Rationality

1 Cf. Elster 1986a: 27.
2 See also DiMaggio and Powell 1991: 21.
3 See Fligstein 1990: 11.
4 These practical structures are not "mythical" in the sense suggested by Meyer and Rowan (1977), nor does the fact that they are tacit and taken for granted mean that they are masked from view, as quite a few neo-institutionalists seem to assume (e.g. DiMaggio 1988; DiMaggio and Powell 1991).
5 Rationality was, as is well known, an essential element of the Enlightenment movement, in which an informed public was to carve out a distinct discursive space founded "upon good sense and sound reason" (Dryden 1926: 238, cited in Eagleton 1984).
6 See, for example, Levine's discussion on the links between rationality and modernity (1985: 142–78); there are many others, e.g. Sica 1988, but

Levine is especially adept in tracing the linkages and what he calls the "flight from ambiguity."

7   But see Udy's interesting discussion, 1959; see also March 1988; Fligstein 1990.

8   This point is developed with elegance in a 1943 article by Schutz (see Schutz 1964).

9   See e.g. Elster's collection of classic essays (1986b).

10   See e.g. Lukes 1991.

11   See Elster 1989; I go on to discuss this issue below.

12   For a classic and much admired position on this, see Tversky and Kahneman 1974.

13   E.g. Granovetter 1978; Granovetter and Soong 1986.

14   See e.g. Schelling 1978: 14.

15   E.g. Simon 1957; March and Simon 1958.

16   E.g. O'Reilly 1982.

17   Hernstein 1990: 356.

18   Simon 1990: 189.

19   Cf. Hilbert 1987.

20   Allison 1971: 38.

21   Jackall 1988.

22   On this point, see Molotch's interesting discussion (1990); cf. Garfinkel 1967.

23   Cf. Etzioni 1988: 136–42.

24   This is similar to the position of Berger and Luckmann (1966), having the same roots in the work of Alfred Schutz.

25   Cf. Zucker 1991.

26   Which, it should be noted, he also very much admires, especially as developed in *The Structure of Social Action*, see Garfinkel 1988.

27   Parsons 1937: 11.

28   Ibid.: 26.

29   Garfinkel 1967: 267–70.

30   Ibid.: 262.

31   See Molotch 1990.

32   Garfinkel 1967: 263, emphasis added. That is to say, as noted above, that there is a distinct tendency, on the part of sociologists especially, to become preoccupied with "deviant" cases or cases that depart from the social scientist's model of rational behavior; see Schutz 1962: 45.

33   Schutz 1962: 46.

34   Ibid.: 1–10.

35   See March and Olsen 1976.

36   Garfinkel 1967: 281.

37   See Drew and Heritage 1992: 18–19.

38   See March and Olsen 1976: 16.

39   See also Meyer and Rowan 1977; Scott 1991: 166–7.

40   See also Fligstein 1990: 304.

41   March and Romelaer 1976: 251.

42 Cyert and March 1963.
43 See also Boden and Molotch 1994.
44 See also the discussion of opportunism and "local hunches" described by Anderson et al. 1989: 42–3.
45 Molotch 1990: 302–3.
46 Weber 1968: 108.
47 Molotch 1990; see also March 1988.
48 Dalton 1959: 68.
49 Simon 1957.
50 Simon 1990: 198.
51 March 1988.
52 Garfinkel 1967: 100.

Chapter 9   The Business of Talk

1 I am grateful to Paul DiMaggio for reminding me of the blooming buzzing words of James Joyce.
2 Smirich and Stubbart 1985: 728.
3 I am borrowing the term "slogans" from Harold Garfinkel, as I have drawn on his insights and encouragement throughout many telephone calls between St Louis and Los Angeles during the writing of this book. It was "personal communication" at its most instructive. The notion of slogans harks back to the discussion of signed objects in chapter 3 and to the ways in which linguistic glosses come *between* observer and object; see also below.
4 This is what Schutz calls the "natural attitude."
5 E.g. Douglas 1986; Etzioni 1988.
6 For example, the work of Jeffrey Pfeffer across a wide range of writings.
7 Silverman 1970.
8 Clegg 1976; Clegg and Dunkerley 1980; Clegg 1989.
9 E.g. Burrell and Morgan 1979; Morgan 1986; Hassard and Pym 1990.
10 Clegg 1990.
11 Mintzberg 1979.
12 Stinchcombe 1990.
13 See Garfinkel and Sacks 1970.
14 See especially Pollner 1991.
15 Even one of the best of recent efforts to summarize the relevance of ethnomethodology to organization theory eventually simply folds into institutional theory; see DiMaggio and Powell 1991.
16 Rules may indeed operate "like an invisible skein that bundles all the technological and social aspects of organizations" together; Perrow 1986: 24. But the link between such rules and action is more like a vibrating membrane, living, breathing and changing.
17 This is Blau's familiar position.

18 Giddens 1984.
19 Organizational members routinely build "informal procedures right into the formal system" of bureaucracy; Mehan et al. 1986: 66.
20 Molotch 1990.
21 Peters and Waterman 1982.
22 For the heading of this section I have borrowed another felicitous phrase from Eudora Welty (1983).
23 Conventional conversation analysts have been slow to acknowledge this point explicitly but it is inherent in the notion of recipient design; see Sacks 1992: 764–72.
24 March and Olsen 1976: 16.
25 In this, the work of Giddens merges with Garfinkel before him; the latter emphasizes reflexivity, the former recursivity, though the essential operation of recursivity – the notion of "another next first time" is integral to both ethnomethodology and to the foundational work of Sacks; see e.g. Garfinkel 1967; Giddens 1984; Sacks 1992.
26 See also Peters 1992: 377.
27 See also Boden 1990a; 1990b; Friedland and Boden 1994.
28 Mintzberg 1973: 44.
29 Blau 1963.
30 Reich 1992: 111.
31 Mintzberg and McHugh 1985.
32 Feldman and March 1981.
33 See Dertouzos et al. 1989: 133–8.
34 I do not intend here the idea of open-plan offices and the kind of sur-veillance of *corps dociles* described by Foucault. What is critical to de-veloping high levels of interaction are the sort of informal workspaces now common in high-tech R&D settings, and the placement of small casual meeting rooms at handy intervals throughout a work setting. "Interaction" means just that: inter-action, and it requires frequent contact and occasional face-to-face exchange; see Boden and Molotch 1994.
35 Zuboff 1988.
36 See e.g. Jordan and Henderson 1992; Suchman 1993.
37 See also Boden and Molotch 1994.
38 Cf. Alexander 1988b: 222.
39 Heritage's excellent phrase has been used quite consciously through-out this study with due appreciation (1984a: 290).
40 Schegloff 1991: 52–7; see also Schegloff's recent elaboration of this rather contentious methodological point (1992).
41 E.g. Drew and Heritage 1992.
42 For a more elaborated discussion of this intensive/extensive equation see Giddens 1990 and Boden 1991.

References

Abrams, P. 1982: *Historical Sociology*. Shepton Mallet: Open Court.

Aldrich, H. E. 1979: *Organizations and Environments*. Englewood Cliffs, NJ: Prentice-Hall.

—— 1992: Incommensurable paradigms? Vital signs from three perspectives. In M. Reed and M. Hughes (eds), *Rethinking Organization: New Directions in Organization Theory and Research*, London: Sage, 17–45.

Aldrich, H. E. and Marsden, P. V. 1988: Environments and organizations. In N. J. Smelser (ed.), *Handbook of Sociology*, Newbury Park: Sage.

Aldrich, H. E. and Pfeffer, J. 1976: Environments of organizations. *Annual Review of Sociology*, 2, 79–105.

Alexander, J. 1988a: *Action and its Environment*. New York: Columbia University Press.

——1988b: The new theoretical movement. In N. J. Smelser (ed.), *Handbook of Sociology*, Newbury Park: Sage.

—— 1990: Commentary: structure, value, action. *American Sociological Review*, 50, 339–45.

Alexander, J., Geisen, B., Munch, R. and Smelser, N. J. (eds) 1987: *The Micro–Macro Link*. Berkeley: University of California Press.

Allison, G. 1971: *Essence of Decision: Explaining the Cuban Missile Crisis*. Boston: Little, Brown.

Anderson, R. J., Hughes, J. A. and Sharrock, W. W. 1989: *Working for Profit: The Social Organization of Calculation in an Entrepreneurial Firm*. Aldershot: Avebury.

Argyris, C. 1965: *Integrating the Individual and the Organization*. New York: John Wiley.

Atkinson, J. M. 1978: *Discovering Suicide: Studies in the Organization of Sudden Death*. Pittsburgh, PA: University of Pittsburgh Press.

—— 1982: Understanding formality: notes on the categorization and production of "formal" interaction. *British Journal of Sociology*, 33, 86–117.

—— 1984: *Our Masters' Voices: The Language and Body Language of Politics*. London: Metheun.

Atkinson, J. M. and Drew, P. 1979: *Order in Court: The Organisation of Verbal Interaction in Judicial Settings*. London: Macmillan.

Atkinson, J. M. and Heritage, J. (eds) 1984: *Structures of Social Action*. Cambridge: Cambridge University Press.

Atkinson, J. M., Cuff, M. and Lee, J. 1973: Right – e:r: prolegomena to the analysis of "meeting talk" with special reference to the problem of "beginnings." Unpublished paper presented at the Didsbury Conversation Analysis Workshop, Working Paper 1.

—— 1978: The recommencement of a meeting as a member's accomplishment. In J. Schenkein (ed.), *Studies in the Organization of Conversational Interaction*, New York: Academic Press, 133–53.

Baccus, M. 1986: Social indication and the visibility criterion of real world theorizing. In H. Garfinkel (ed.), *Ethnomethodological Studies of Work*, London: Routledge, 20–60.

Ballé, C. 1990: *Sociologie des Organisations*, Collection Que sais-je? 2497, Paris: PUF.

Barley, S. 1983: Semiotics and the study of occupational and organizational cultures. *Administrative Science Quarterly*, 28, 393–413.

Barnard, C. 1938: *The Functions of the Executive*. Cambridge, MA: Harvard University Press.

Baron, J. N. and Bielby, W. T. 1980: Bringing firms back in: stratification, segmentation and the organization of work. *American Sociological Review*, 45, 737–65.

Becker, H. S. 1986: *Doing Things Together: Selected Papers*. Evanston, IL: Northwestern University Press.

Benson, J. K. 1983: A dialectical method for the study of organizations. In G. Morgan (ed.), *Beyond Method*, Beverly Hills: Sage, 331–46.

Berger, J., Eyre, D. P. and Zelditch Jr., M. 1989: Theoretical structures and the micro–macro problem. In J. Berger, M. Zeldirch Jr and B. Anderson (eds), *Sociological Theories in Progress: New Formulations*, Newbury Park, CA: Sage, 11–32.

Berger, P. and Luckmann, T. 1966: *The Social Construction of Reality: A Treatise in the Sociology of Knowledge*. New York: Doubleday.

Bittner, E. 1965: The concept of organization. *Sociological Research*, 31, 240–55.

—— 1967a: Police discretion in emergency apprehension of mentally ill persons. *Social Problems*, 14, 278–92.

—— 1967b: The police on skid-row: a study of peace keeping. *American Sociological Review*, 32, 699–715.

Blau, P. M. 1963: *The Dynamics of Bureaucracy* (1955). Chicago: University of Chicago Press.

Blau, P. M. 1970: A formal theory of differentiation in organizations. *American Sociological Review*, 35, 201–18.

Blau, P. M. and Scott, W. R. 1962: *Formal Organizations*. London: Routledge and Kegan Paul.

Boden, D. 1983: Talk international: turn-taking in seven Indo-European languages. Paper presented at the Annual Meetings of the American Anthropological Association, Chicago.

—— 1984: The business of talk. Unpublished Ph.D. dissertation, Department of Sociology, University of California, Santa Barbara.

—— 1990a: The world as it happens: ethnomethodology and conversation analysis. In George Ritzer (ed.), *Frontiers of Social Theory: The New Synthesis*, New York: Columbia University Press, 185–213.

—— 1990b: People are talking: conversation analysis and symbolic interaction. In Howard S. Becker and Michal McCall (eds), *Symbolic Interaction and Cultural Studies*, Chicago: University of Chicago Press.

—— 1991: Trust, modernity and the interaction order. Unpublished MS, Department of Sociology, University of Lancaster.

—— 1994: Agendas and arrangements: everyday negotiations in meetings. In Alan Firth (ed.), *Negotiation in the Workplace*, Oxford: Pergamon Press.

Boden, D. and Molotch, H. 1994: The compulsion of proximity. In Roger Friedland and Deirdre Boden (eds), *NowHere: Space, Time and Modernity*, Berkeley: University of California Press.

Boden, D. and Zimmerman D. H. (eds) 1991: *Talk and Social Structure: Studies in Ethnomethodology and Conversation Analysis*. Cambridge: Polity.

Boje, D. M. 1991: The storytelling organization: a study of story performance in an office-supply firm. *Administrative Science Quarterly*, 36, 106–12.

Bonazzi, G. 1989: *Storia del Pensiero Organizzativo*. Milan: Franco Angeli.

Bonnson, N. 1982: The irrationality of action and action availability: decisions, ideologies, and organizational actions. *Journal of Management Studies*, 19, 29–44.

Boomer, D. S. and Dittmann, A. T. 1965: Hesitation pauses and juncture pauses in speech. *Language and Speech*, 5, 148–58.

Bouchikhi, H. 1990: *Structuration des organisations: Concepts constructivistes et étude de cas*. Paris: Economica.

Boudon, R. 1989: Subjective rationality and the explanation of social behavior. *Rationality and Society*, 1, 173–97.

Bourdieu, P. 1977: *Outline of a Theory of Practice*. Cambridge: Cambridge University Press.

Brun-Cottan, F. 1990: Coordinating cooperation. Paper presented at the 89th meeting of the American Anthropological Association, New Orleans.

Burrell, W. G. and Morgan, G. 1979: *Sociological Paradigms and Organizational Analysis*. London: Heinemann.

Button, G. 1987: Answers as interactional products: two sequential practices used in interviews. *Social Psychology Quarterly*, 50, 160–71.

—— 1991: Conversation-in-a-series. In D. Boden and D. H. Zimmerman (eds), *Talk and Social Structure: Studies in Ethnomethodology and Conversation Analysis*, 251–77.

Button, G. and N. Casey. 1984: Generating topic: the use of topic initial elicitors. In J. Maxwell Atkinson and John Heritage (eds), *Structures of Social Action: Studies in Conversation Analysis*, Cambridge: Cambridge University Press, 167–90.

—— 1985: Topic nomination and topic pursuit. *Human Studies*, 8, 3–55.

Button, G. and Lee, J. 1987: *Talk and Social Organization*. Clevedon: Multilingual Matters.

Carroll, G. R. 1987: *Publish and Perish: The Organizational Ecology of Newspaper Industries*, vol. 8 of Monographs in Organizational Behavior and Industrial Relations. Greenwich, CT: JAI Press.

Chandler, A. D. Jr 1962: *Strategy and Structure: Chapters in the History of the American Industrial Enterprise*. Cambridge, MA: MIT Press.

Chanlat, J. F. (ed.) 1990: *L'individu dans l'organisation: les dimensions oubliées*. Québec: Les Presses de l'Université Laval.

—— 1991: L'analyse des organisations: un regard sur la production de langue française contemporaine (1950–1990). Cahier de recherche no. 91–09. École des Hautes Études Commerciales, Montreal, 1–39.

Chomsky, N. 1957: *Syntactic Structures*. The Hague: Mouton.

Cicourel, A. V. 1964: *Method and Measurement in Sociology*. New York: Free Press.

—— 1968: *The Social Organization of Juvenile Justice*. New York: Wiley.

—— 1974: *Cognitive Sociology*. New York: Macmillan.

—— 1980: Three models of discourse. *Discourse Processes*, 3, 100–32.

—— 1981: The role of cognitive-linguistic concepts in understanding everyday social interactions. *Annual Review of Sociology*, 7, 87–116.

—— 1985: Text and discourse. *Annual Review of Anthropology*, 14, 159–85.

Clayman, S. 1987: *Generating news:* the interactional organization of news interviews. Unpublished Ph.D. dissertation, University of California, Santa Barbara.

—— 1989: The production of punctuality: social interaction, temporal organization, and social structure, *American Journal of Sociology*, 95, 659–91.

Clegg, S. 1976: *Power, Rule and Domination: A Critical and Empirical Understanding of Power in Sociological Theory and Organizational Life*. London: Routledge and Kegan Paul.

—— 1981: Organization and control. *Adminstrative Science Quarterly*, 26, 545–62.

—— 1989: *Frameworks of Power*. London: Sage.

—— 1990: *Organizations: Organization Studies in the Postmodern World*. London: Sage.

Clegg, S. and Dunkerley, D. 1980: *Organization, Class and Control*. London: Routledge and Kegan Paul.

Cohen, I. J. 1989: *Structuration Theory*. London: Macmillan.

Cohen, M., March, J. G. and Olsen, J. H. 1972: A garbage can model of organizational choice. *Administrative Science Quarterly*, 17, 1–25.

Colignon, R. A. 1989: Reification: the "holistic" and "individualistic" views of organizations. *Theory and Society*, 18, 83–123.

Collins, R. 1981a: On the microfoundations of macrosociology. *American Journal of Sociology*, 86, 984–1014.

—— 1981b: Micro translation as a theory building activity. In K. Knorr-Cetina and A. V. Cicourel (eds), *Advances in Social Theory and Methodology*, New York: Routledge and Kegan Paul, 81–108.

—— 1984: Statistics versus words. *Sociological Theory*, 1, 329–36.

—— 1987: Interaction ritual chains, power and property: the micro-macro connection as an empirically based theoretical problem. In Alexander et al. (eds), *The Micro-Macro Link*, Berkeley: University of California Press.

—— 1988a: *Theoretical Sociology*. Orlando, FL: Harcourt Brace Jovanovich.

—— 1988b: The micro contribution to macrosociology. *Sociological Theory*, 6, 242–53.

Coser, L. 1975: Structure and conflict. In P. Blau (ed.), *Approaches to the Study of Social Structure*, New York: Free Press, 210–19.

Crozier, M. 1963: *Le phénomène bureaucratique*. Paris: Éditions du Seuil.

Cyert, R. M. and March, J. G. 1963: *A Behavioral Theory of the Firm*. Englewood Cliffs, NJ: Prentice-Hall.

Daft, R. L. 1983: Symbols in organizations: A dual-content framework for analysis. In L. Pondy et al., *Organizational Symbolism*, Greenwich, CT: JAI Press, 199–206.

—— 1990: Can organization studies begin to break out of the natural science straightjacket? *Organization Science*, 1, 1–9.

Dalton, M. 1959: *Men Who Manage*. New York: John Wiley.

Davidson, J. 1984: Subsequent versions of invitations, offers, requests, and proposals dealing with potential or actual rejection. In J. M. Atkinson and J. Heritage (eds.), *Structures of Social Action*, Cambridge: Cambridge University Press, 102–28.

Deal, T. E. and Kennedy, A. A. 1982: *Corporate Cultures: The Rites and Rituals of Corporate Life*. Reading, MA: Addison-Wesley.

Dertouzos, M. L. et al. 1989: *Made in America: Regaining the Productive Edge*. Cambridge, MA: MIT Press.

DiMaggio, P. J. 1988: Interest and agency in institutional theory. In L. Zucker (ed.), *Institutional Patterns and Organization: Culture and Environment*, Cambridge, MA: Ballinger, 3–21.

DiMaggio, P. J. and Powell, W. W. 1983: The iron cage revisited: institutional isomorphism and collective rationality in organizational fields. *American Sociological Review*, 48, 147–60.

—— 1991: Introduction. In W. W. Powell and P. J. DiMaggio, *The New Institutionalism in Organizational Analysis*, Chicago: University of Chicago Press.

Dingwall, R. and Strong, P. 1985: The interactional study of organizations. *Urban Life*, 14, 205–31.

DiTomasi, Nancy 1982: Sociological reductionism from Parsons to Althusser. *American Sociological Review*, 47, 14–28.

Donnelon, A., Gray, B. and Bougon, M. 1986: Communication, meaning, and organized action. *Administrative Science Quarterly*, 31, 43–55.

Douglas, M. 1986: *How Institutions Think*. Syracuse, NY: Syracuse University Press.

Drew, P. 1987: Po-faced responses to teases. *Linguistics*, 25, 219–53.

Drew, P. and Heritage, J. 1992: *Talk at Work*. Cambridge: Cambridge University Press.

Drew, P. and Holt, E. 1988: Complainable matters: the use of idiomatic expressions in making complaints. *Social Problems*, 35, 398–417.

Drucker, P. 1974: *Management: Tasks, Responsibilities, Practices*. New York: Harper and Row.

Duncan, O. D. 1984: *Notes on Social Measurement: Historical and Critical*. New York: Russell Sage Foundation.

Durkheim, E. 1982: *The Rules of Sociological Method* (1895), ed. S. Lukes, trans. W. D. Halls. New York: Free Press.

Eagleton, T. 1984: *The Function of Criticism*. London: Verso.

—— 1985: *Against the Grain*. London: Verso.

Eberle, T. 1992: A new paradigm for the sociology of knowledge: the social construction of reality after 25 years. *Schweizerische Zeitschrift für Soziologie*, 18, 493–502.

Elster, J. 1983: *Explaining Technical Change*. Cambridge: Cambridge University Press.

—— 1986a: Introduction. In J. Elster (ed.), *Rational Choice*, Oxford: Blackwell, 1–33.

—— (ed.) 1986b: *Rational Choice*. Oxford: Blackwell.

—— 1989: *The Concrete of Society*. Cambridge: Cambridge University Press.

Etzioni, A. 1964. *Modern Organizations*. Englewood Cliffs: Prentice-Hall.

—— 1988: *The Moral Dimension: Toward a New Economics*. New York: Free Press.

Feldman, M. 1989: *Order Without Design: Information Production and Policy Making*. Stanford, CA: Stanford University Press.

Feldman, M. S. and March, J. G. 1981: Information in organizations as symbol and signal. *Administrative Science Quarterly*, 26, 171–86.

Fele, Giolo 1991: *L'Insorgere del Conflitto: Uno studio sull'organizzazione sociale del disaccordo nella conversazione*. Milano: Franco Angeli.

Fine, G. A. 1984: Negotiated orders and organizational culture. *Annual Review of Sociology*, 10, 239–62.

Fine, G. A. and Kleinman, S. 1983: Network and meaning: an interactional approach to structure. *Symbolic Interaction*, 5, 97–110.

Finholt, T. and Sproull, L. S. 1990: Electronic groups at work. *Organization Science*, 1, 41–64.

Fligstein, N. 1990: *The Transformation of Corporate Control*. Cambridge, MA: Harvard University Press.

Frank, R. H. 1990: Patching up the rational choice model. In R. Friedland and A. F. Robertson (eds), *Beyond the Marketplace: Rethinking Models of Economy and Society*, Chicago: Aldine.

Frankel, R. M. 1984: From sentence to sequence: understanding the medical encounter through micro-interactional analysis. *Discourse Processes*, 7, 135–70.

—— 1989: "I wz wondering – uhm could Raid uhm effect the brain permanently d'y know?": some observations on the intersection of speaking and writing in calls to a poison control center. *Western Journal of Speech Communication*, 53, 195–226.

Freeman, J. 1978: The unit of analysis in organizational research. In Marshall W. Meyer et al. (eds), *Environments and Organizations*, San Francisco: Jossey-Bass, 335–51.

Freeman, J., Carroll, G. R. and Hannan, M. T. 1983: The liability of newness: age dependence in organizational death rates. *American Sociological Review*, 48, 692–710.

French, P. and Local, J. 1983: Turn-completion incomings. *Journal of Pragmatics*, 7, 17–38.

Friedland, R. and Alford, R. 1991: Bringing society back in: symbols, practices and institutional contradictions. In W. W. Powell and P. DiMaggio (eds), *The New Institutionalism in Organizational Analysis*, Chicago: University of Chicago Press, 232–63.

Friedland, R. and Boden, D. 1994: *NowHere: Space, Time and Modernity*. Berkeley: University of California Press.

Friedland, R. and Palmer, D. 1994: Space, corporation, and class: towards a grounded theory. In R. Friedland and D. Boden, *NowHere: Space, Time, and Modernity*, Berkeley: University of California Press.

Galaskiewicz, J. 1985: Professional networks and the institutionalization of a single mind set. *American Sociological Review*, 50, 639–58.

Garcia, A. 1991: Dispute resolution without disputing: how the interactional organization of mediation hearings minimizes argument. *American Sociological Review*, 56, 818–35.

Garfinkel, H. 1967: *Studies in Ethnomethodology*. Englewood Cliffs, NJ: Prentice-Hall.

—— 1974: On the origins of the term 'ethnomethodology'. In R. Turner (ed.), *Ethnomethodology*, Harmondsworth: Penguin, 15–18.

—— (ed.) 1986: *Ethnomethodological Studies of Work*. London: Routledge and Kegan Paul.

—— 1988: Evidence for locally produced, naturally accountable phenomena of order, logic, reason, meaning, method, etc. in and as of the essential quiddity of immortal ordinary society, (I of IV): an announcement of studies. *Sociological Theory*, 6, 103–9.

Garfinkel, H. and Sacks, H. 1970: On formal structures of practical action. In J. C. McKinney and E. A. Tiryakian (eds), *Theoretical Sociology*, New York: Appleton Century Crofts, 338–66.

Garfinkel, H., Lynch, M. and Livingston, E. 1981: The work of a discovering science construed from materials from the optically discovered pulsar. *Philosophy of the Social Sciences*, 11, 131–58.

Giddens, A. 1976: *New Rules of Sociological Method*. London: Macmillan.

—— 1979: *Central Problems in Social Theory: Action, Structure and Contradiction in Social Analysis*. Berkeley: University of California Press.

—— 1981: *Contemporary Critique of Historical Materialism*. Berkeley: University of California Press.

—— 1984: *The Constitution of Society: Outline of the Theory of Structuration*. Cambridge: Polity.

—— 1987: Time and social organization. In A. Giddens, *Social Theory and Modern Social*, Cambridge: Polity.

—— 1990: *The Consequences of Modernity*. Cambridge: Polity.

Giglioli, P. P. 1972: *Language and Social Context Anthology*. Harmondsworth: Penguin.

Goffman, E. 1961: *Encounters*. Indianapolis: Bobbs–Merrill.

—— 1972: *Relations in Public*. New York: Harper and Row.

—— 1974: *Frame Analysis*. New York: Harper-Colophon.

—— 1976: Replies and responses. *Language in Society*, 5, 257–313.

—— 1981: *Forms of Talk*. Philadelphia: University of Pennsylvania Press.

—— 1983a: The interaction order. *American Sociological Review*, 48, 1–17.

—— 1983b: Felicity's condition. *American Journal of Sociology*, 89, 1–51.

Goodwin, C. 1979: The interactive construction of a sentence in natural conversation. In G. Psathas (ed.), *Everyday Language: Studies in Ethnomethodology*, New York: Irvington Press.

—— 1981: *Conversational Organization: Interaction between Speakers and Hearers*. New York: Academic Press.

—— 1987: Unilateral departure. In G. Button and J. R. E. Lee (eds), *Talk and Social Organization*, Clevedon: Multilingual Matters, 206–16.

Goodwin, C. and Goodwin, M. H. 1993: Seeing as a situated activity: formulating planes. In D. Middleton and Y. Engeström (eds), *Cognition and Communication at Work*, Cambridge: Cambridge University Press.

Goodwin, C. and Heritage, J. 1990: Conversation analysis. *Annual Review of Anthropology*, 19: 283–307.

Gouldner, A. W. 1954: *Patterns of Industrial Bureaucracy*. Glencoe, IL: Free Press.

—— 1955: Metaphysical pathos and the theory of bureaucracy. *American Political Science Review*, 49, 496–507.

—— 1959: Organizational analysis. In R. K. Merton, L. Broom and L. S. Coltrell Jr (eds), *Sociology Today*, New York: Basic Books.

—— 1970: *The Coming Crisis in Western Sociology*. New York: Basic Books.

Granovetter, M. S. 1978: Threshold models of collective behavior. *American Journal of Sociology*, 83, 1420–43.

—— 1985: Economic action and social structure: the problem of embeddedness. *American Journal of Sociology*, 91, 481–510.

Granovetter, M. S. and Soong, R. 1986: Threshold models of interpersonal effects on consumer demand. *Journal of Economic Behavior and Organization*, 7, 83–99.

Gray, B., Brown, M. G. and Donnellon, A. 1985: Organizations as constructions and destructions of meaning. *Journal of Management*, 11, 83–98.

Greatbatch, D. L. 1986: Aspects of topical organization in news interviews: the use of agenda-shifting procedures by interviewees, *Media, Culture and Society* 8, 441–55.

—— 1988: A turn-taking system for British news interviews. *Language in Society*, 17, 401–30.

Grimshaw, A. D. 1981: *Language as a Social Resource*. Stanford: Stanford University Press.

—— 1989: *Collegial Discourse: Professional Conversation among Peers*. Norwood, NJ: Ablex.

—— (ed.) 1990: *Conflict Talk: Sociolinguistic Investigations of Arguments in Conversation*. Cambridge: Cambridge University Press.

Gronn, P. C. 1983: Talk as the work: the accomplishment of school administration. *Administrative Science Quarterly*, 28, 1–21.

—— 1985: Committee talk: negotiating "personal development" at a training college. *Journal of Management Studies*, 22, 245–68.

Gurwitsch, A. 1979: *Human Encounters with the Social World*. Pittsburgh, PA: Dusquesne University Press.

Halkowski, T. 1989: The interactional organization of a congressional hearing. Paper presented at the American Sociological Association meetings, San Francisco.

Halkowski, T. 1990a: Hearing talk: the social organization of a congressional hearing. Unpublished Ph.D. dissertation, Department of Sociology, University of California, Santa Barbara.

Halkowski, T. 1990b: 'Role' as an interactional device. *Social Problems*, 37, 564–77.

Hall, R. 1987: *Organization, Structure and Process*, 3rd edn. Englewood Cliffs, NJ: Prentice-Hall.

Hall, R. H., Haas, J. E. and Johnson, N. J. 1967: Organizational size, complexity, and formalization. *American Sociological Review*, 32, 903–11.

Hannan, M. and Freeman, J. 1977: The population ecology of organizations: a causal analysis. *American Journal of Sociology*, 82, 929–64.

—— 1989: *Organizational Ecology*. Cambridge, MA: Harvard University Press.

Harper, R. R. 1988: Not any old numbers: an examination of practical reasoning in an accountancy environment. *Journal of Interdisciplinary Economics*, 2, 297–306.

Harper, R. R., Hughes, J. A. and Shapiro, D. 1991: Harmonious working and CSCW: computer technology and air traffic control. In J. Bowers and S. Benford (eds), *Studies in CSCW: Theory, Practice, Design*, North-Holland.

Hassard, J. 1991: Multiple paradigms and organizational analysis: a case study. *Organization Studies*, 12, 275–99.

—— 1993: *Sociology and Organization Theory: Positivism, Paradigms and Postmodernity*. Cambridge: Cambridge University Press.

Hassard, J. and Pym, D. (eds) 1990: *The Theory and Philosophy of Organizations*. London: Routledge.

Heath, C. 1986: *Body Movement and Speech in Medical Interaction*. Cambridge: Cambridge University Press.

Heath, C. and Luff, P. 1991: Collaborative activity and technological design: task coordination in London Underground control rooms. In Proceedings of the Second European Conference on Computer-Supported Cooperative Work, Amsterdam.

Hechter, M. 1983: *Microfoundations of Macrosociology*. Philadelphia: Temple University Press.

Heritage, J. 1983: Accounts in Action. In P. Abell and G. N. Gilbert (eds), *Accounts and Action*, Aldershot: Gower.

—— 1984a: *Garfinkel and Ethnomethodology*. Cambridge: Polity.

—— 1984b: A change in state token and aspects of its sequential placement. In J. M. Atkinson and J. Heritage (eds), *Structures of Social Action*, Cambridge: Cambridge University Press, 299–345.

—— 1985: Recent developments in conversation analysis. *Sociolinguistics*, 15, 1–19.

—— 1987: Ethnomethodology. In A. Giddens and J. Turner (eds), *Social Theory Today*, Cambridge: Polity, 224–72.

Heritage, J. and Drew, P. 1992: Introduction. In P. Drew and J. Heritage (eds), *Talk at Work*, Cambridge: Cambridge University Press.

Heritage, J. and Greatbatch, D. 1986: Generating applause: a study of rhetoric and response and party political conferences. *American Journal of Sociology*, 92, 110–57.

—— 1991: On the institutional character of institutional talk: the case of news interviews. In D. Boden and D. H. Zimmerman (eds), *Talk and Social Structure: Studies in Ethnomethodology and Conversation Analysis*, Cambridge: Polity, 93–137.

Heritage, J. and Watson, D. R. 1979: Formulations as conversational objects. In G. Psathas (ed.), *Everyday Language: Studies in Ethnomethodology*, New York: Irvington, 123–62.

Heritage, J., Clayman, S. and Zimmerman, D. H. 1988: Discourse and message analysis: the micro-structure of mass media messages. In R. P. Hawkins, J. M. Wiemann and S. Pingree (eds), *Advancing Communication Science: Merging Mass and Interpersonal Processes*, Newbury Park: Sage, 77–109.

Hernstein, R. J. 1990: Rational choice theory: necessary but not sufficient. *American Psychologist*, 45, 356–67.

Hilbert, R. 1987: Bureaucracy as belief, rationalization as repair: Max Weber in a post-functionalist age. *Sociological Theory*, 5, 70–86.

—— 1990: Ethnomethodology and the micro–macro order. *American Sociological Review*, 55, 794–808

—— 1992: *The Classical Roots of Ethnomethodology: Durkheim, Weber, and Garfinkel*. Chapel Hill, NC: University of North Carolina Press.

Hobbes, T. 1968: *Leviathan* (1651), ed. C. B. McPherson. Harmondsworth: Penguin.

Homans, G. 1964: Bringing men back in. *American Sociological Review,* 29, 809–18.

Jackall, R. 1988: *Moral Mazes: The World of Corporate Managers.* Oxford: Oxford University Press.

Jefferson, G. 1972: Side sequences. In D. Sudnow (ed.), *Studies in Social Interaction,* New York: Free Press, 294–338.

—— 1973: A case of precision timing in ordinary conversation: overlapped tag-positioned address terms in closing sequences. *Semiotica,* 9, 47–96.

—— 1974: Error correction as an interactional resource. *Language in Society,* 2, 181–99.

—— 1978: Sequential aspects of story telling in conversation. In J. Schenkein (ed.), *Studies in the Organization of Conversational Interaction.* New York: Academic Press, 219–48.

—— 1979: A technique for inviting laughter and its subsequent acceptance/declination. In G. Psathas (ed.), *Everyday Language: Studies in Ethnomethodology,* New York: Irvington, 79–96.

—— 1983: Two explorations of the organization of overlapping talk in conversation. In *Tilburg Papers in Language and Literature,* Tilburg, Netherlands.

—— 1984a: Notes on "latency" in overlap onset. Paper presented at the British Sociological Association's International and Multidisciplinary Conference on Interaction and Language Use, Plymouth, England.

—— 1984b: On stepwise transition from talk about a trouble to inappropriately next-positioned matters. In J. M. Atkinson and J. Heritage (eds), *Structures of Social Action,* Cambridge: Cambridge University Press, 191–222.

—— 1989: Preliminary notes on a possible metric which provides for a "standard maximum" silence of approximately one second in conversation. In D. Roger and P. Bull (eds), *Conversation: An Interdisciplinary Perspective,* Clevedon: Multilingual Matters, 156–97.

—— 1990: List-construction as a task and a resource. In G. Psathas (ed.), *Interactional Competence,* Washington, DC: University Press of America, 63–92.

Jefferson, G. and Lee, J. 1981: The rejection of advice: managing the problematic convergence of a "trouble-telling" and a "service encounter." *Journal of Pragmatics,* 55, 399–422.

Jefferson, G. and Schegloff, E. A. 1975: Sketch: some orderly aspects of overlap in natural conversation. Paper presented at the Annual Meetings of the American Anthropological Association, December.

Jordan, G. and Henderson, A. 1992: Interaction analysis: foundations and practice. Unpublished MS, Xerox Palo Alto Research Center and Institute for Research on Learning, Palo Alto, CA.

Kahneman, D., Slovic, P. and Tversky, A. (eds) 1982: *Judgement under Uncertainty: Heuristics and Biases.* Cambridge: Cambridge University Press.

Kamens, D. 1977: Legitimacy myth and educational organization: the relationship between organizational ideology and formal structure. *American Sociological Review*, 42, 208–19.

Kanter, R. M. 1977: *Men and Women of the Corporation*. New York: Basic Books.

Katz, D. and Kahn, R. L. 1966: *The Social Psychology of Organizations*. New York: John Wiley.

Kaufman, F. 1944: *The Methodology of the Social Sciences*. New York: Humanities.

Kurke, L. B. and Aldrich, H. E. 1983: Mintzberg was right!: a replication and extension of *The Nature of Managerial Work*. *Management Science*, 29, 975–84.

Lawrence, P. R. and Lorsch, J. W. 1967: *Organization and Environment: Managing Differentiantion and Integration*. Boston: Graduate School of Business Administration, Harvard University.

Leavitt, H. J. 1951: Some effects of certain group communication patterns on group performance, *Journal of Abnormal and Social Psychology*, 46, 38–50.

—— 1987: *Corporate Pathfinders*. New York: Viking Penguin.

Levine, D. 1985: *The Flight from Ambiguity: Essays in Social and Cultural Theory*. Chicago: University of Chicago Press.

Lieberson, S. 1984: *Making It Count*. Berkeley: University of California Press.

Lynch, M. 1982: Technical work and critical inquiry: investigations in a scientific laboratory. *Social Studies of Science*, 12, 499–534.

Lynch, M. 1985: *Art and Artifact in Laboratory Science*. London: Routledge and Kegan Paul.

Lukes, S. 1991: The rationality of norms. *European Journal of Sociology*, 32, 142–9.

McHoul, A. 1978: The organization of turns at formal talk in the classroom. *Language in Society*, 7, 183–213.

March, J. G. 1962: The business firm as a political coalition. *Journal of Politics*, 24, 662–78.

—— 1978: Bounded rationality, ambiguity, and the engineering of choice. *Bell Journal of Economics*, 9, 587–608.

—— 1981: Footnote on organizational change. *Administrative Science Quarterly*, 26, 563–77.

—— 1988: *Decisions and Organizations*. Oxford: Blackwell.

March, J. G. and Olsen, J. P. 1976: *Ambiguity and Choice in Organizations*. Bergen: Universitetsforlaget.

March, J. G. and Romelaer, P. J. 1976: Position and presence in the drift of decisions. In J. G. March and J. P. Olsen (eds), *Ambiguity and Choice in Organizations*, Bergen: Universitetsforlaget.

March, J. G. and Simon, H. A. 1958: *Organizations*. New York: JohnWiley.

Maynard, D. W. 1980: Placement of topic changes in conversatioin. *Semiotica*, 30, 263–90.

Maynard, D. W. 1984: *Inside Plea Bargaining*. New York: Plenum.
—— 1985: On the functions of social conflict among children. *American Sociological Review*, 50, 207–23.
—— 1988: Language, interaction and social problems, *Social Problems*, 35, 311–34.
—— 1991: The perspective-display series and the delivery and receipt of diagnostic news. In D. Boden and D. H. Zimmerman (eds), *Talk and Social Structure*, Cambridge: Polity, 164–92.
—— 1992: On clinicians co-implicating recipients in the delivery of diagnostic news. In P. Drew and J. Heritage (eds), *Talk at Work: Interaction in Institutional Settings*. Cambridge: Cambridge University Press, 331–58.
Maynard, D. W. and Clayman, S. 1991: The diversity of ethnomethodology. *Annual Review of Sociology*, 71: 385–418.
Maynard, D. W. and Wilson, T. P. 1980: On the reification of social structure. In S. G. McNall and G. N. Howes (eds), *Current Perspectives in Social Theory*, vol. 1, Greenwich, CT: JAI Press, 287–322.
Maynard, D. W. and Zimmerman, D. H. 1984: Topical talk, ritual and the social organization of relationships. *Social Psychology Quarterly*, 47, 301–16.
Mead, G. H. 1934: *Mind, Self and Society*. Chicago: University of Chicago Press.
Mehan, H. 1978: Structuring school structure. *Harvard Educational Review*, 48, 311–88.
—— 1979: *Learning Lessons: Social Organization in the Classroom*. Cambridge, MA: Harvard University Press.
—— 1987: Language and power in organizational process. *Discourse Processes*, 10, 291–301.
Mehan, H. and Wood, H. 1975: *The Reality of Ethnomethodology*. New York: Wiley.
Mehan, H., Hertweck, A. and Meihls, J. L. 1986: *Handicapping the Handicapped: Decision-making in Students' Educational Careers*. Stanford: Stanford University Press.
Mellinger, W. M. 1990: Negotiated orders: the social organization of paramedic calls for emergency field services. Unpublished Ph.D. dissertation, Department of Sociology, University of California, Santa Barbara.
Merleau-Ponty, M. 1945: *La phénomenologie de la perception*. Paris: Gallimard.
Merritt, M. 1976: On questions following questions in service encounters. *Language in Society*, 5, 315–57.
Meyer, J. W. and Rowan, B. 1977: Institutionalized organizations: formal structures as myth and ceremony. *American Journal of Sociology*, 83, 340–63.
Meyer, J. W. and Scott, W. R. 1983: *Organizational Environments: Ritual and Rationality*. Beverly Hills, CA: Sage.
Meyer, J. W., Ramirez, F. O. and J. Boli 1987: Ontology and rationalization in the Western cultural account. In J. Boli and G. Thomas (eds), *Institutional Structure: Constituting State, Society, and the Individual*, Newbury Park, CA: Sage, 12–37.

Meyer, M. W. 1979: Organizational structure as signalling. *Pacific Sociological Review*, 22, 481–500.

Meyer, M. W. et al. 1978: *Environments and Organizations*. San Francisco: Jossey-Bass.

Mintzberg, H. 1973: *The Nature of Managerial Work*. New York: Harper and Row.

——1979: *The Structuring of Organizations*. Englewood Cliffs, NJ: Prentice-Hall.

——1983: *Structure in Fives: Designing Effective Organizations*. Englewood Cliffs, NJ: Prentice-Hall.

Mintzberg, H. and McHugh, A. 1985: Strategy formation in an adhocracy. *Administrative Science Quarterly*, 30, 160–97.

Mintzberg, H., Raisinghani, D. and Theoret, A. 1976: The structure of "unstructured" decision processes. *Administrative Science Quarterly*, 21, 246–75.

Mishler, E. G. 1975: Studies in dialogue and discourse: an exponential law of successive questioning. *Language in Society*, 4, 31–51.

Moerman, M. 1977: The preference for self-correction in a Tai conversational corpus. *Language*, 53, 872–82.

Molotch, H. 1990: Sociology, economics and the economy. In H. Gans (ed.), *Sociology in America*, ASA Presidential Series, Newbury Park: Sage, 293–309.

Molotch, H. and Boden, D. 1985: Talking social structure: discourse, dominance and the Watergate hearings. *American Sociological Review*, 50, 273–388.

Morgan, G. 1980: Paradigms, metaphors, and puzzle solving in organization theory. *Administrative Science Quarterly*, 25, 605–22.

—— 1986: *Images of Organization*. Beverly Hills: Sage.

Moser, P. K. (ed.) 1990: *Rationality in Action: Contemporary Approaches*. Cambridge: Cambridge University Press.

Mulkay, M. 1984: Conversations and texts. Paper presented at the British Sociological Association's International and Multidisciplinary Conference on Interaction and Language Use, Plymouth, England.

Olson, M. 1971: *The Logic of Collective Action*. Cambridge, MA: Harvard University Press.

O'Reilly, C. 1982: Variation in decision-makers' use of information sources: the impact of quality and accessibility of information. *Academy of Management Journal*, 25, 113–24.

Padgett, J. F. 1980: Bounded rationality in budgetary research. *American Political Science Review*, 74, 354–71.

Parkinson, C. N. 1957: *Parkinson's Law and Other Studies in Administration*. Cambridge, MA: Riverside Press.

Parsons, T. 1937: *The Structure of Social Action*. New York: Free Press.

—— 1951: *The Social System*. Glencoe, IL: Free Press.

Peirce, C. S. 1985: *Collected Papers of Charles Saunders Peirce*. Cambridge, MA: Harvard University Press.

Perrow, C. 1986: *Complex Organizations* (1972), 3rd edn. New York: McGraw-Hill.

Peters, T. 1992: *Liberation Management.* New York: Knopf.

Peters, T. J. and Waterman, R. H. 1982: *In Search of Excellence.* New York: Harper and Row.

Pettigrew, A. W. 1979: On studying organizational cultures. *Administrative Science Quarterly*, 24, 570–81.

Pfeffer, J. 1978: The micropolitics of organizations. In M. Meyer (ed.), *Environments and Organizations*, San Francisco: Jossey-Bass, 29–50.

—— 1981: Management as symbolic action: the creation and maintenance of organizational paradigms. In L. L. Cummings and Barry M. Staw (eds), *Research in Organizational Behavior*, vol 3, Greenwich, CT: JAI Press, 1–52.

—— 1982: *Organizations and Organizational Theory.* Boston: Pitman.

Pfeffer, J. and Salancik, G. 1977: Administrator effectiveness: the effects of advocacy and information on achieving outcomes in an organizational context. *Human Relations*, 30, 641–56.

—— 1978: *The External Control of Organizations: A Resource Dependency Perspective.* New York: Harper and Row.

Pollner, M. 1987: *Mundane Reason.* Cambridge: Cambridge University Press.

Pollner, M. 1991: Left of ethnomethodology: the rise and decline of radical reflexivity. *American Sociological Review*, 56, 370–80.

Pomerantz, A. 1975: Second assessments: a study of some features of agreements/disagreements. Unpublished doctoral dissertation, University of California, Irvine.

—— 1984: Agreeing and disagreeing with assessments: some features of preferred/dispreferred turn shapes. In J. M. Atkinson and J. Heritage (eds), *Structures of Social Action*, Cambridge: Cambridge University Press, 57–101.

Pondy, L. 1978: Leadership as a language game. In M. W. McCall and M. M. Lombardo (eds), *Leadership: Where Else Can We Go?* Durham, NC: Duke University Press, 87–99.

—— 1983: The role of metaphors and myths in organization and in the facilitation of change. In Louis R. Pondy, Peter J. Frost, Gareth Morgan and Thomas C. Dandridge (eds), *Organizational Symbolism*, Greenwich, CT: JAI Press, 157–66.

Pondy, L. R., Hammer, T. H. and Bacharach, S. B. 1977: The other hand clapping: an information-processing approach to organizational power. In *Reward Systems and Power Distribution*, Ithaca, NY: School of Industrial and Labor Relations, Cornell University, 59–91.

Powell, W. W. 1988: International effects on organizational structure and performance. In L. Zucker (ed.), *Institutional Patterns and Organizations: Culture and Environment*, Cambridge, MA: Ballinger, 115–36.

Powell, W. W. and Friedkin, R. 1986: Politics and programs: organizational factors in public television decision making. In P. DiMaggio (ed.), *Nonprofit Enterprise in the Arts*, New York: Oxford University Press.

Rawlings, B. 1982: Turn-taking as an organizational matter. Paper presented at the Tenth World Congress of Sociology, Mexico City.

Rawls, A. W. 1987: The interaction order *sui generis*: Goffman's contribution to social theory. *Sociological Theory*, 5, 136–49.

Reich, R. B. 1992: *The Work of Nations: Preparing Ourselves for Twenty-First Century Capitalism*. New York: Vintage.

Ren, J. 1989: Turn-taking in Mandarin Chinese. Unpublished Masters thesis, Department of Sociology, University of California, Santa Barbara.

Ritzer, G. 1985: The rise of micro-sociological theory. *Sociological Theory*, 3, 88–98.

—— 1988: The micro–macro problem and prospects. *Contemporary Sociology*, 17, 703–6.

—— (ed.), 1990: *Frontiers of Social Theory: The New Synthesis*. New York: Columbia University Press.

Roth, G. 1968: Introduction. In G. Roth and C. Wittich (eds), *Max Weber: Economy and Society: An Outline of Interpretive Sociology*, New York: Bedminster, xxvii-civ.

Sacks, H. 1963: On sociological description. *Berkeley Journal of Sociology*, 8, 1–16.

—— 1965–71: Lectures, unpublished, transcribed. University of California, Irvine.

—— 1966: *No One to Turn To*. Unpublished Ph.D. dissertation, Department of Sociology, University of California, Berkeley.

—— 1972a: An initial investigation of the usability of conversational data for doing sociology. In D. Sudnow (ed.), *Studies in Social Interaction*, New York: Free Press, 31–47.

—— 1972b. On the analyzability of stories by children. In J. J. Gumperz and D. Hymes (eds), *Directions of Sociolinguistics*, New York: Holt, Rinehart and Winston, 325–45.

—— 1974: An analysis of the course of a joke's telling in conversation. In R. Bauman and J. Scherzer (eds), *Explorations in the Ethnography of Speaking*, Cambridge: Cambridge University Press.

—— 1979: Hotrodder: a revolutionary category. In G. Psathas (ed.), *Everyday Language: Studies in Ethnomethodology*, New York: Irvington.

—— 1984: Notes on methodology. In J. M. Atkinson and J. Heritage (eds), *Structures of Social Action*, Cambridge: Cambridge University Press, 21–7.

—— 1987: On the preference for agreement and contiguity in sequences in conversation. In G. Button and J. R. E. Lee (eds), *Talk and Social Organization*, Clevedon: Multilingual Matters, 54–69.

—— 1989: *Lectures* (1964–1965), ed. G. Jefferson and with a memoir by E. A. Schegloff. *Human Studies*, 12(3–4).

—— 1992: *Lectures on Conversation*, vols 1 and 2, ed. G. Jefferson. Oxford: Blackwell.

Sacks, H. and Schegloff, E. A. 1979: Two preferences in the organization of reference to persons in conversation and their interaction. In G. Psathas (ed.), *Everyday Language: Studies in Ethnomethodology*, New York: Irvington Press, 15–21.

Sacks, H., Schegloff, E. A. and Jefferson, G. 1974: A simplest systematics for the organization of turn-taking for conversation. *Language*, 50, 696–735.

Sahlins, M. 1985: *Islands of History*. Chicago: University of Chicago Press.

Saussure, F. de 1974: *Course in General Linguistics* (1916), ed. C. Bally and A. Sechebaye. London: Collins.

Schegloff, E. A. 1968: Sequencing in conversational openings. *American Anthropologist*, 70, 1075–95.

—— 1972: Notes on conversational practice: formulating place. In D. Sudnow (ed.), *Studies in Social Interaction*. New York: Free Press, 75–119.

—— 1979: Identification and recognition in telephone conversation openings. In G. Psathas (ed.), *Everyday Language*, New York: Irvington, 23–78.

—— 1980: Preliminaries to preliminaries: "can I ask you a question?" *Sociological Inquiry*, 50, 104–52.

—— 1982: Discourse as an interactional achievement: some uses of "uh-huh" and other things that come between sentences. In D. Tannen (ed.), *Analyzing Discourse: Text and Talk, Georgetown University Roundtable on Languages and Linguistics 1981*, Washington, DC: Georgetown University Press, 71–93.

—— 1986: The routine as achievement. *Human Studies*, 9, 111–52.

—— 1987a: Between macro and micro: contexts and other connections. In J. Alexander, B. Geisen, R. Munch and N. Smelser (eds), *The Micro–Macro Link*, Berkeley: University of California Press.

—— 1987b: Analyzing single sequences of interaction: an exercise in conversation analysis, *Social Psychology Quarterly*, 50, 101–14.

—— 1991: Reflections on talk and social structure. In D. Boden and D. H. Zimmerman (eds), *Talk and Social Structure*, Cambridge: Polity, 44–70.

—— 1992: Repair after next turn: the last structurally provided defense of intersubjectivity in conversation. *American Journal of Sociology*, 97, 1295–345.

Schegloff, E. A. and Sacks, H. 1973: Opening up closings. *Semiotica*, 7, 289–327.

Schegloff, E. A., Jefferson, G. and Sacks, H. 1977: The preference for self-correction in the organization of repair in conversation. *Language*, 53, 361–82.

Schelling, T. C. 1978: *Micromotives and Macrobehavior*. New York: W. W. Norton.

Schutz, A. 1962: *Collected Papers I*. The Hague: Martinus Nijhoff.

—— 1964: *Collected Papers II*. The Hague: Martinus Nijhoff.

Schwartzman, H. 1988: *The Meeting*. New York: Plenum.

Scott, W. R. 1987a: *Organizations: Rational, Natural and Open Systems* (1983). Englewood Cliffs, NJ: Prentice-Hall.

—— 1987b: The adolescence of institutional theory. *Administrative Science Quarterly*, 32, 493–511.

—— 1991: Unpacking institutional arguments. In W. W. Powell and P. J. DiMaggio (eds), *The New Institutionalism in Organizational Analysis*, Chicago: University of Chicago Press, 164–82.

Scott, W. R. and Black, B. 1986: *The Organization of Mental Health Services: Societal and Community Systems.* Beverly Hills, CA: Sage.

Selznick, P. 1948: Foundations of a theory of organization. *American Sociological Review*, 13, 25–35.

—— 1949: *TVA and the Grass Roots.* New York: Harper and Row.

Sharrock, W. and Button, G. 1990: The social actor: social action in real time. In G. Button (ed.), *Ethnomethodology and the Human Sciences*, Cambridge: Cambridge University Press, 137–76.

Sica, A. 1988: *Weber, Irrationality, and Social Order.* Berkeley: University of California Press.

Sigman, S. 1980: On communication rules from a social perspective. *Human Communication Research*, 7, 37–51.

Silverman, D. 1970: *The Theory of Organizations.* London: Heinemann.

Silverman, D. and Jones, J. 1976: *Organizational Work: The Language of Grading: the Grading of Language.* London: Macmillan.

Simmel, G. 1978: *The Philosophy of Money*, ed. D. Frisby, trans. T. Bottomore and D. Frisby. London: Routledge.

Simon, H. A. 1957: *Models of Man, Social and Radical: Mathematical Essays on Rational Human Behavior in a Social Setting.* New York: John Wiley.

—— 1962: *Administrative Behavior: A Study of Decision-Making Processes in Administrative Organization* (1947), 2nd edn. New York: Free Press.

—— 1972: Theories of bounded rationality. In C. B. McGuire and R. Radner (eds), *Decision and Organization*, Amsterdam: North Holland, 161–76.

—— 1990: Alternative visions of rationality. In P. Moser (ed.), *Rationality in Action*, Cambridge: Cambridge University Press.

Smelser, N. J. 1988: Social structure. In N. J. Smelser (ed.), *Handbook of Sociology*, Newbury Park: Sage.

Smirich, L. 1983: Organizations as shared meanings. In L. Pondy et al. (eds), *Organizational Symbolism*, Greenwich, CT: JAI Press, 55–65.

Smirich, L. and Stubbart, C. 1985: Strategic management in an enacted world. *Academy of Management Review*, 10, 724–36.

Smith, D. 1978: *The Everyday World as Problematic.* Toronto: University of Toronto Press.

Smith, D. K. and Alexander, R. C. 1988: *Fumbling the Future: How Xerox Invented, Then Ignored, the First Personal Computer.* New York: Williams Morrow.

Sproull, L. S. 1981: Beliefs in organizations. In P. C. Nystrom and W. H. Starbuck (eds), *Handbook of Organizational Design*, vol. 2, New York: Oxford University Press.

Sproull, L. S. and P. D. Larkey (eds) 1982: *Advances in Information Processing in Organizations.* Greenwich, CT: JAI Press.

Starbuck, W. H. 1983: Organizations as action generators. *American Sociological Review* 48, 91–102.

Staw, B. 1981: The escalation of commitment to a course of action. *Academy of Management Review*, 6, 577–87.

Stinchcombe, A. 1965: Social structure and environment. In J. G. March (ed.), *The Handbook of Organizations*, Chicago: Rand McNally, 142–93.

Stinchcombe, A. 1990: *Information and Organizations*. Berkeley: University of California Press.

Suchman, L. 1987: *Plans and Situated Actions: The Problem of Human/ Machine Communication*. Cambridge: Cambridge University Press.

Suchman, L. 1993: Constituting shared workspaces. In Yrjo Engestrom and David Middleton (eds), *Communication and Cognition at Work*, Cambridge: Cambridge University Press.

Suchman, L. and Jordan, B. 1990: Interactional troubles in face-to-face survey interviews. *Journal of the American Statistical Association*, 85, 232–41.

Sudnow, D. 1967: *Passing On*. Englewood Cliffs, NJ: Prentice-Hall.

—— (ed.) 1972: *Studies in Social Organization*. New York: Free Press.

Sztompka, P. 1991: *Society in Action: The Theory of Social Becoming*. Cambridge: Polity.

Ten Have, P. 1991: Talk and institution: a reconsideration of the "asymmetry" of doctor–patient interaction. In D. Boden and D. H. Zimmerman (eds), *Talk and Social Structure*, Cambridge: Polity, 138–63.

Thompson, J. D. 1967: *Organizations in Action*. New York: McGraw-Hill.

Tichy, N. M., Tushman, M. L. and Fombrum, C. 1979: Social network analysis for organizations. *Academy of Management Review*, 4, 507–19.

Tilly, Charles 1984: *Big Structures, Large Processes and Huge Comparisons*. New York: Russell Sage Foundation.

Trudgill, P. 1974: *Sociolinguistics: An Introduction*. Harmondsworth: Penguin.

Turner, B. 1990: The rise of organizational symbolism. In J. Hassard and D. Pym (eds), *The Theory and Philosophy of Organizations*, London: Routledge, 83–96.

Turner, J. H. 1987: Analytical theorizing. In A. Giddens and J. H. Turner (eds), *Social Theory Today*, Cambridge: Polity, 156–94.

—— 1988: *A Theory of Social Interaction*. Stanford: Stanford University Press.

Turner, R. 1974: *Ethnomethodology*. Harmondsworth: Penguin.

Tversky, A. and Kahneman, D. 1974: Judgment under uncertainty: heuristics and basics. *Science*, 185, 1124–31.

Udy, S. H. 1959: "Bureaucracy" and "rationality" in Weber's organization theory: an empirical study. *American Sociological Review*, 24, 791–5.

Van Maanen, J. 1979: The fact of fiction in organizational ethnography. *Administrative Science Quarterly* 24, 539–49.

Van Maanen, J. and Schein, E. 1979: Toward a theory of organizational socialization. In B. Staw (ed.), *Research in Organization Behavior*, Greenwich, CT: JAI Press, 209–44.

Weber, M. 1964: *The Theory of Social and Economic Organization* (1947). New York: Free Press.

—— 1968: *Economy and Society: An Outline of Interpretive Sociology*, ed. G. Roth and C. Wittich. New York: Bedminster Press.

Weick, K. E. 1976: Educational organizations as loosely coupled systems. *Administrative Science Quarterly*, 21, 1–19.

—— 1979: *The Social Psychology of Organizing* (1969). Reading, MA: Addison-Wesley.

—— 1985: Cosmology episodes. *Organizational Dynamics*, 51–64.

Welty, E. 1983: *One Writer's Beginnings*. Cambridge, MA: Harvard University Press.

West, C. 1982: Why can't a woman be more like a man: an interactional note on organizational game playing for managerial women, *Work and Occupations*, 9, 5–19.

—— 1984: *Routine Complications: Troubles in Talk between Doctors and Patients*. Bloomington: Indiana University Press.

Whalen, J., Zimmerman, D. H. and Whalen, M. R. 1988: When words fail: a single case study. *Social Problems*, 335–62.

Whalen, M. and Zimmerman, D. 1987: Sequential and institutional contexts in calls for help. *Social Psychology Quarterly*, 50, 172–85.

—— 1990: Describing trouble: practical epistemology in citizen calls to the police. *Language in Society*, 19, 465–92.

Wieder, L. 1988: *Language and Social Reality: The Case of Telling the Convict Code* (1974). Washington, DC: University Press of America.

Williamson, O. 1975: *Markets and Hierarchies*. New York: Free Press.

Wilson, T. P. 1982: Qualitative "oden" quantitative Methoden in den Sozialforschung. *Kölner Zeitschrift für Soziologie und Socialpsychologie*, 487–508.

—— 1987: Sociology and the mathematical method. In A. Giddens and J. Turner (eds), *Social Theory Today*, Cambridge: Polity, 383–404.

—— 1989: Agency, structure and the explanation of miracles. Paper presented at the Midwest Sociology Society Annual Meetings, St Louis.

Wilson, T. P. and Zimmerman, D. H. 1980: Ethnomethodology, sociology and theory. *Humboldt Journal of Social Relations*, 7, 52–88.

Wilson, T. P. and Zimmerman, D. H. 1986: The structure of silence between turns in two-party conversation, *Discourse Processes*, 9, 375–90.

Wilson, T. P., Wiemann, J. and Zimmerman, D. H. 1984: Models of turn-taking in conversational interaction. *Journal of Language and Social Psychology*, 15, 159–83.

Wittgenstein, L. 1958: *Philosophical Investigations*. Oxford: Blackwell.

Wolf, Eric 1982: *Europe and the People Without History*. Berkeley: University of California Press.

Woodward, J. 1965: *Industrial Organizations, Theory and Practice*. London: Oxford University Press.

Zerubavel, E. 1987: The language of time: toward a semiotics of temporality. *Sociological Quarterly*, 28, 343–56.

Zimmerman, D. H. 1969: Tasks and troubles: the practical bases of work activities in a Public Assistance agency. In D. Hansen (ed.), *Explorations in Sociology and Counseling*, New York: Houghton-Mifflin, 237–66.

—— 1971: The practicalities of rule use. In J. Douglas (ed.), *Understanding Everyday Life*, Chicago: Aldine, 285–95.

Zimmerman, D. H. 1974: Preface. In D. L. Wieder, *Language and Social Reality*, The Hague: Mouton, 9–26.

—— 1984: Talk and its occasion: the case of calling the police. In D. Schiffrin (ed.), *Meaning, Form and Use in Context*, Washington, DC: Georgetown University Press, 210–28.

—— 1988: On conversation: the conversation analytic perspective. In J. A. Anderson (ed.), *Communications Yearbook 11*, Newbury Park: Sage, 406–32.

Zimmerman, D. H. and Boden, D. 1991: Structure-in-action. In D. Boden and D. H. Zimmerman (eds), *Talk and Social Structure*, Cambridge: Polity, 3–21.

Zimmerman, D. H. and Pollner, M. 1970: The everyday world as a phenomenon. In H. Pepinksy (ed.), *People and Information*, New York: Praeger.

Zimmerman, D. H. and Wieder, D. L. 1970: Ethnomethodology and the problem of order: comment on Denzin. In J. D. Douglas (ed.), *Understanding Everyday Life*, Chicago: Aldine, 286–98.

Zuboff, S. 1988: *In the Age of the Smart Machine*. New York: Basic Books.

Zucker, L. 1977: The role of institutionalization in cultural persistence. *American Sociological Review*, 42, 726–43.

—— 1988a: Where do institutional patterns come from? Organizations as actors in social systems. In L. Zucker (ed.), *Institutional Patterns and Organizations: Culture and Environment*, Cambridge, MA: Ballinger, 23–49.

—— (ed.) 1988b: *Institutional Patterns and Organizations: Culture and Environment*. Cambridge, MA: Ballinger.

—— 1989: Combining institutional theory and population ecology. *American Sociological Review*, 54, 542–5.

—— 1991: The role of institutionalization in cultural persistence. In W. W. Powell and P. J. DiMaggio (eds), *The New Institutionalism in Organizational Analysis*, Chicago: University of Chicago Press, 83–107.

Index